CAPITAL INVESTMENT ANALYSIS

Using Discounted Cash Flows

CAPITAL INVESTMENT ANALYSIS

Using Discounted Cash Flows

Third Edition

George L. Casler
New York State College of Agriculture and Life Sciences,
Cornell University

Bruce L. Anderson
New York State College of Agriculture and Life Sciences,
Cornell University

Richard D. Aplin
New York State College of Agriculture and Life Sciences,
Cornell University

JOHN WILEY & SONS

New York • Chichester • Brisbane • Toronto • Singapore

Library of Congress Cataloging in Publication Data:

ISBN 0-471-84231-1

Printed in the United States of America

10 9 8 7 6 5 4 3 2

Library of Congress Cataloging in Publication Data

Casler, George L.
Capital investment analysis.

Rev. ed. of: Capital investment analysis/Richard D. Aplin, George L. Casler, Cheryl P. Francis
Includes bibliographical references.
1. Capital investments—Evaluation. 2. Discounted cash flow.
I. Anderson, Bruce L. II. Aplin, Richard D. (Richard David). Capital investment analysis. III. Title
HG4028.C4A64 1984 658.1'52 83-18570
ISBN 0-88244-272-4 (pbk.)

CONTENTS

		Page
PREFACE		ix
1.	CAPITAL INVESTMENT DECISIONS	1
	Major Steps in Evaluating Capital Expenditure Proposals	1
2.	COMMONLY USED MEASURES OF INVESTMENT WORTH	3
	Urgency	4
	Payback Period	4
	Pros and Cons of Payback	5
	Return on Investment (ROI)	6
	Pros and Cons of ROI	7
	Summary of Commonly Used Measures of Investment Worth	7
3.	TIME VALUE OF MONEY	9
	Alternative Uses of Money (A)	9
	Risk and Uncertainty (R)	10
	Inflation (I)	10
	Conclusion	10
4.	PRESENT VALUE OF A FUTURE SUM OF MONEY	11
	Compound Interest	11
	Present Value	12
	Compound Interest and Present Value	14
	Present Value Tables	15
	Timing of Cash Flows and Frequency of Compounding	16
	A Note on Time Lines	17
	Present Value Examples	17
	Determination of Bond Price	18
	Yield of Loan	19
	Summary	20

		Page
5.	FINANCIAL INFORMATION RELEVANT TO EVALUATING CAPITAL INVESTMENTS: CASH FLOWS	21
	Ad Hoc Analyses Usually Needed	21
	The Meaning of Cash Flows	21
	Net Investment	22
	Net Cash Inflows or Benefits	22
	Projecting Future Cash Flows	23
	Relevant Costs	23
	Relevant Income	24
	Handling Depreciation and Interest	24
	Loan Payments	25
6.	DISCOUNTED CASH FLOW MEASURES OF INVESTMENT WORTH	27
	Net Present Value Method of Evaluating Investments	27
	Illustrations	29
	A Warning	30
	Internal Rate of Return Method of Evaluating Investments	30
	Procedure and Rationale	31
	Guidelines for Determining Internal Rate of Return	34
	Relative Advantages and Disadvantages of Net Present Value and Internal Rate of Return Methods	34
	Advantages of Net Present Value Method	35
	Advantages of the Internal Rate of Return Method	35
	Summary of Relative Merits	36
7.	ADJUSTING CASH FLOWS FOR INCOME TAXES	37
	Ordinary Income Taxes	37
	Depreciation	37
	After Tax Cash Flows	39
	Method #1: "Income Statement Method"	39
	Method #2: "No Name Method"	40
	Method #3: "Component Method"	40
	Present Value Calculations	41
	Component Method	42
	Accelerated vs. Straight Line Depreciation	42
	Investment Credit	43
	Terminal Values	43
	The Complete Example	44
	Present Value Calculations	44
	Capital Gain Income	44
8.	THE COST OF CAPITAL	47
	Rationale for a Weighted Average Cost of Capital	48
	Computing a Weighted Average Cost of Capital	50
	Estimating the Costs of Capital From Various Sources	51
	Cost of Debt	51
	Cost of Equity Captial in Proprietorships and Partnerships	51
	Adjustment for Taxes	53
	Cost of Equity Capital in Corporations	54
	Cost of Preferred Stock	54
	Cost of Common Stock	54
	Cost of Retained Earnings	56
	Cost of Equity Capital in Cooperatives	57
	Cost of Revolving Funds	57
	Cost of Permanent Capital	59
	A Final Comment on the Cost of Equity Capital	59

		Page
	Overall Cost of Capital	59
	Cost of Unusually Large Amounts of Capital in a Given Period	60
	Cost of Capital Not a Profit Goal	61
9.	SOME SPECIAL PROBLEMS IN PROJECTING CASH FLOWS AND IN ANALYZING INVESTMENTS	63
	Expected Terminal or Salvage Values	63
	Estimated Terminal Value of New Asset	63
	Salvage Values of Old Asset Being Retired	63
	Illustration	64
	Working Capital	64
	Analyzing Investment Alternviates with Unequal Lives	65
	Analyzing Using Common Terminal Dates	66
	View as a Continuous Replacement Cycle	66
	Annual Equivalent Cash Flows	67
	Summary	68
	Other Uses of Annual Equivalent Cash Flows	69
10.	HANDLING UNCERTAINTY	71
	Break-even Approach	71
	Adjusting the Discount Rate	74
	Using a Range of Possible Outcomes	75
	Probability Distribution Approach	76
	Decision Trees	77
	Example: Herein Lies the Rub (Skakespeare)	78
	The Procedure	79
	A Few Comments About Decision Trees	83
	Investor's Aversion to Uncertainty	84
	A Parting Reminder	84
11.	HANDLING INFLATION	85
	Real Flows and Money Flows	85
	Inflation and the Discount Rate	89
	Computing the After-tax Real Discount Rate	90
	An Example	91
	The Balloon Manufacturing Company	92
	Solution to Balloon Manufacturing Company	93
	Summary	96
12.	ACQUISITION OF ASSETS WITH A FINANCIAL LEASE VS. PURCHASE AND LOAN	97
	Illustration	98
	Example A	98
	Lease	98
	Purchase and Loan	99
	Example B: The Tax Rate	100
	Lease	100
	Purchase and Loan	100
	Lessee Pays No Taxes	100
	Lease	100
	Purchase and Loan	100
	A Note on Terminal Values	101
	Example C: A More Realistic Case	101
	Lease	101
	Purchase and Loan	102
	Comparison	102
	Qualitative Factors Influencing the Lease vs. Purchase Decision	102

Page

13. CAPITAL RATIONING 103

14. SUMMARY AND CONCLUSIONS 107

APPENDIX A. GUIDELINES FOR DETERMINING THE INTERNAL RATE OF RETURN OF AN INVESTMENT 109

APPENDIX B. PROBLEMS INVOLVING THE APPLICATION OF DISCOUNTED CASH FLOW MEASURES OF INVESTMENT WORTH 113

Notes 113
Problems 114

APPENDIX C. TABLES 133

Table I - Compound Interest 134
Table II - Present Value of \$1 135
Table III - Present Value of \$1 Received Annually at the End of Each Year for n Years 138
Table IV - e^{-rt} Values for Continuous Discounting 141
Table V - Present Value of Depreciation Charges, Sum-of-the-Year's Digits Method, No Salvage 142
Table VI - Present Value of Depreciation Charges, Double Declining Balance Method with Switchover to Straight Line, No Salvage 143
Table VII - Present Value of Accellerated Cost Recovery 144

PREFACE

PREFACE TO THE THIRD EDITION

This edition benefits from our continuing experience in the classroom and with business managers as well as from contact with colleagues at Cornell and other colleges and universities.

No claim is made that we are pushing out the frontiers of knowledge in the application of discounted cash flow measures of investment worth. Our intent is to provide methodology useable to business managers. We believe that the material presented is correct -- even if some people believe it is outmoded or perhaps old-fashioned.

Perhaps the greatest divergence between our book and some of the recent literature is in the area of handling uncertainty and the choice of an appropriate rate for of discounting cash flows -- two intertwined problems that cannot be fully separated. While we acknowledge that the use of a default-free discount rate and separate handling of uncertainty is a logical approach, we are not convinced that the concept of weighted average cost of capital is outmoded. There are still many business managers who may be ready for our approach but not ready for more sophisticated approaches.

The material on adjusting cash flows for income taxes has been revised to be consistent with 1981 and 1982 federal tax laws. We make no claim that the book will be consistent with federal tax laws by the time it is printed.

A chapter on acquisition of assets with a financial lease vs. a purchase and loan has been added. This important decision can effectively be analyzed with present value techniques. A section on the use of decision trees to help analyze sequential investment decisions has been added to the chapter on uncertainty.

The chapter on inflation has been revised. A section has been added to clarify the computation of the real, after-tax discount rate from the before tax nominal rate. We believe inflation has been ignored or inadequately handled by most authors. Current and likely future rates of inflation and our experience working with managers on real problems strongly suggests that the impact of inflation on capital investment decisions cannot be ignored.

We would like to thank Darlene Jennings for typing the manuscript.

August 1983

PREFACE TO THE FIRST EDITION

Business executives and academicians have devoted considerable attention in recent years to measures available to management for evaluating the economic worth of investments. The superiority of the discounted cash flow or present value methods has been clearly demonstrated. The authors are convinced that the correct application of the discounted cash flow measures of investment worth can help most managers crystalize the relevant factors and help them toward more intelligent decision making. Although increasing numbers of firms have been using the discounted cash flow measures in the past ten years, the majority of firms apparently still have not adopted them as guides to making decisions on capital investments.

This publication is aimed at explaining the rationale behind the present value methods and at demonstrating their application to an audience unfamiliar with the measures. If this publication fills a void in the literature -- and the authors think (and hope) that it does -- it does so by combining a presentation of the rationale behind the present value methods in non-technical terms with numerous illustrations of their application.

This publication has been developed from the authors' experiences in teaching the discounted cash flows measures of investment worth to undergraduates in business management courses and to groups of adults such as business executives, farmers, representatives of lending institutions and to Agricultural Extension Agents.

The authors wish to express their appreciation to the undergraduates at Cornell and to the managers, bankers, county agents and others who have explored this topic with the authors in the classroom and in management seminars and workshops. Undoubtedly this publication benefited in significant, but unidentifiable, ways from the interchanges experienced by the authors in teaching present value techniques to these groups.

The authors wish to particularly thank three of their colleagues at Cornell University. Professor R. B. How reviewed the manuscript and made suggestions that led to improvements. Professor B. F. Stanton, who also carefully reviewed a draft, encouraged the authors not only to publish the manuscript but to get on with it. Our debt to Professor R.S. Smith perhaps can best be explained by telling you that we at first wanted to list him as a co-author, but concluded that he would not stand for it. Secondly we thought of dedicating the publication to him, but concluded that our wives would not stand for that. So we end up merely publicly saying "Thanks Bob for your stimulation, encouragement and help at practically every step of the way".

Lastly, we want to thank our faithful and reliable secretaries, Mrs. Cheryl Morse, Miss Sandra Pond and Mrs. Violet Calvano, for their patience and help in typing successive drafts.

Earlier editions of this book have been published under the title "Evaluating Proposed Capital Investments with Discounted Cash Flow Methods" by the Department of Agricultural Economics at Cornell University. The current edition has been improved as a result not only of our experiences in using the earlier publication as a teaching aid, but of the experiences of our friends and colleagues at other universities who have used it in their teaching programs.

November 1972

1

CAPITAL INVESTMENT DECISIONS

Capital investment decisions may be the most important judgments undertaken by management. Frequently large sums of money are involved in expenditures for land, equipment, buildings and other assets. Most such expenditures affect operations over a series of years. Capital expenditures often are large, permanent commitments that influence the long-run flexibility and earning power of the business. This emphasizes the importance of basing capital investment decisions on reliable forecasting and evaluation procedures.

Decisions on capital expenditures also are among the most difficult managerial problems. A major source of difficulty stems from the fact that the effects of most capital investments occur over a considerable period of time in the future. Because our knowledge of the future is imperfect, it is imperative that considerable effort be made to predict as reliably as possible the probable costs and benefits of each investment alternative. Another difficulty arises because, in the case of many capital expenditures, most, if not all, of the capital must be laid out immediately whereas the benefits accrue to the business over time. Thus, once management has reliable estimates of costs and benefits, it has the problem of balancing added returns that will accrue to the business in future years against a capital expenditure that will be made immediately if the decision is made to invest.

The problem of evaluating the profit potential of capital expenditure proposals has been receiving increased attention by business managers, economists and accountants in recent years. The objective of this publication is to introduce managers and future managers to some of the contemporary thinking in this area in a non-technical manner.

MAJOR STEPS IN EVALUATING CAPITAL EXPENDITURE PROPOSALS

Sound decisions on capital expenditures require that management give careful attention to the following steps:

1) Making a thorough search for possible profitable investment opportunities.
2) Evaluating the profit potential of the various capital expenditure proposals:

    a) Determining the amount of capital required by each alternative.
    b) Forecasting the added earnings or benefits that would likely result from each investment alternative.

   c) Using a realistic method to evaluate the economic worth of the alternative investment proposals in view of the availability, cost and alternative uses of capital.

3) Making the decision based on the foregoing evaluation of the economic worth of the investment proposals, any significant intangible factors, and managerial judgment.
4) Post-auditing decisions to improve management's forecasting, evaluation, and decision making procedures in the future.

All steps are vitally important. In accomplishing any particular step, the decision maker is at the mercy of the quality of the job that has been done in the previous steps. For example, no measure for evaluating the economic worth of investments is any better than the information -- the forecasts of benefits and costs associated with the investment alternatives -- that the investor has to feed into the formula or yardstick of investment worth that he or she uses. Without question the greatest errors in the management of capital come from insufficient consideration of alternatives and from poor forecasts as to the extent and duration of the benefits to be realized from an investment proposal rather than from the yardstick of investment worth used. In recent years, however, more powerful measures of investment worth have become available to management. Although imagination, hard work, and good judgment remain as all important ingredients in making sound capital expenditure decisions, the correct application of the newer measures of investment worth described herein should crystallize the relevant factors and help management toward intelligent decision making. In short, some measures of investment worth provide the investor with a better basis for applying managerial judgment than do others.

2

COMMONLY USED MEASURES OF INVESTMENT WORTH

In this publication, we focus on measures available to management for evaluating the economic worth of investments. We assume that management has made a thorough search for investment opportunities and has reliable estimates of the costs and benefits that would be associated with each investment alternative. 1/ We further assume that the primary objective of the business is to maximize the economic well-being (wealth) of the owners. In making this last assumption, we recognize that decision makers in many firms frequently have other objectives, some of which may conflict with the assumed goal of maximizing owners' economic interests. In such instances, the other objectives must be considered in the decision making process. But usually it will be useful to determine first which decisions on investment alternatives will maximize the wealth (economic well-being) of the firm to its owners. 2/ Then if another objective suggests different decisions, management can render a judgment knowing better that some goals are in conflict and having some measure of how much it will "cost" to satisfy some objective other than the maximization of the economic interest of the owners.

In some cases, management only needs to determine whether to accept or reject a capital expenditure project. But in certain circumstances, it may be necessary to rank projects in terms of their economic desirability in order that they may be compared with each other. The need to rank capital expenditure proposals arises when two or more projects are "mutually exclusive"--that is, by their nature only one of them can be undertaken. For example, a manager is deciding between two pieces of equipment, each of which will perform essentially the same function. Or an entreprenuer is analyzing alternative uses for a particular piece of property. The need for ranking capital expenditure alternatives also arises when the business does not have access to unlimited funds with which to undertake

1/ We recognize that some, and in a few investments all, of the benefits are intangible--it is impossible to make dollar estimates of the benefits. This publication is aimed at assisting managers in evaluating the many capital expenditure proposals where most, if not all, of the benefits can be quantified.

2/ It should be noted that the assumed objective of the firm is to maximize its value to the owners. The reader should realize that maximization of profits is not always synonymous with maximization of owners' wealth. Wealth maximization is a more inclusive goal than profit maximization. It takes into account earnings per dollar invested by the owners and the risk associated with these earnings as well as other factors that affect the value of the firm.

acceptable projects. In this case, it often is necessary to rank proposed investments so that the limited capital funds available may be allocated among competing projects to the firm's best advantage.

The approaches widely used by business managers in judging the economic desirability of capital expenditure projects and in ranking them include: (1) Urgency, (2) payback period, and (3) return on investment (ROI). 3/ Each of these measures has a number of variations. We will discuss only one variation -- hopefully the most widely used -- of each of these measures in this section to provide a basis for understanding the merits as well as the weaknesses of each. Later more powerful measures will be explained and illustrated in detail.

URGENCY

Many managers, especially those of small businesses, go to little effort to make a quantitative analysis of their investment alternatives. Such managers rely on their subjective evaluations of the alternatives that come to their attention. Often urgency or postponability is the key factor in their decisions. This approach is much like that used by many car owners -- stop-gap action frequently is taken so that the car can be back in service quickly without any consideration that the repair of the moment is only one of a series that are coming up.

Although many "urgent" or "necessary" proposals are likely to be profitable, the danger exists that some "postponable" projects may be even more profitable investments than the "urgent" ones. Although common sense action in some instances, such as replacing a motor that is instrumental in keeping a production line going, is too obvious to warrant formal pro-and-con analysis, many investments are large and far-reaching enough in their effects to make urgency an unsound and dangerous approach. Guesses, hunches, and intuition should be secondary to economic considerations and formal analysis in evaluating most capital expenditure decisions.

PAYBACK PERIOD

"The machine looks like a good investment; it will pay for itself in three years." When managers make such a comment regarding capital expenditure proposals, they are thinking in terms of the payback period of the project.

The payback period, sometimes called "payout" or "payoff," is one of the simplest and apparently one of the most widely used quantitative methods of measuring the economic value of an investment. The payback period is simply the time it takes the firm to recover the initial investment out of the earnings expected to result from the investment.

The formula for the payback period is:

$$P = \frac{C}{E}$$

where: P is the payback period,
C is the amount of capital required by the investment,
and E is the additional average annual after-tax earnings, before depreciation, expected from the investment.

3/The ROI method also is called "financial statement method," "accounting method rate of return," "rate of return on assets method," "book value method" and "simple rate of return."

For example, if an investment in a machine would require a capital expenditure of \$10,000 and is expected to result in added earnings (or cost savings) of \$3,000 a year, the payback period is 3 1/3 years (i.e., \$10,000 ÷ \$3,000 = 3.3 years).

At this stage of our discussion, it is important to recognize that the annual cash inflow, E, in the payback formula should represent added earnings without a deduction for depreciation. Since the formula is concerned with the recovery of the initial investment, it would be improper and would result in double counting to subtract depreciation as an expense, since depreciation also is concerned with capital recovery.

Ordinarily, management sets some maximum payback period as being acceptable, say four years, and it rejects all investment proposals for which the payback period is greater than this maximum. Managers frequently vary their maximum payback period guidelines according to the type of investment being considered. For example, it would seem unreasonable to require a new building to "pay for itself" as quickly as many types of equipment.

The payback period can be used to rank investment alternatives. Investment proposals having the shortest paybacks are given the highest ranking.

PROS AND CONS OF PAYBACK

The payback period has some serious weaknesses as a measure of investment worth. It can lead to incorrect ranking of investments and can suggest unsound decisions. 4/

One major limitation of the payback is that it fails to consider the entire economic life of the investment proposal -- it ignores profits earned after the initial investment has been recovered. Suppose we are considering two investments, each costing \$10,000 and each returning a cash inflow of \$3,000 a year. Further assume that the first is expected to provide earnings for ten years, the second for five years. Both would pass equally well the requirement of a five-year payback, while the first investment obviously is the better investment.

Strictly applied, the payback period is not a measure of profitability. Since it considers how quickly investment dollars may be recouped, it is really a measure of liquidity. The main objective of making an investment is profitability, not merely recapturing the original outlay. To carry it to the absurd, if we really were interested in a short payback, we wouldn't invest funds at all -- the payback time would be zero. Of course, managers who use the payback method as a guideline do not apply the measure as blindly as the above discussion infers. They recognize that given the payback period, the longer the expected useful life of the asset, the greater the profitability. But if a measure of investment worth that allows management to consider the entire economic life of the investment is available -- and it is -- why not use it rather than the payback?

The payback period method has another serious defect as a measure of the economic worth of investment alternatives. The establishment of the cut-off criterion -- the maximum acceptable payback -- is usually an entirely subjective decision. Except under certain conditions usually not met in practice, the establishment of the maximum acceptable payback has no objective basis and no necessary relation to the assumed primary objective of the business which is to maximize the economic well-being of the owners.

A third weakness of the payback period as a measure of investment worth -- and one that can suggest incorrect decisions to management -- is the fact that it fails to consider properly the timing of the cash outflows and inflows. It ignores the fact that a dollar in

4/The reader interested in a detailed demonstration and discussion of the weaknesses of the payback method is referred to Harold Bierman, Jr. and Seymour Smidt, The Capital Budgeting Decision, Macmillan Publishing Co., 5th edition, 1980, Chapter 2.

hand today is more valuable to us than a dollar that we will receive sometime in the future.5/ As discussed later, most managers have one or more reasons for preferrring a dollar today over a dollar sometime in the future. Consequently, to make valid comparisons between the capital outlays required by an investment and the resulting benefits -- added cash inflows-- in future years, management must attempt to reflect the time value of money.

Although the payback period has some serious limitations, some favorable things can be said of it. The payback is certainly superior to the urgency approach. It requires conscious estimates of capital outlays and of annual cost savings or expected additions to revenue, which is a crucial step in any analysis of investment alternatives. It is simple. It is a conservative measure that may have particular usefulness when a firm is extremely short of cash or credit ability or when the project being analyzed carries extreme risk of obsolescence. The payback can be used as a coarse screen to weed out obviously desirable investments (e.g., an investment that can be expected to have a productive life many, many times its payback period) and obviously undesirable investments (e.g., a project whose payback period is as long as its expected useful life). Although prudent use of the payback period as a measure of investment worth may be helpful to management, it has serious shortcomings as the primary measure of the desirability of investment proposals. 6/

RETURN ON INVESTMENT (ROI)

Return on investment (ROI) analysis apparently is widely used by managers in evaluating the economic worth of investment proposals. Although there are numerous variations, the ROI is commonly computed with the formula:

$$R = \frac{E - D}{C}$$

where: R is the average annual rate of return,
E is the additional average annual after-tax earnings, before depreciation, expected from the investment,
D is the additional average annual depreciation (i.e., straight-line depreciation),
and C is the amount of capital required by the investment.7/

5/Actually, the payback period counts as equals (assigns weights of 1) all cash flows up to the payback point and ignores (places no weight on) cash flows earned after the payback date.

6/ The payback of an investment can provide useful information. Although the payback period is a crude, weak, and often misleading measure of the economic worth of an investment, managers may want to compute the payback period to supplement the other measures used to judge the desirability of investment projects.

7/ A variation of this method involves using one-half the original investment as the denominator rather than the total investment required by a project. Those who advocate the use of half the total investment argue that this reflects the average amount invested in the asset over its expected life. They reason that depreciable assets do not require a permanent investment of the original amount. Rather the funds are gradually recovered as the earnings are realized. The rankings of competing investments will be the same regardless of whether the total or average investment is used. One must merely recognize that rates of return using the average base will be substantially higher than those that are computed using the total original investment. Of course, the desirable rate of return used as a cut-off for accepting projects must be accordingly higher when average investment is used as the investment base.

Assume that a machine costs \$10,000 and is expected to increase after-tax profits of the business an average of \$3,000 a year for five years. Assuming zero salvage value of the machine at the end of its expected useful life and using straight-line depreciation for the sake of simplicity (depreciation = \$2,000 per year), the ROI of the investment would be:

$$R = \frac{\$3,000 - \$2,000}{\$10,000} = 10 \text{ percent}$$

The rate of return of a project is then compared with some rate that has been determined by management to be the cut-off criterion or the minimum desired rate of return (e.g., 10 percent). Alternative investments can be ranked using the rate of return -- the higher the rate of return of a particular project, the higher its ranking.

PROS AND CONS OF ROI

The ROI method is superior to the payback period as a measure of investment worth because it considers the added earnings of an investment over its entire expected useful life, not merely the added earnings up to the payback date. But ROI has some serious limitations. One of its weaknesses is that the rate of return computed is not directly comparable to figures used in the financial world in quoting interest rates on borrowed funds, yields on bonds and the like. Such rates are usually computed on the basis of capital in use from year to year rather than on average or initial investment. Thus it does not permit the direct comparison of projected returns on investments with the cost of borrowing money or with the returns that might be obtained on ownership capital if invested in financial securities.

A second limitation of ROI, and one that can be serious in some instances, is that it fails to take into consideration the timing of the capital outlays and benefits. Since this measure of investment worth does not enable management to reflect the fact that a dollar invested in a project today is more valuable than a dollar of benefits to be received sometime in the future -- a weakness of the payback period method also -- it can suggest incorrect decisions to management. This can occur particularly when the earnings or savings from an investment are likely to start at a relatively low level but increase significantly over time (e.g., a new product or new enterprise). In such a case, an investment could have an acceptable average rate of return but still be undesirable when the time value of money is considered. 8/

SUMMARY OF COMMONLY USED MEASURES OF INVESTMENT WORTH

We conclude that two measures widely used by managers in appraising the economic worth of investments -- payback period and ROI methods -- although better than nothing, have some serious limitations as guides to management. Two weaknesses common to both approaches are (1) the failure to consider the fact that a dollar in hand today is more valuable than a dollar to be received sometime in the future and (2) the inability to develop a cut-off criterion that is meaningful in terms of the cost of capital funds to the firm.

Two measures of investment worth that do not have these weaknesses, the so-called "net present value" and "yield of investment" or "internal rate of return" methods -- both referred to as "discounted cash flow measures" -- are available to managers. The remainder of this publication is aimed at explaining and illustrating the rationale and application of these two measures of investment worth.

8/ For a more complete explanation and a demonstration of the dangers of using the ROI method, see Bierman and Smidt, The Capital Budgeting Decision, 5th edition, Chapter 2.

3

TIME VALUE OF MONEY

Does money have a time value?
Is a dollar in hand today worth more to a manager than
a dollar to be received sometime in the future?

Managers would answer "yes" to these questions -- which are really the same question. Moreover, if queried, they would be likely to give more than one reason for their answer. The most commonly given reasons for preferring a dollar today to a dollar to be received sometime in the future are (1) alternative uses for today's dollar; (2) uncertainty; and (3) inflationary trends. Although each of these is a valid reason for placing more weight on today's dollars than on dollars to be received in the future, there are differences in the appropriate way to reflect the various factors in capital expenditure decision making.

We can think of the time value of money as having three separate and distinct components which can be represented as follows:

$$T = A + R + I$$

where T = the time value of money,
A = alternative uses of money or the pure time value of money,
R = an allowance or premium for risk or uncertainty,
and I = an allowance or premium for inflation.

The term "A" is the pure time value of money -- the return the investor would require for the use of his funds in the absence of uncertainty and inflation. "R" is a premium for the risk or uncertainty associated with investment proposals and may vary with the proposal being considered. "I" is a premium for inflation. It will vary according to the current and expected rate of inflation over the life of the proposal. A brief discussion of each component follows. More detailed discussions of uncertainty and inflation appear in Chapters 10 and 11.

ALTERNATIVE USES OF MONEY (A)

One reason that a dollar in hand today is more valuable than a dollar to be received five years from now stems from the investment possibilities for today's dollar. We can invest the dollar we have today to earn for us, thereby having considerably more than a dollar five years from now. The fact that money begets money is certainly one reason that expected future receipts must be brought back to today's worth -- must be discounted -- to make them comparable to investment outlays made today. The usual reason for discounting the cash inflows (benefits) expected from an investment is to determine whether the investment can be expected to yield more cash than alternative uses of the same amount of money.

RISK AND UNCERTAINTY (R)

A second reason given for preferring today's dollar to tomorrow's dollar is uncertainty. We live in an uncertain world, and frequently the more distant the future, the more uncertainty. Moreover, more uncertainty is associated with some capital expenditure projects than others. Thus, management must attempt to recognize uncertainty in analyzing the profit potential of investments. Although applying a higher discount rate to more risky investments is sometimes done in an attempt to allow for uncertainty, other methods of handling uncertainty such as those discussed in Chapter 10 are usually more appropriate.

INFLATION (I)

A third reason for a dollar in hand today being more valuable than a dollar to be received sometime in the future is the probability of continued inflationary tendencies. In view of the history of our economy, a manager should consider the likelihood of wages and the prices of other inputs continuing to rise as well as possible changes in the prices of products. If the manager expects changes in input or product prices, he or she may need to reflect such anticipated changes in the budgets of the costs and benefits likely to be associated with each investment alternative.

Regardless of the effect of inflation on prices of inputs and products and the resulting effect on net income, the fact remains that because of inflation a dollar of net income in the future will buy less than a dollar of net income at present. This has a meaning different from saying that a dollar in the future is worth less than a dollar now because of the fact that "money begets money." Using a higher discount rate to allow for inflationary possibilities is not appropriate except as discussed in Chapter 11.

CONCLUSION

It should be emphasized that management should apply the techniques discussed herein to reflect the time value of money because of alternative uses of money, rather than to allow for uncertainty and inflation. The additional reasons for money having a time value usually should be handled in other ways as will be discussed in Chapters 10 and 11.

4

PRESENT VALUE OF A FUTURE SUM OF MONEY

Several measures are available to assist managers in appraising the economic worth of investments. We have noted that two widely used measures, payback and return on investment, have some serious limitations as guides to management. A weakness of both is that they fail to consider the fact that a dollar in hand today is more valuable than a dollar to be received sometime in the future -- that money has a time value.

One basic reason that a dollar we have today is worth more than a dollar that we will receive sometime in the future is the idea that money begets money -- that a dollar we have today is worth more to us than a dollar we will not receive until sometime in the future because we can put today's dollar to work for us so it will grow. This idea is basic to the discounted cash flow techniques used by some managers to help them evaluate the economic worth of investment opportunities. The discounted cash flow techniques incorporate the time value of money concept. Since these techniques are based on the concept of the present value of a future sum of money, it is necessary to explain what is meant by "present value" before we proceed to explain the discounted cash flow measures.

The concept of present value is not difficult to comprehend. Money on hand today is more valuable than if it were to be received at a later date because the money on hand can be invested and therefore will "grow" over a period of time. For now, it will be less confusing if you forget about the complications of inflation and uncertainty and just focus on the general concept of the time value of money. To understand the concept of present value, it helps first to understand the concept of compound interest.

COMPOUND INTEREST

Compound interest means that interest is received on the interest earned but not withdrawn in previous periods as well as on the initial principal. The total amount of interest earned will depend on (1) the interest rate, (2) the frequency of compounding and (3) the number of years or periods. The formula for compound interest is:

$$A = P\,(1 + r)^n$$

where: A = future accumulated sum,
P = amount of money invested today,
r = rate of interest per period,
and n = number of years or periods.

Unless otherwise stated, the frequency of compounding is once per period.

Suppose that P = \$1.00, r = 9 percent and n = five years. Interest is compounded once per period, in this case annually.

$A = \$1.00\ (1.09)^5 = \$1.5386$ rounded to four decimal places or about \$1.54 when rounded to the nearest cent.

The year-by-year calculations will lead to the same result:

Year	Amount at beginning of year	1 + r	Amount at end of year
1	\$1.00	1.09	\$1.09
2	1.09	1.09	1.1881
3	1.1881	1.09	1.2950
4	1.2950	1.09	1.4116
5	1.4116	1.09	1.5386

Compound interest tables are available to save time in making the calculations. Table I in Appendix C provides compound interest factors for a variety of rates and periods. The user selects the rate and number of years or periods and picks the compound interest factor from the table. The factor for nine percent, five years is 1.5386. This factor, when multiplied by P, the amount invested today, results in A, the future accumulated sum.

It may help to understand the compound interest table if you use the following symbol to indicate a compound interest factor:

$$c_{n,i}$$

The small "c" denotes the fact that we are dealing with a compound interest factor, the subscript "n" indicates the number of years and "i" stands for the compound interest rate. Therefore,

$$c_{n,i} = (1 + r)^n$$

Substituting the compound interest factor into the original formula, we obtain:

$$A = Pc_{n,i}$$

Now if the factor from the compound interest table is substituted for n,i and P is known, A can be computed. For example, if P = \$1, n = 5 years and i = 9%.

$$A = \$1(1.5386) = \$1.5386$$

PRESENT VALUE

Using the example above, we can say that \$1.09 one year hence is the equivalent of \$1.00 today or that one dollar today is the present value of \$1.09 a year in the future. Similarly we can also say that \$1.54 to be received five years in the future is the equivalent of \$1.00 today. One dollar today is the present value of \$1.54 five years in the future (i.e., we have to invest \$1.00 today at 9 percent interest in order to have \$1.54 five years from now). Both statements are true providing the interest rate is 9 percent, compounded annually. By the same token we can compute the present value of \$1.00 to be realized at any future date.

The formula for present value is:

$$P = A \frac{1}{(1 + r)^n} = \frac{A}{(1 + r)^n}$$

where: P = present value of a future sum of money,
A = future sum of money,
r = rate of interest per period,
and n = number of years or periods.

The present value formula can be derived from the compound interest formula by algebraic manipulation. Present value is the inverse of compound interest.

Using our example, we can say that \$1.00 now is the present value of \$1.54 five years from now if the interest rate is nine percent compounded annually. Suppose we want to know the present value of \$1.00 to be paid or received five years from now. Think about this by referring to the compound interest example. Will the present value be greater or smaller than the future value, that is, the \$1.00 five years from now? At any interest rate above zero, the present value will be smaller than the future value. We can compute the present value by dividing the future value by the compound interest factor from Table I. This is exactly what the present value formula tells us to do.

$$P = \frac{\$1.00}{(1.09)^5} = \frac{\$1.00}{1.5386} = \$0.6499 \text{ or about } \$0.65$$

The present value of \$1.00 five years from now if the interest rate is nine percent compounded annually is \$0.65. If the \$0.65 was invested now at nine percent compounded annually, it would grow to \$1.00 at the end of five years.

The present value of a future sum can also be calculated by using the present value factor for appropriate interest rate and year from Table II. The factors in Table II are computed from the present value formula but in reality each factor in Table II is the inverse of the factor in the compound interest table for the same rate and number of years.

Use of the following symbol to indicate a present value factor may clarify Table II, the present value of \$1:

$$a_{n,i}$$

The small "a" denotes that we are dealing with a present value factor, the subscript "n" indicates the year in which the lump sum is received and "i" stands for the discount rate. Therefore,

$$a_{n,i} = \frac{1}{(1 + r)^n}$$

Substituting the present value factor into our original present value formula, we obtain:

$$P = Aa_{n,i}$$

If the factor from Table II is substituted for n,i and A is known, P can be computed. For example, if A = \$1, n = 5 years and i = 9%:

$$P = \$1(.6499) = \$.6499$$

Turning to higher finance, suppose an investment promises to return a total of $100 at the end of five years. What's the present value assuming that our interest rate is nine percent? Since $1.00 invested today at nine percent compounded annually would grow to $1.5386 in five years, we can find the present value of $100 at nine percent in five years by dividing $100 by $1.5386. This gives $64.99. Therefore, a sum of $64.99 that earns nine percent interest compounded annually will be worth $100 at the end of five years. The present value of $100 received five years from now discounted at nine percent is $64.99. The answer can also be calculated by multiplying $100 by 0.6499, which is the present value factor for nine percent, five years from Table II.

COMPOUND INTEREST AND PRESENT VALUE

A time line may help you understand the relationship between compound interest and present value.

If $100 is compounded at nine percent annually for five years it will grow to $153.86. If $64.99, which is the present value of $100 five years from now discounted at nine percent annually, is compounded at nine percent annually for five years it will grow to $100.00

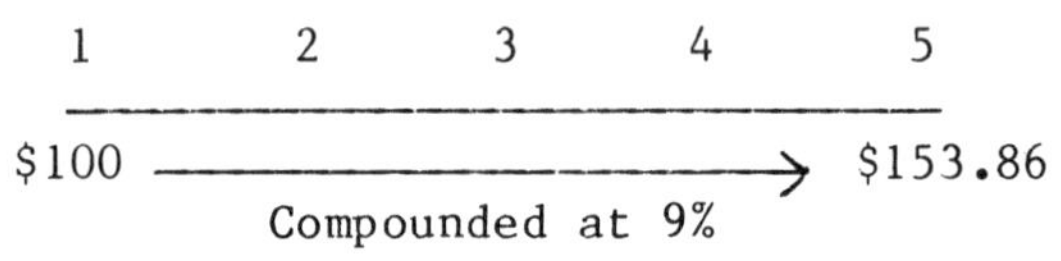

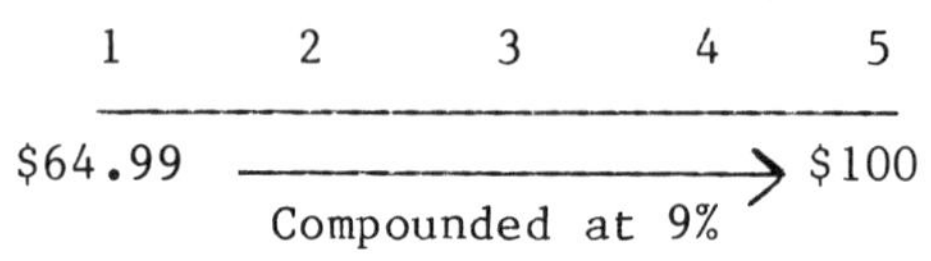

Conversely, if $153.86 is discounted at nine percent annually for five years, the present value will be $100. If $100 is discounted at nine percent annually for five years, the present value will be $64.99.

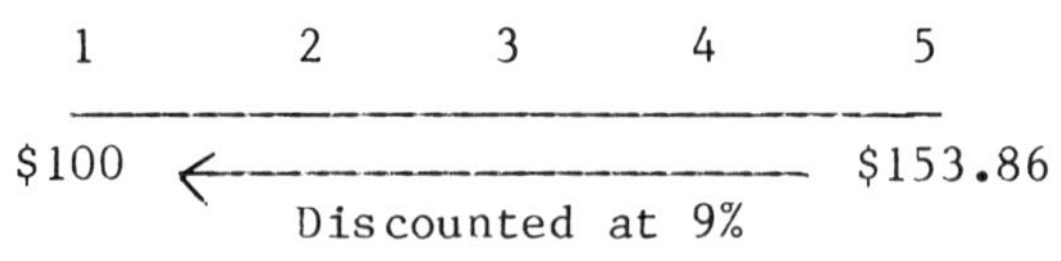

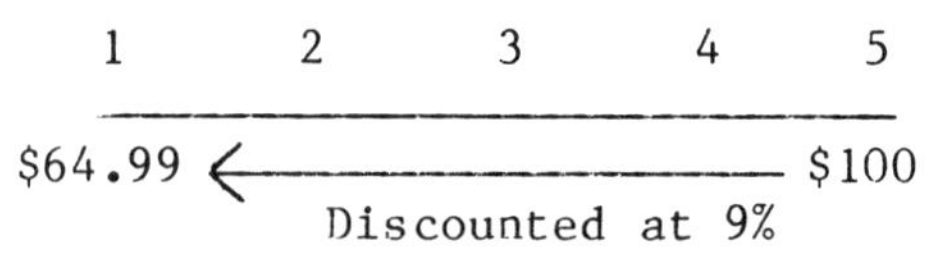

As the diagrams illustrate, compound interest is concerned with projecting forward an amount to be received from money invested today. Present value indicates the current worth of money to be paid or received in the future.

The reader is reminded that determining present value is just the reverse process from determining an accumulated amount under compound interest. When using compound interest, the present sum of money is known. We are interested in determining the amount of money that we will have sometime in the future if we invest and allow compound interest to accrue. When accumulating under compound interest, we advance or roll forward in time. The difference between our original amount and our accumulated amount is called "compound interest." When determining present value, the sum of money to be received in the future is known, and we are interested in determining present worth of that future sum. In determining present values -- when discounting -- we retreat or roll back in time. The difference between the future amount and the present value is called "compound discount."

PRESENT VALUE TABLES

The equivalent present value of any series of future cash outflows (e.g., capital outlays) and inflows (e.g., added earnings from an investment) can be determined by using the present value formula. Fortunately, we have tables of present value available so that we do not have to do such tedious calculations. Two tables are included in Appendix C (Tables II and III). One -- entitled The Present Value of $1 -- gives the present value of a dollar received or spent at one point in time, up to 50 years for various rates of discount. We have used this table in one of our examples. The other table --entitled The Present Value of $1 Per Year -- provides the present value of a dollar received each year for a number of years for various rates of discount -- the present value of a series of payments.

While present value tables simplify the calculations for those who use an ordinary calculator, if you have a calculator with the appropriate financial functions, it may be quicker to use the calculator alone and not use the tables.

A simple illustration may help clarify the difference between the two present value tables. Assume that your grandfather has promised to give you $1,000 five years from now. You want to determine the present worth of the $1,000. Let us further assume that your time value of money is 8 percent. In this case, since you will receive the $1,000 only once, Table II -- the present value of $1 -- is the appropriate table. Reading from the 8 percent column for year n = 5, we find the factor 0.6806 and determine that the present value of the gift is $1,000 x .6806 = $680.60. In other words, you would have to invest $680.60 today at 8 percent interest compounded annually in order to have $1,000 five years from now. So, if your grandfather would give you $680.60 now and you could invest it at 8 percent, it would be as good as receiving the $1,000 five years from now. In fact, it might be better because grandpa might not be here five years from now. But for now, we are ignoring uncertainty.

Now assume that you have an unusually generous grandfather. He announces that he is going to give you $1,000 per year for the next five years and that you will receive the first gift one year from now. What is the present value of this gift? In this situation, we could use Table II -- the present value of $1. The present value of the gift is shown below.

Year	(1) Amount to be received	(2) Present value of $1 received at 8%*	(3) Present value of gift**
1	$1,000	0.9259	$925.90
2	$1,000	0.8573	857.30
3	$1,000	0.7938	793.80
4	$1,000	0.7350	735.00
5	$1,000	0.6806	680.60
		Total present value of gift at 8% =	$3,992.60

*From Appendix C, Table II, the 8 percent column.
**Amount to be received (column 1) times present value of $1 to be received in a particular year (column 2).

However, since you will be receiving the same amount of money each year, we can save some multiplication and addition by using Table III -- present value of $1 received per period. Reading the 8 percent column for n = 5 in Table III, we see that the present value of a dollar received each year for five years (first payment in year one) is $3.9927. Each figure in Table III is the sum of the present value figures in Table II for periods up through and including the number of years and for the interest rate in which we are interested. The $1,000 per year for five years x 3.9927 = $3,992.70 which is the answer (within rounding error) we obtained by using Table II and more calculations.

We will use the following symbol to indicate a series of payments of equal amounts, sometimes called an annuity:

$$a_{1-n,i}$$

The subscript "1-n" indicates that the period for which the annuity will be received runs from the end of year 1 to the end of year n, and a and i have the same meaning as before. Keep in mind that we are now dealing with a series of payments rather than a lump sum at one point in time.

The formula to compute the present value of a series of equal payments is:

$$P = A_{1-n}\, a_{1-n,i}$$

The subscript "1-n" on A means that the amount A is received each year for n years, starting one year from now.

Returning to your unusually generous grandfather, if A = \$1,000, n = 5 and i = 8%, P = \$1,000(3.9927) = \$3,992.70.

You should keep in mind that the only purpose of Table III is to reduce the number of calculations when there is a series of payments of equal amounts.

TIMING OF CASH FLOWS AND FREQUENCY OF COMPOUNDING

It should be noted that our illustrations and the present value tables provided in this book assume that cash flows accrue in lump sums at the beginning and end of yearly periods (i.e., assumption of annual discounting). Of course business transactions actually occur throughout the year. Commonly the cash flows, particularly the net cash inflows (e.g., the benefits of lower payroll costs expected from a labor saving investment), will accrue to the firm throughout the year, not just at the end of the year. The present value techniques do not rest on the assumption of cash flows accruing in lump sums at the beginning or end of yearly periods. Present value tables are available to reflect any appropriate assumption concerning the timing of cash flows, including the assumption of continuous discounting.

The authors' experiences have indicated that the assumption of annual discounting usually provides sufficient precision. Only on rather infrequent occasions have they thought turning to monthly or continuous (as an approximation of daily) discounting was warranted. Remember that the manager of a business is discounting estimates (hopefully good estimates) of cash flows and consequently the degree of precision implied by monthly or continuous discounting may not be justified. One should also be mindful that annual discounting tends to lead to conservative estimates of the worth of investments -- in most instances the assumption of monthly or continuous discounting would result in the investment looking slightly more desirable than it does with the assumption of yearly discounting used in tables II and III.

If the assumption of monthly payments and discounting is appropriate, Table III can be used by dividing the annual discount rate and the annual payment by 12 and multiplying the number of years by 12. For example, assume we want to compute the present value of \$1200 per year for two years at 12 percent but also want to assume monthly payments. Using the 1 percent column and 24 periods, we find a present value factor of 21.2434 which, when multiplied by \$100, results in a present value of \$2,124. If annual payments were assumed, the present value would be \$1200 x 1.6901 = \$2028. Our Table III is limited in the combinations of interest rates and number of periods available for the assumption of monthly payments. However, tables are available for almost any reasonable rate of interest and number of payments. Those who have a calculator with the appropriate financial functions can easily compute present values for monthly or daily discounting if they believe it is necessary.

For those who insist on using the assumption of continuous cash flows and discounting, we have provided Table IV. To use Table IV we make use of the following formula:

$$P.V. = \frac{1 - e^{-rt}}{r}$$

where P.V. = present value factor,
e = 2.71828, the base of the natural system of logarithms,
r = rate of interest,
and t = number of years.

To use Table IV, we must know the value of e^{-rt} with which we are concerned. An example will illustrate the use of continuous payments and discounting and the use of Table IV.

Suppose we want the present value factor for 6 percent, 10 years:

$$P.V. = \frac{1 - e^{-(.06)(10)}}{.06} = \frac{1 - e^{-0.6}}{.06}$$

From Table IV we find that the value for $e^{-0.6}$ is 0.5488. Substituting, we have:

$$P.V. = \frac{1 - 0.5488}{.06} = \frac{0.4512}{.06} = 7.5200$$

The value 7.5200 can be compared with 7.3601 (from Table III) which is the present value of $1 per year for 10 years, assuming annual payments at the end of each year. The continuous factor is larger than the annual factor because the inflows are received earlier and compounded continuously.

The reader should keep in mind that while the assumption of annual cash flows and discounting may be conservative, the assumption of continuous discounting is likely to be optimistic for many business investment decisions.

A NOTE ON TIME LINES

Constructing a time line often will help visualize a problem and reduce confusion. The following time line covers three years:

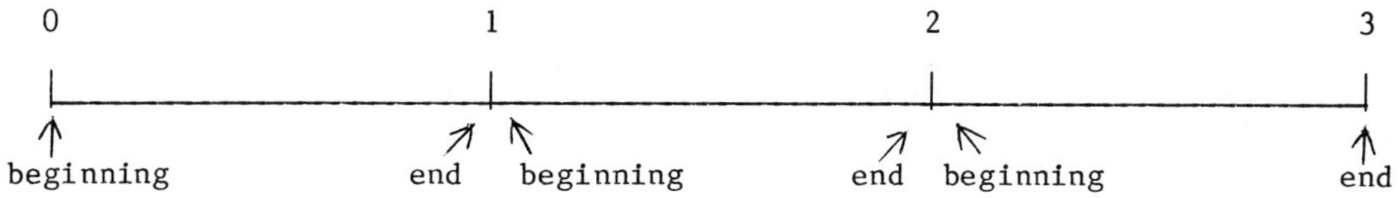

Time zero is always "now" and has nothing to do with the beginning of a calendar year, except by coincidence. The end of year 1 is one year after time zero, the end of year 2 is two years after "0", etc. The end of year 1 is for all practical purposes, the beginning of year 2.

PRESENT VALUE EXAMPLES

Perhaps applying present value to buying a bond and making a loan will help you understand the essence of present value -- namely that it provides a means for making valid comparisons between an immediate outlay and a later inflow of cash.

DETERMINATION OF BOND PRICE

Investment in a bond resembles most other conventional investments in that it consists of an initial outlay of cash followed by future cash inflows or returns. These monetary returns, in the case of a bond, are known with certainty at the time of purchase if the bond is to be held to maturity. The cash inflows are composed of a sequence of previously determined interest payments plus the payment of the bond's face value at maturity. The price which a buyer will be willing to pay for the bond is equal to the present value of the face amount due at maturity plus the present value of the future series of interest payments when both have been discounted at the prevailing market rate of interest. The market rate of interest, as opposed to the stated rate of interest, is the rate of return being earned by bonds of quality and maturity similar to those of the bond under consideration. This rate could be more tightly defined as the coupon rate on bonds of similar quality and maturity selling at par.

Let us illustrate this with the example of a $10,000 bond with a 9 percent coupon rate which matures in 5 years. Assume first that the prevailing rate of interest on similar bonds is 9%. Since the investor wants to gain an equitable return on his money, and the current market rate of interest is 9%, he will look for a 9% yield on his bond. By paying face value ($10,000), he will receive this 9% yield (interest of $900 per year for 5 years). The fact that the buyer would pay face value is borne out by the present value calculations.

Present value of annual interest payments = $900 x 3.8897* =	$3,500.73
Present value of amount due at maturity = $10,000 x 0.6499** =	6,499.00
Total present value of future receipts = bond price =	$9,999.73

*Present value of $1 received annually for five years at 9 percent as shown in Appendix C, Table III.

**Present value of $1 received in year five at 9 percent as shown in Appendix C, Table II.

The total present value of future receipts is equal to the face value of the bond, within rounding error caused by the use of four-place present value factors. Now suppose that the rate of return on bonds of similar quality and equal maturity has risen to 10%. No thoughtful investor will purchase a $10,000 bond earning 9% when he can buy a similar bond with a return of 10%.

In order to be competitive with the current market, the price of our bond must be discounted so that it too will earn a return of 10%. The price which a purchaser would be willing to pay may be determined through present value techniques as follows:

Present value of annual interest payments = $900 x 3.7908* =	$3,411.72
Present value of amount due at maturity = $10,000 x 0.6209** =	6,209.00
Bond price which purchaser would be willing to pay =	$9,620.72

*Present value of $1 received annually for five years at 10 percent as shown in Appendix C, Table III.

**Present value of $1 received in year five at 10 percent as shown in Appendix C, Table II.

The investor would purchase the bond, with the same interest and maturity cash inflows as before, only at a lower price. This lower price determines that the effective yield on the bond will now be 10%, and therefore competitive with the market.

Perhaps working through the schedule of cash flows during the life of our hypothetical bond will help demonstrate to the reader that paying $9,620.72 for this bond will yield a 10 percent return annually on the outstanding investment plus the $10,000 at maturity.

Initial investment =	$9,620.72
Plus return on investment for year 1 = $9,620.72 x .10 =	+962.07
Total	$10,582.79
Less interest collected year 1 = $10,000 x .09	-900.00
Equals investment balance at beginning of year 2 =	$ 9,682.79
Plus return on investment for year 2 = $9,682.79 x .10 =	+968.28
Total	$10,651.07
Less interest collected year 2 = $10,000 x .09 =	-900.00
Equals investment balance at beginning of year 3 =	$ 9,751.07
Plus return on investment for year 3 = $9,751.07 x .10 =	+975.11
Total	$10,726.18
Less interest collected year 3 = $10,000 x .09	-900.00
Equals investment balance at beginning of year 4 =	$ 9,826.18
Plus return on investment for year 4 = $9,826.18 x .10 =	+982.62
Total	$10,808.80
Less interest collected year 4 = $10,000 x .09 =	-900.00
Equals investment balance at beginning of year 5 =	$ 9,908.80
Plus return on investment for year 5 = $9,908.80 x .10 =	+990.88
Total	$10,899.68
Less interest collected year 5 = $10,000 x .09	-900.00
Remainder =	$ 9,999.68
Less principal collected year 5 =	-10,000.00
Equals investment balance at end of year 5 =	$ -0.32

Through the same logic, the reader should be able to reason that if the market rate of interest were lower (say 8% in our case) than the bond's stated rate of interest, the bond would be sold at a premium. Since other similar bonds are yielding 8%, our bond with its 9% coupon rate would be more valuable than the others. The market would bid up the price of our bond to approximately $10,399, where it too would give an 8% return.

YIELD OF LOAN

In the case of a loan which provides for repayment of principal and interest in equal annual installments, the rate of return to the lender is the rate of interest used to discount the flow of future installments. For example, suppose we had the possibility of lending $1,000 at a 10 percent rate of interest. Assume the loan was to be repaid in three annual installments. In this situation the borrower would have to pay $402.11 at the end of each of three years. As shown below, $1,000 is the present value of the 3 payments at 10 percent interest compounded annually.

Present value of three installment payments at 10 percent:
$402.11 x 2.4869* = $1,000

*Present value at 10 percent of $1 received annually for three years.

It is enlightening to demonstrate that three annual payments of $402.11 are exactly enough to provide for the repayment of the $1,000 principal plus 10 percent interest on the unpaid principal each year:

Amount of loan (i.e., initial investment)	$1,000.00
Plus interest on unpaid balance year 1 = $1,000 x 10%	100.00
Total	$1,100.00

Less installment collected end of year 1 =	-402.11
Equals unpaid balance beginning year 2 =	$ 697.89
Plus interest on unpaid balance year 2 = $697.89 x 10% =	69.79
Total	$ 767.68
Less installment collected end of year 2 =	-402.11
Equals unpaid balance beginning of year 3 =	$ 365.57
Plus interest on unpaid balance year 3 = $365.57 x 10%	36.56
Total	$ 402.13
Less installment collected year 3 =	-402.11
Balance	$ 0.02

Both the bond and the loan examples required an initial outlay. Both produced annual cash inflows that provided for recovery of the investment and for a rate of return on unrecovered investment. The examples demonstrate that present value provides a means for establishing equivalence between an immediate outlay and the stream of future earnings that the outlay will generate. In both examples, the initial investment is equal to the present value of the expected future proceeds.

SUMMARY

We have argued that the concept of the time value of money is an important one in evaluating capital expenditure projects because capital funds have alternative uses and, therefore, the timing of the benefits from an investment has a definite effect on its profitability. The dollar that we lay out today is not equivalent to a dollar that we will save in labor costs three years from now. The application of present value thinking permits managers to take into account the timing of the benefits of an investment. The discounted cash flow measures, which will be explained shortly, incorporate the present value concept.

5

FINANCIAL INFORMATION RELEVANT TO EVALUATING CAPITAL INVESTMENTS: CASH FLOWS

AD HOC ANALYSES USUALLY NEEDED

Since any investment requires an outlay of funds, it will normally be undertaken only if there is a belief that it will produce a subsequent inflow of funds that will provide for recovery of the initial commitment plus a yield or rate of return. The forecasting of the impact of each investment proposal in terms of the capital commitment and ensuing benefits is a crucial and difficult step in the capital expenditure decision-making process. Although some measures of investment worth are superior to others, no degree of refinement in later steps can overcome errors in these forecasts.

It is not the purpose of this publication to discuss the process of forecasting benefits of investment alternatives. We will merely mention several things that managers should keep in mind when forecasting the likely results of investments.

Although in some cases the firm's accounting system may provide the data required to analyze investment alternatives, usually an ad hoc analysis is needed to measure the full impact of the proposed investment on costs and revenues. This stems from the fact that accounting records reflect the past and, in analyzing the impacts of proposed investments, managers are interested in anticipated or future revenues and/or costs. Moreover, investments often involve a rearrangement of production inputs. In addition, when analyzing proposed investments, the relevant revenues and costs are the incremental revenues and costs, not total revenues or total costs. We are interested in the changes in revenues, the changes in costs, and, in turn, the changes in net cash inflows that are likely to result from making a particular capital expenditure. Traditional accounting records of a business report some revenue and expense items that are likely to be unaffected by the investment under consideration. Ad hoc analyses using budgeting techniques are usually required to measure the full impact of an investment on costs and revenues.

THE MEANING OF CASH FLOWS

Revenue and cost information relevant to evaluating capital investments should be expressed in terms of cash flows. For the most part, the costs and benefits that will be associated with an investment will take the form of cash flows into and out of the business during the expected economic lifetime of the investment. For example, the capital expenditure itself involves an outflow of funds -- either borrowed or owned --

from the business. The benefits of an investment will be in the form of cash inflows into the business either as a result of revenues increasing more than expenses, costs decreasing, or both.

NET INVESTMENT

It is important to identify the correct net investment associated with an investment proposal. For example, assume that a manager is analyzing the desirability of replacing an old machine that has an undepreciated book value of $25,000. The price of the new machine is $30,000 F.O.B. the manufacturing plant. There will be $500 for shipping charges associated with the delivery of the new machine and $1,000 installation charges for the new machine (including costs of removing old machine). If he buys the new machine, the old machine can be sold in the second-hand market (or a trade-in allowance will be made) for $10,000. The "net investment" or net capital outlay required by the proposed investment is $30,000 + $500 + $1,000 - $10,000 = $21,500. The net outflow of cash from the firm if the old machine is replaced by the new is $21,500. Note carefully that the $15,000 book loss on the old machine (i.e., $25,000 book value less $10,000 trade-in allowance) is irrelevant (except for its effect on income taxes, if any, and the consequent impact on cash outflows in the form of taxes). It represents neither an inflow or outflow that has any bearing on the decision. It represents an outflow that occurred when the machine was purchased. It is history and should be ignored in making decisions regarding the future except to the extent it will affect future income taxes. There is a strong tendency to tack a book loss on to the cost of the new investment -- but this is wrong! We are only interested in those fund flows that would result from the decision to buy the new machine.

In many investment proposals, not all the capital items are purchased at the beginning of the planning period (year 0). This can occur because some projects are developed in stages and not all capital items are needed immediately. Outflows for delayed capital items are handled in the same manner as the outflows for items purchased immediately except that they are discounted for the appropriate rate and time period to reflect the fact that the capital outflow will take place at some time in the future. Such outflows can be combined with annual cash operating outflows and inflows for the appropriate year. However, it usually is easier and less confusing to discount these capital outflows separately.

As an example, suppose that Baco Noir presently has no grapes but is considering the development of a vineyard. He would have some immediate cash outflows for land, vines, trellises, etc. When the grapes start producing in year 5 he will need a $65,000 grape harvester. At a 10 percent rate of discount, the present value of the outflow at the end of year 4 (or beginning of year 5) for the harvester would be $65,000 x 0.6830 = $44,395.

Frequently, investment projects will require that some capital items be replaced before the end of the planning period. For example, a project including capital outlays for equipment includes a building in which the equipment would be located. The potential investor wants to use a 15-year planning period and knows that the building would be usable for 15 years. He also knows that the equipment is likely to be worn out by the end of the tenth year. Therefore, the cash flows at the end of year ten (or beginning of year 11) would include the cost of replacing the equipment. The salvage value of the replaced equipment would either be deducted from the outflows for the new equipment or included as an inflow at the end of year 10.

NET CASH INFLOWS OR BENEFITS

In discussing the net cash inflows, proceeds, or benefits associated with an investment, it is useful to distinguish between two types of investments. One type consists of cost-reducing investments. An example would be the purchase of a machine to do work presently being done by hand labor. The "cash inflow" (or benefit) with which we are concerned on this type of investment consists of the amount by which the annual operating expenses will be reduced if the machine is purchased -- the net cost difference resulting from the investment. For example, if the use of the machine will allow us to escape in the first year $5,000 in labor costs that will have to be paid if we do not buy the machine, but increases our expenses for maintenance, repairs, and electricity by about $500 a year, the net benefits of the investment are said to be a net cash inflow (or net cash proceeds) of $4,500 in the first year. Costs that remain unchanged regardless of the decision are ignored.

The other type of investment consists of revenue-increasing investments, such as the expansion of the business (e.g., expanding a farm enterprise or opening another store). The "cash flows" in this case may consist of both changes in revenues and changes in costs. In such a case, the benefits can be expressed in terms of net cash inflows (or net cash proceeds) that will be equal to the expected additional revenue minus expected additional cash operating expenses other than interest. For example, a dairy farmer is considering a 20-cow herd expansion, which will require an additional investment of $50,000 immediately. Revenue in each of the next ten years is expected to increase by approximately $6,000 a year more than cash expenses for feed, labor, etc. are expected to increase. In this example, when analyzing whether the investment to expand dairy enterprise seems desirable, we would have a cash outflow of $50,000 immediately and net cash inflows of $6,000 in each of the succeeding 10 years.

PROJECTING FUTURE CASH FLOWS

As stated earlier, careful and reasonable projections of future cash flows are crucial to accurate evaluations of investment proposals. Our work with students and managers suggests that this is one of the most difficult and least understood parts of investment analysis. In the words of one student, "Almost anyone can learn to discount cash flows. The difficult part is projecting reasonable cash flows so that we can discount them." While we agree that the uncertainties of the future often make cash flow forecasting imprecise, we are concerned about the lack of understanding of the conceptual basis for projecting changes in receipts and expenses likely to result from a particular capital investment project. A complete treatment of the subject is outside the scope of this publication. Therefore, only a few of the crucial concepts will be discussed.1/

RELEVANT COSTS

Projected cash outflows should include only those costs that will be affected by the investment proposal under consideration. Costs that will not be altered by this investment are irrelevant and should be ignored. The terms committed costs and differential costs may be helpful to your thinking. Committed costs (sometimes called sunk or unaffected costs) are those costs that result from some past decision and will not be changed as a result of the decision currently under consideration. Differential costs (sometimes called incremental or avoidable costs) are those costs that will change or differ as a result of the decision now under consideration.

For example, suppose that Apple Grain, a grower of apples and grain, is considering the purchase of additional land and the development of a new orchard. The outlay for the land, trees, fertilizer, spray materials, added hired labor and everything else required to operate the new orchard are differential costs. For the purposes of this decision, the investment and costs of operating the orchard he already owns are irrelevant and can be considered committed. The fact that Apple has decided to purchase a mechanical pruner for the big trees in his old orchard and will purchase it even if the new orchard is not planted is irrelevant to the proposed orchard investment. The cash outflows for the pur-

1/ A good reference is Charles T. Horngren, Introduction to Management Accounting, 5th edition, Prentice Hall, 1981, Chapters 4 and 5.

chase and operation of the pruner in the old orchard must not be included in the cash flow budget for the proposed orchard.

Another classification of costs that may be helpful in projecting cash flows is opportunity costs vs. outlay costs. Outlay costs are costs that require an expenditure (outlay) of cash at some point in time. An opportunity cost is the value of a resource in some alternative use. For example, the opportunity cost of the labor of the owner-operator of a business is the amount that could be earned in alternative employment. Returning to our orchard example, the purchase of land to plant an orchard is an outlay cost and would be included in cash outflows, probably in year 0. Now suppose that instead of buying additional land on which to plant the orchard, Apple plans to plant trees on 50 acres of land which would otherwise be used for corn production in the future. There is no outlay cost because no land is purchased. However, there is an opportunity cost equivalent to the income over avoidable costs that could be earned from growing corn on the land each year during the planning period selected for the orchard. (We assume that corn is the highest paying alternative use for the land.) This opportunity cost (i.e., the net income given up by not growing corn) must be added to the annual orchard costs when projecting the cash flows. An alternative which may be a simpler way of handling the opportunity cost would be to enter as a cash outflow in year 0 the amount that the land could be sold for at that time or the amount that it would take to purchase a similar plot of land. Presumably, either of these values (which should be the same or at least close together), are the present values of the income that could be earned from operating the land in its highest paying use and therefore can be considered an approximation of the opportunity cost of the land to orchard production.

RELEVANT INCOME

While the preceding discussion has been in terms of costs, the same concepts can be applied to income. Only that income which will be affected by the investment proposal under consideration is included in projected cash flows. For example, the sale of fruit from the new orchard is income resulting from the orchard development. Increased sales of fruit from the old orchard due to a more complete pruning job with the mechanical pruner are not relevant income when considering the decision of whether to invest in the new orchard.

HANDLING DEPRECIATION AND INTEREST

It should be recognized that cash flows are not identical with profits or income as shown on accounting records and the operating statement. <u>In estimating cash flows, depreciation and other non-cash expenses are not included</u>. Depreciation, while recorded as an expense in the income statement, is not a cash outflow and is not considered in forecasting cash flows associated with an investment alternative. Including depreciation as a cash flow would be double counting. The cash outflow takes place at the time that the capital expenditure is made. Depreciation merely represents the recovery of this original expenditure over a period of years -- the accountant's attempt to allocate the original outlay over the expected useful life of the asset. It would be incorrect to include as a "cost" in an investment analysis both the initial outlay and the subsequent depreciation of it. Although depreciation per se is not considered in forecasting cash flows, the effect of depreciation as a tax shield must be considered in adjusting cash flows to an after-tax basis. (See Chapter 7.)

Interest expense and other financing costs normally are not considered in forecasting cash flows for the purposes of measuring the economic worth of an investment even though they involve cash disbursements. These expenses constitute part of the cost of capital, to be treated in Chapter 8, and help to determine minimum acceptable rates of return on investments. Since the methods of investment worth most helpful to managers take into account the cost of capital -- both borrowed and owned, financing costs such as interest are not included in estimating cash flows.

We will assume in our examples that cash, equal to the purchase price of an investment item, flows out of the business at the time the item is acquired rather than assuming that the cash outflow occurs as payments (principal and interest) on any loan used to acquire the item.1/ You should be aware that some analysts prefer to include down payments and loan payments in cash outflows rather than to assume that all the cash flows out at the time the item is purchased. Some of the implications of including principal and interest payments in cash flows are discussed in the next section.

LOAN PAYMENTS

It has been argued by some analysts that principal and interest payments should be included in cash flows. Those who advocate this method see the down payment, rather than the initial (total) capital investment, as the cash outflow required to acquire the capital asset. This argument is based partly on the idea that the investor is interested in the return that can be made on equity capital rather than on the total investment in the capital asset. The debt payments, both principal and interest, are then included in the expected annual cash flows associated with the project. These analysts argue that to the extent debt capital has a cost less than the required rate of return on equity (which is used as the discount rate), the leverage effect of the debt financing should be included in the investment analysis. We see several difficulties with this type of approach:

1. The amount of equity vs. debt capital used in the evaluation can significantly affect the desirability of projects. This becomes particularly relevant when comparing alternative projects, especially if differing proportions of debt and equity capital are used in the analysis.

2. In many situations, a capital asset is acquired entirely with debt capital -- the investor uses none of his or her cash to acquire the investment. Of course, part of the equity of the firm is used as a base for the loan with which to purchase the asset but it would be impossible to ascertain exactly how much. In such cases, it would be impossible to calculate the internal rate of return of the investment, although it would still be possible to calculate the net present value. However, the basic argument for using this method of analysis usually rests on the internal rate of return to be made on the owner's equity. If this rate cannot be computed, the argument has no meaning.

3. Capital investment proposals that are large in relation to the current size of the business often require that the entire business be refinanced. In such a case it would be very difficult and probably impossible to separate the loan payments related to the proposed investment from those related to the original business.

In addition, if the discount rate is based on the blend of debt and equity to be used in the future after the investment is made the leverage effect of financing the proposed investment will be included in the computation of the discount rate.

Finally, the analyst or investor who insists on including the loan payments in annual cash flows must remember when adjusting the payments to an after-tax basis that only the interest portion of the loan is an expense that may be claimed on the tax return.

1/For example, suppose that you are considering the purchase of a $100,000 combine and will borrow 75 percent of the money at 14 percent interest on a five year loan with annual payments of $21,846. We would assume in our analysis of this proposed investment that the $100,000 is an outflow at time zero rather than assuming that the down payment of $25,000 is an outflow at time zero and that $21,846 flows out each year, years one through five.

6

DISCOUNTED CASH FLOW MEASURES OF INVESTMENT WORTH

So far we have stressed the following viewpoints:

(1) The two measures of investment worth most widely used by managers, the payback and ROI suffer from serious weaknesses and can suggest incorrect decisions.

(2) A dollar received at some future date is worth less than a dollar in hand today.

(3) Therefore, no sums of money are comparable unless the comparison is made at the same point in time.

(4) The use of discounted cash flow methods requires that all relevant financial information be converted to actual cash flows (money receipts and payments), and that information which has no effect on cash flows be ignored.

We are now ready to consider two measures of investment worth that allow managers to reflect these concepts. These measures, both of which are called "discounted cash flow methods," are: (1) the net present value method and (2) the internal rate of return method. The underlying logic and mechanics of these two measures will be explained in succeeding pages using simple, hypothetical investment proposals as illustrations. These measures are applied to a number of real world investment problems of various types in Appendix B.

NET PRESENT VALUE METHOD OF EVALUATING INVESTMENTS

The net present value method of evaluating an investment, which allows management to reflect the time value of money, involves four steps. First each step will be explained. Then we will apply the steps to a simple illustrative investment.

The first step involves the determination of an "appropriate" discount rate. The discount rate should reflect the minimum acceptable rate of return. We will discuss later the answer to the question, "What is the appropriate discount rate?" As we will see, the appropriate discount rate depends in part on how the problems posed by uncertainty and inflation are handled in the analysis. A commonly-held viewpoint, until a few years ago, was that the appropriate discount was an estimate of the firm's weighted average cost of capital. 1/ Today, many question this. For now, let's leave it that the first step involves determining the minimum acceptable rate of return. The discount rate chosen by the decision maker represents the "cut off criterion" in judging whether or not an investment is desirable. Consequently the selection of the "correct" discount rate by management is of crucial concern. Later we will deal in some detail with the concept of the cost of capital and the selection of the appropriate discount factor.

The next step involves computing the present value of the net cash inflows -- the benefits -- that are expected to result if the capital expenditure is made. The present value of the net cash inflows (or net cash proceeds of an investment) discounted at the firm's minimum acceptable rate of return represents the maximum amount that a firm could afford to pay for the opportunity of making the investment without being financially worse off. This interpretation of the present value of the net cash inflows is crucial to understanding the net present value method.

The third step in the net present value method involves computing the present value of the cash outlays required by the investment. All of the capital outlays associated with some investments occur immediately, in which case the present value of the outlays is merely the net amount of additional capital needed if the investment is made (i.e., the present value of a dollar expended today is $1.00).

In the fourth step, the present value of the capital outlays -- as determined in Step 3 -- is subtracted from the present value of the net cash inflows -- as determined in Step 2. The difference is referred to as the net present value of the investment.

Criterion for Acceptance or Rejection. Management should accept all independent investments that have positive net present values and reject as undesirable all investments that have a negative net present value. 2/, 3/ This criterion for judging the desirability of investment proposals is based on the fact that the present value of net cash inflows when discounted with the minimum acceptable rate of return represents the maximum amount that the investor could afford to pay for the benefits expected and just "break even" (Step 2). If an investment has a positive net present value, it means that the investor could afford to pay more for the opportunity of making the investment than he

1/ Our definition of the cost of capital is a weighted average based on both debt and equity sources of capital. Cost of capital is not the rate of interest on borrowed money. The cost of capital is discussed in Chapter 8.

2/ The net present value method expressed in a formula is:

$$P = \frac{A_1}{(1+r)} + \frac{A_2}{(1+r)^2} + \ldots + \frac{A_n}{(1+r)^n} + \frac{S}{(1+r)^n}$$

where: P = present value of net cash inflows,

$A_1, A_2 \ldots A_n$ = cash inflow after taxes in years 1, 2, ... n,

r = the discount rate or minimum acceptable rate of return

n = expected economic life of the asset,

and S = salvage value of the asset in year n.

If $P > C$, the investment appears desirable, where

C = the present value of the capital expenditure required by the investment.

3/ There are a few exceptions to this criterion -- for example, in the case of "mutually exclusive investments" (i.e., for some reason only one of two or more investments can be undertaken) or in the case of capital rationing.

has to pay (i.e., present value of net cash inflows is greater than capital outlay required). An investment with a positive net present value will yield a return greater than the rate of return used as the standard in testing the proposal. On the other hand, if an investment proposal has a negative net present value, it would seem undesirable from an economic viewpoint because the investment outlays required exceed the maximum amount the firm could afford to pay without being financially worse off (i.e., the present value of the benefits expected).

ILLUSTRATIONS

To illustrate the net present value method, assume that a firm is considering an investment which would require a capital expenditure of $6,000 immediately and that it is expected to produce net cash inflows, through savings in cost of $1,500 a year for five years and have a salvage value of $1,500 at the end of the fifth year. Let's further assume that management, at least for this type of investment, has an 8 percent minimum acceptable rate of return. The net present value of this hypothetical investment can be computed as follows:

Present value of net cash inflows:

Year	(1) Cash inflows		(2) 8% discount factor*		(3) Present value of inflows**
1	$1,500	X	0.9259	=	$1,389
2	1,500	X	0.8573	=	1,286
3	1,500	X	0.7938	=	1,191
4	1,500	X	0.7350	=	1,103
5	3,000	X	0.6806	=	2,042

Present value of net cash inflows	$7,011
Minus present value of capital outlay	-6,000
Net present value of investment	$1,011

*Present value of $1 at 8 percent for respective years, Appendix C, Table II.
**Equals figure in column 1 times present value factor in column 2.

Since the net present value of the investment is positive (i.e., $1,011), the investment appears desirable as it will yield a return of something more than the 8 percent standard used in testing the proposal. Another way of viewing this comparison is to say that the firm could invest $1,011 more (or a total of $7,011) and still earn an 8 percent return on this investment. But it only needs to invest $6,000 -- thus the conclusion that the investment appears to be a sound one.

As a means of further illustrating the net present value technique, let's consider a decision involving the choice of equipment. Often equipment is available from several suppliers which offer essentially the same product insofar as function is concerned. However, there may be considerable variation between machines in original outlay and subsequent operating costs. The problem here becomes one of determining which type of equipment will be most advantageous from the standpoint of minimizing costs. For example, assume that a company is confronted with a choice of purchasing Machine A or Machine B. Both machines are suited to the needs of the firm, have expected lives of ten years and the same productive capacities. If Machine A is purchased the firm will incur a higher initial outlay but lower annual operating costs than with Machine B. A comparison of the two machines shows:

	Machine A	Machine B
Initial cost of equipment	$15,000	$12,000
Annual cash operating costs	8,000	8,700

Assume that the firm has a minimum acceptable rate of return or a cost of capital of 8 percent. We will ignore the impact of income taxes, which will be treated in a later section.

Since the revenues of the firm are assumed to be the same regardless of which machine is selected, the only difference between the two machines lies in the initial capital outlays and the future operating costs. Consequently the decision involves ascertaining which machine will minimize anticipated future costs. We compute the present value of the total expenditures involved with each machine. The more desirable investment will be the machine having the lowest present value of total future costs. The present value analysis is shown below.

	Machine A	Machine B
Present value of initial investment	$15,000	$12,000
Present value of annual operating costs		
$8,000 x 6.7101*	53,681	
$8,700 x 6.7101*		58,378
Total present value of costs	$68,681	$70,378

*6.7101 is the present value of $1 received annually in years 1 through 10 when the relevant time value of of money is 8 percent, Appendix C, Table III.

Since both machines have the same expected lives, we conclude from the above analysis that Machine A is the better investment since the present value of the costs associated with it are $70,378 - $68,681 = $1,697 lower than those of B.

At times it may be convenient to work only with the differences between alternative investments. If we take this approach in this illustration, the desirability of purchasing Machine A instead of B would involve determining whether the opportunity of saving $700 a year in operating costs for ten years justifies an additional capital outlay of $3,000. Analysis of just these differences gives exactly the same answer as the above analysis -- Machine A has a present value advantage of $1,697:

Present value of savings in operating costs associated with Machine A:

$700 x 6.7101 =	$4,697
Less additional investment required by Machine A =	-3,000
Net present value of difference	$1,697

A WARNING

One thing worthy of note emerges from the two proceding examples. The present value of costs of mutally exclusive alternatives -- as computed above -- are useful in decision making only if the lengths of life are the same for each alternative. The correct application of the net present value method to mutually exclusive investment alternatives with unequal lives is treated later. (See section entitled "Analyzing Investments with Unequal Lives.")

INTERNAL RATE OF RETURN METHOD OF EVALUATING INVESTMENTS

A second measure of investment worth that allows the decision maker to reflect the time value of money concept is the "internal rate of return method." This method is also called the "discounted rate of return," "yield of investment," "time-adjusted rate of return" or "marginal efficiency of capital" method. Like the net present value method considered previously, this measure incorporates the present value concept and offers management guidelines superior to measures such as payback and return on investment. We will discuss the relative merits of the internal rate of return approach as compared to the net present value method in a later section.

PROCEDURE AND RATIONALE

The internal rate of return (IRR) approach involves finding the discount rate that will make the present value of the cash inflows (the benefits) expected from an investment equal to the present value of the cash outlays required by the investment. This rate of discount is referred to as the "internal rate of return." The investment criterion is as follows: If the IRR of the investment is greater than the investor's minimum acceptable rate of return, the investment is desirable. 4/

Although short-cut procedures are available for use under some circumstances, basically the IRR must be found by trail and error. We discount with appropriate figures from present value tables until the IRR is found. First a discount rate is selected arbitrarily and the present value of the cash flows is determined for that rate. If the present value of the benefits thereby obtained is higher than the present value of the outflows (the capital outlay), a higher discount rate is selected on the next trial. This process is continued until the discount factor that makes the present value of the benefits equal to present value of outlays is found.

Computer programs to compute the internal rate of return are available but we will use our calculator to compute IRR. To illustrate the IRR method, let's start with the first example used to illustrate the net present value approach. This particular investment opportunity has the following cash flow:

Year	Cash flows	Item
0	$-6,000	Amount of capital expenditure
1	1,500	Net savings, year 1
2	1,500	Net savings, year 2
3	1,500	Net savings, year 3
4	1,500	Net savings, year 4
5	3,000	Net savings plus salvage value, year 5

We want to compute the IRR of this investment. Let's start by trying 5 percent. We compute the net present value of this investment using 5 percent as the discount rate.

4/The internal rate of return method expressed in a formula is:

$$C = \frac{A_1}{(1+r)} + \frac{A_2}{(1+r)^2} + \ldots + \frac{A_n}{(1+r)^n} + \frac{S}{(1+r)^n}$$

where: C = the present value of the capital expenditure required by the investment,

A_1, A_2, ..., A_n = cash inflow after taxes in years 1, 2, ..., n,

r = rate of return (or discount) that will exactly equate the income stream the cash inflows) to the capital outlay required by the investment,

n = expected economic life of the project,

and S = estimated salvage value of the asset in year n.

If $r > i$, where i = the investor's minimum acceptable rate of return, the investment is judged desirable.

Year	(1) Cash flows	(2) 5% Present-value factor*	(3) Present value**
1	$1,500	0.9524	$1,429
2	1,500	0.9070	1,361
3	1,500	0.8638	1,296
4	1,500	0.8227	1,234
5	3,000	0.7835	2,351
	Present value of cash inflows		$7,671
	Minus present value of capital outlay		-6,000
	Net present value or amount by which present value of cash inflows (benefits) exceeds present value of capital outlay at 5 percent =		$1,671

*Present value of $1 at 5 percent for respective years, Appendix C, Table II.
**Equals cash flows (column 1) times present value factor (column 2).

We are searching for the rate of discount that makes the sum of the present values of the cash flows equal to zero--the rate of return that makes the net present value zero. We have found that the net present value using 5 percent is a positive $1,671. We want to change the discount rate so that the net present value is zero. To decrease the net present value of the cash flows we should increase the rate of discount (thus causing the present value of the future cash flows that are positive to be smaller).

We might try next 15 percent as the rate of discount:

Year	Cash flows	15% Present-value factor	Present value
1	$1,500	0.8696	$1,304
2	1,500	0.7561	1,134
3	1,500	0.6575	986
4	1,500	0.5718	858
5	3,000	0.4972	1,497
Present value of cash inflows			$5,779
Minus present value of cash outflows			-6,000
Net present value at 15 percent =			$- 221

We see that with the 15 percent rate the present value of the cash inflows is about $221 less than the $6,000 initial investment or that the net present value = -$221. This indicates that a 15 percent rate of discount is too high. On the other hand, at a 5 percent rate of discount the present value of the cash inflows is considerably larger (by $1,671) than the $6,000 initial investment. Consequently, we know that the IRR of this particular investment is between 5 and 15 percent, and much closer to 15 percent than 5 percent. Interpolation over wide ranges is inaccurate because present value factors are not linear. Therefore we need to try a discount rate somewhat lower than 15 percent but much higher than 5 percent. Let's try 13 percent.

Year	Cash flows	13% Present-value factor	Present value
1	$1,500	0.8850	$1,328
2	1,500	0.7831	1,175
3	1,500	0.6931	1,040
4	1,500	0.6133	920
5	3,000	0.5428	1,628
	Present value of cash inflows		$6,091
	Minus present value of cash outflows		-6,000
	Net present value at 13 percent =		$ 91

The net present value of the investment at a 13 percent discount rate is $91, indicating that the IRR of the investment is slightly higher than 13 percent. At this point, we can say that the IRR of this investment is between 13 and 15 percent and closer to the former. For some purposes, knowing this may be good enough. Continuing the search (i.e., trying 14 percent) and interpolating would yield an estimate of 13.6 percent (13.558 to be more exact). But given the fact that the cash flows are forecasts of the future -- and consequently only approximations -- estimates of the internal rate of return in fractions of percent infer greater precision than actually exists. Consequently it may be appropriate to say that the expected internal rate of return of the investment is about 13 or 14 percent. If the investor's minimum acceptable rate of return or cost of capital were less than 13 percent, it would be a desirable investment.

By such a trial and error process, the approximately correct discount rate can be determined. This rate of discount is referred to as the "internal rate of return" of the investment. Remember that it is that rate of discount at which the benefits expected from a proposal have a discounted present value exactly equal to the present value of the outlays required.

As Bierman and Smidt point out, the internal rate of return of an investment has an interesting interpretation that can help us understand the method. "It represents the highest rate of interest an investor could afford to pay, without losing money, if all the funds to finance the investment were borrowed and the loan (principal and accrued interest) was repaid by application of the cash proceeds from the investment as they were earned." 6/ Because of this interpretation, it can be argued that an investment for which the yield is greater than the investor's minimum acceptable rate of return is desirable.

In the case of our hypothetical investment, if money were borrowed at an effective rate of 13.56 percent, the cash inflow produced by the project would exactly repay the hypothetical loan plus interest as demonstrated below:

Year	Unrecovered investment at beginning of year	Cash inflow during year	Return on unrecovered investment at 13.56%/yr*	Amount of Capital recovered at end of year	Unrecovered investment at end of year
1	$6,000	$1,500	$813	$ 687	$5,313
2	5,313	1,500	720	780	4,533
3	4,533	1,500	615	885	3,648
4	3,648	1,500	494	1,006	2,642
5	2,642	3,000	358	2,642	0

*Assumes unrecovered investment at beginning of each year earns interest for whole year and annual cash inflows are received at end of each year.

As seen, the cash inflows represent recovery of the initial investment plus annual interest at 13.56 percent on unrecovered capital over the life of investment. The IRR of the investment is computed on the basis of capital in use from year to year rather than on average or initial investment.

To clarify the trail and error procedure used to determine the internal rate of return of an investment and to illustrate the relationship between the net present value and the internal rate of return measures, it is helpful to use a graph where we plot the net present values of an investment against various alternative discount rates. In Figure 1, the vertical axis represents the net present value of the just discussed investment at various possible rates of discount, which are measured along the horizontal axis. The IRR is the point at which the net present value line crosses the horizontal axis since the IRR of an investment is that rate of discount that makes the net present value of an investment zero.

6/ Harold Bierman and Seymour Smidt, The Capital Budgeting Decision, The Macmillan Publishing Co., 5th edition, 1980, p. 31.

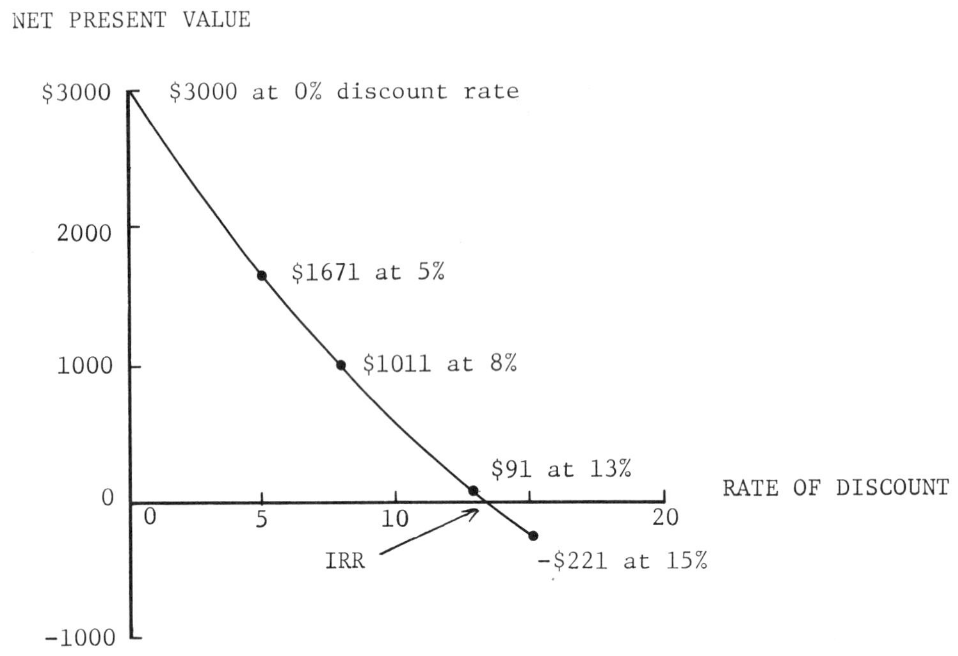

Figure 1. Relationship between Net Present Value and Internal Rate of Return

As shown, the net present value line drops as the discount rate increases. At discount rates lower than 13.6 percent, the net present value of our hypothetical investment is positive. At discount rates higher than 13.6 percent, the net present value is negative.

The IRR method suggests to the business manager that an investment should be made if the internal rate of return is greater than the firm's minimum acceptable rate of return. In the case of our hypothetical investment, the IRR method suggests that the investment is desirable if the firm's minimum acceptable rate of return is less than 13.6 percent. On the other hand, the net present value method suggests than an investment is desirable if the net present value is positive. We note that our illustrative investment has a positive net present value at any discount rate of less than 13.6 percent. Thus, in our hypothetical case, the two methods suggest the same decision, and normally -- if applied appropriately -- the two measures will be in agreement.

GUIDELINES FOR DETERMINING INTERNAL RATE OF RETURN

As explained earlier, we must determine the internal rate of return of an investment essentially by a trial and error process. Some guidelines for facilitating the trial and error search are discussed in Appendix A.

RELATIVE ADVANTAGES AND DISADVANTAGES OF NET PRESENT VALUE AND INTERNAL RATE OF RETURN METHODS

Both discounted cash flow measures of investment worth -- the net present value and internal rate of return methods -- offer managers powerful guides in making capital expenditure decisions. The payback period, ROI and other measures are less appropriate because they do not employ the time value of money concept. But what are the relative merits of the net present value and internal rate of return methods? It should be emphasized at the outset that both these discounted cash flow measures will suggest the same decision in most situations. But the net present value method and IRR method in some instances will lead to contradictory conclusions in ranking investment alternatives unless the IRR method is modified so that it involves an incremental type of analysis. Moreover, there are other advantages of each of these two measures which may lead the investor to favor one of these methods over the other.

Since the two discounted cash flow measures usually will suggest the same decision and since a thorough discussion of some of the relative merits becomes highly technical, we will merely summarize the advantages of each measure as we see them. The reader interested in a more thorough consideration is referred to other texts, especially The Capital Budgeting Decision, 5th edition, by Harold Bierman, Jr., and Seymour Smidt (Chapter 3) and Financial Management and Policy, 5th edition, by James C. Van Horne (Chapter 5).

ADVANTAGES OF NET PRESENT VALUE METHOD

The net present value method has at least three principal advantages as compared to the internal rate of return method:

(1) Unless an incremental analysis is used, 7/ the IRR method can suggest incorrect decisions on mutually exclusive investments whereas the net present value method will not. 8/ This is because the IRR method implicitly assumes that net cash inflows from an investment are reinvested at a rate of return equal to the internal rate of return of the investment being considered while the net present value method assumes that net cash inflows are reinvested at the firm's minimum acceptable rate of return. Therefore an incremental analysis must be made of the internal rate of return on the difference in cash flows between proposals. In short, the net present value method is an easier and more direct method of analyzing mutually exclusive alternatives than the IRR method.

(2) In some complex investments, an investment can have two different internal rates of return. This occurs in so-called "non-conventional investments" -- investments that have one or more periods of cash outflows interspersed with periods of cash inflows or proceeds.

(3) It is easier to use the net present value method than the IRR method.

ADVANTAGES OF THE INTERNAL RATE OF RETURN METHOD

The IRR method, on the other hand, has some advantages over the net present value method.

For one thing, it helps dramatize the desirability of an investment. To illustrate with an extreme example, two investments may both have net present values of $1,000 using a cost of capital of 10 percent as the discount rate. But one may require a capital outlay of only $5,000 to generate this positive net present value, whereas the other investment may require a capital outlay of $50,000 to generate the same net present value. Although theoretically all investments with a positive net present value should be undertaken, the practical manager likes to know how much "elbow room" there is before the firm is financially worse off because of having made the investment. The IRR method provides such insight.

7/ See, for example, James C. Van Horne, Financial Management and Policy, Prentice-Hall, Inc., 1980, Chapter 5.

8/ For an explanation of what is meant by "mutually exclusive" investments, see first page of Chapter 2.

Another advantage of the IRR method over the net present value method is that most managers find it easier to think in terms of internal rates of return (or yields) than in terms of net present value. The notion of rate of return is a common one in the business world as compared to the notion of net present value.

Lastly, extra care must be taken in using the net present value method in comparing alternative investments from which the benefits extend over unequal time periods -- that is, the investments have unequal lives. However, investments with unequal lives can be analyzed with the net present value method by using the concept of "annual equivalent flows" which will be treated later. (See section entitled "Analyzing Investments with Unequal Lives.")

SUMMARY OF RELATIVE MERITS

Both the net present value and IRR methods have advantages as compared to one another. The authors tend to prefer the net present value method to the IRR method, but they frequently apply both to the same investment alternatives. The important things to keep in mind are (1) that both methods are guides to which management should apply its judgement; (2) both -- if used correctly -- will suggest the same decision under most circumstances, and (3) both are superior to other measures of investment worth.

7

ADJUSTING CASH FLOWS FOR INCOME TAXES

A manager whose business or personal income is subject to income taxes should evaluate investment alternatives on an after-tax basis. Thus far we have bypassed the handling of corporate or individual income taxes in estimating cash flows by assuming that either the cash inflows had been adjusted for taxes or that the firm was exempt from income taxes. In this section we will illustrate how the effect of income taxes can be reflected in the net cash inflows for investment analysis purposes.

We do not intend to provide detailed information about business income taxes. Those unfamiliar with the application of income taxes to businesses should seek additional references such as tax guides published by IRS.

ORDINARY INCOME TAXES

Since federal and state income taxes are based upon net income (and not "cash inflows" as we have defined them), it is necessary to consider depreciation in determining the basis for the tax. Why? Because even though depreciation expense does not create a cash outflow at the time it is incurred, it is deductible from revenues in determining taxable income. Therefore, an amount of income equal to depreciation is shielded from taxes. Since depreciation reduces taxable income, it reduces taxes and the net cash outflow that would otherwise be incurred to make tax payments. The result is that after tax cash flows are greater than they would be if depreciation was not a deductible expense for tax purposes. The concepts and calculations that are appropriate to depreciation also apply to other "book" type expenses such as amortization of goodwill or amortization of patent expense.

DEPRECIATION

The Economic Recovery Tax Act of 1981 (ERTA) provided that for federal income tax purposes, depreciation on most assets acquired after 1980 is computed using the Accelerated Cost Recovery System which frequently is described with the acronym ACRS, pronounced "acres". ACRS provides for four classes of personal property: 3 year, 5 year, 10 year, and 15 year public utility and for a 15 year class which applies to most real property. Some real estate is included in the 10 year class. Most equipment is included in the 5 year class. Automobiles and trucks under 13,000 lbs. are included in the 3 year class. The reader should consult publications from IRS or one of commercial tax services to find the appropriate class for investment items not discussed here. Each class of property may be depreciated with either rapid depreciation using the percentages in the table below or with one of three straight line options. Property is depreciated without regard to salvage value.

RAPID (REGULAR) RECOVERY PERCENTAGES UNDER ACRS

Recovery Year	Type of Property 3-Year	5-Year	10-Year	15-Year Public Utility	15-Year Real Estate 1/
	-----Percentage-----				
1	25	15	8	5	12
2	38	22	14	10	10
3	37	21	12	9	9
4	--	21	10	8	8
5	--	21	10	7	7
6	--	--	10	7	6
7	--	--	9	6	6
8	--	--	9	6	6
9	--	--	9	6	6
10	--	--	9	6	5
11-15 (per year)	--	--	--	6	5

1/ Percentage deductions in this column apply only to 15-year property placed in service during the first month of the tax year. Fifteen-year property placed in service later in the tax year will earn 1 percent per month in the first year.

A provision of ERTA provides that the taxpayer may elect to expense a portion of depreciable assets acquired in any year. This usually is called the "Section 179 election" because the election is provided for in that section of the Internal Revenue Code. The limit on the amount that may be expensed is $7,500 in 1984 and 1985 and $10,000 in 1986 and later. The property for which such an election is made must be eligible for ACRS and for investment credit. If the Section 179 election is made, investment credit may not be claimed on the amount expensed.

The Tax Equity and Fiscal Responsibility Act of 1982 (TEFRA) provides that for assets acquired after 1982, the basis for depreciaion must be reduced by 50 percent of any allowable regular investment credit, energy investment credit or the credit for rehabilitating certified historic structures. The taxpayer has the option of reducing the regular investment credit by two percentage points rather than reducing the basis but this option does not apply to the other two credits. Including investment credit in cash flows will be presented in a later section.

Some states do not allow taxpayers to use ACRS when filing state tax returns. In the interest of simplicity, our examples will assume that ACRS is used for both federal and state income tax purposes.

For assets acquired prior to ERTA, depreciation usually is claimed using either straight line or one of two accelerated methods, declining balance or sum-of-the-years'-digits. While these methods currently are being used by many firms, they are almost irrelevant for planning purposes because very few assets acquired will be eligible for such methods.

AFTER TAX CASH FLOWS

We will demonstrate three methods that may be used to adjust annual cash flows to an after-tax basis. For each of these illustrations, assume that we are considering the purchase of a piece of equipment which is expected to produce annual net cash inflows of $7,000 a year before taxes. Assume further that the firm is in the 52 percent (federal plus state) marginal income tax bracket. The cost of the asset is $30,000 and it is expected to have a terminal value of $2,000 at the end of the 15 year planning period. The asset is 5 year ACRS property and it will be depreciated with the percentages for 5 year rapid cost recovery. The illustrations of computation of added after-tax cash flows will be based on the first year's depreciation of $30,000 (.15) = $4,500. Calculations for subsequent years would use depreciation based on the applicable percentage. After year five, there will be no depreciation tax shield because the asset will be fully depreciated.

For simplicity, our example will use the two point reduction in investment credit rather than the reduction in basis. You should be aware that in many cases, the reduction in basis is the superior option. A good exercise for you would be to compare the two alternatives for our example. Just reduce the basis for depreciation by one-half the Federal investment credit before computing depreciation and depreciation tax savings.

Method #1: "Income Statement Method"

Added cash inflow before taxes, year 1	$7,000
Less: Depreciation = $30,000 (.15) =	4,500
Estimated increase in taxable income from investment =	$2,500
Expected increase in taxes: $2,500 x .52	1,300
Increase in net income after taxes =	1,200
Plus: Depreciation	4,500
Added cash inflow after taxes, year 1	$5,700

The added cash inflow to which the discount factor should be applied would be $5,700 rather than the $7,000 increase in before-tax cash flow or the $1,200 increase in net income after taxes.

The "income statement approach" may be further documented by comparing the current income statement of the firm as a whole to the firm's projected income statement for the first year after the machine has been purchased. Assume that sales increase $27,000 and operating costs increase by $20,000, giving a $7,000 increase in net cash inflow before taxes.

Income Statement

	Without Machine	With Machine Year 1	Difference
1. Sales (Receipts)	$200,000	$227,000	$27,000
2. Less: Costs (Expenses)	140,000	160,000	20,000
3. Depreciation	10,000	14,500	4,500
4. Taxable Income	50,000	52,500	2,500
5. Income Tax	26,000	27,300	1,300
6. Profit	24,000	25,200	1,200
7. Cash Flow (3+6)	$ 34,000	$ 39,700	$ 5,700

The difference in after-tax cash inflow is $5,700, the same as in the calculations above.

Method #2: "No Name Method"

This technique is a variation of the income statement approach. Instead of calculating the profit or net income after taxes and then adding the depreciation expense back to this figure, this approach simply calculates the amount of the tax and subtracts it from the cash inflow before taxes.

Added cash inflow before taxes, year 1	$7,000
Less: Depreciation = $30,000 (.15) =	4,500
Estimated increase in taxable income from investment	2,500
Expected increase in taxes: $2,500 x .52	1,300
Added cash inflow before taxes, year 1	$7,000
Less: Increase in income taxes =	1,300
Added cash inflow after taxes, year 1	$5,700

Again, the result is an added net cash inflow after taxes of $5,700 in year 1.

Method #3: "Component Method"

The component method is based on the following three equations:

1) After-tax receipts = Before-tax receipts (1 - tax rate)

2) After-tax expenses = Before-tax expenses (1 - tax rate)

3) Tax savings from depreciation = (depreciation) (tax rate)

These rules of the component method may be derived from the income statement approach. Remember that net cash flows before taxes are composed of cash receipts less cash expenses. The income statement format gives us:

Receipts, before taxes
Less: Expenses, before taxes
Less: Depreciation
Taxable income

Less: Taxes
Net income after taxes

Plus: Depreciation
Net cash inflow after taxes

To solve algebraically for the component formulas, we introduce the following notation:

Let R = receipts, before taxes,

E = expenses, before taxes

D = depreciation,

t = marginal tax rate,

Z = after tax cash inflow

The above income statement gives us

$$(R - E - D) - t(R - E - D) + D = Z$$

and regrouping the terms shows that

$$R - E - D - tR + tE + tD + D = Z$$

$$R - tR - E + tE - D + tD + D = Z$$

$$R(1 - t) - E(1 - t) + tD \qquad = Z$$

or Receipts, before taxes (1 - tax rate)

Less: Expenses, before tax (1 - tax rate)

Plus: Depreciation (tax rate)

Equals: Net cash inflow after taxes

Thus, the three component equations may be used to determine any change in after-tax income by calculating incremental after-tax cash flows. In our example for year 1 we find:

After-tax cash receipts = \$27,000 (1 - .52) =	\$12,960
Less: After-tax cash expenses = \$20,000 (1 - .52) =	9,600
Plus: Tax savings from depreciation = \$4,500 (.52) =	2,340
Equals: Annual net cash inflow after taxes =	\$ 5,700

The resulting \$5,700 agrees with the answer determined with the previous methods.

A simplified version of the component method combines the receipt and expense components into before tax cash net inflow and applies (1 - t). Using our example:

After tax cash inflow = \$7,000 (1 - .52) =	\$3,360
Plus: Tax savings from depreciation = \$4,500 (.52) =	2,340
Equals: Annual net cash inflow after taxes =	\$5,700

PRESENT VALUE CALCULATIONS

Now we will compute the present value of the after-tax cash flows for this example. At this point we will not include investment credit and salvage value. The after-tax cost of capital or discount rate is assumed to be 8 percent. First we will use the no-name method and then the component method.

No Name Method

Year	Before-tax cash inflow	Depreciation	Taxable income	.52 Tax	After-tax cash inflow	Factor	Present Value
1	\$7,000	\$4,500	\$2,500	\$1,300	\$5,700	0.9259	\$ 5,278
2	7,000	6,600	400	208	6,792	0.8573	5,823
3	7,000	6,300	700	364	6,636	0.7938	5,268
4	7,000	6,300	700	364	6,636	0.7350	4,877
5	7,000	6,300	700	364	6,636	0.6806	4,517
6-15	7,000	0	7,000	3,640	3,360	4.5668	15,344

Present value of net cash inflow after taxes = \$41,107

Component Method

Use of the present value of depreciation table for 5 year rapid ACRS (Table VII) simplifies the mechanics of the component method. To utilize this table, it is necessary to determine the appropriate discount rate and then to multiply the capital outlay to be depreciated times the tax rate and then by the appropriate present value factor. The annual depreciation and tax saving are not calculated. The present value of the depreciation tax savings is computed with one calculation. The calculation of the present value of the after-tax cash inflows using Table VII and the component method follows:

After-tax cash inflow, yrs. 1-15 = $7,000 (1 - .52) (8.5595) =		$28,760
Plus:	Tax savings from depreciation, yrs. 1-5 = $30,000 (.52) (0.7915)* =	12,347
Equals:	Present value of net cash inflow after taxes =	$41,107

*Factor for 8 percent, 5 year rapid ACRS, from Table VII.

Present values of after-tax cash flows using ACRS for 3, 10 and 15 year property may be calculated by using the appropriate factors from Table VII. Tables V and VI may be used for items eligible for sum-of-the-years' digits and double declining balance depreciation. Most items acquired after 1980 are not eligible for these methods.

A note of caution must be stated about the use of Table VI. The table assumes that there is no salvage value for income tax purposes. In using declining balance depreciation, salvage value is not deducted before starting to compute depreciation. Salvage value is accounted for by stopping depreciation when the salvage value is reached or by taking it into account at the time of switchover to straight line. To include such computations in a table would require a separate table for each possible salvage percentage. If an assumption of zero salvage value is not logical, then Table VI should not be used. Internal Revenue Service regulations allow salvage values under 10 percent of the original investment to be disregarded in computing depreciation for non-ACRS property. Therefore Table VI may be used unless salvage value is expected to be greater than 10 percent because the zero salvage value assumption can be made.

Use of Table V (for sum-of-the-years' digits) does not have the salvage value problem. One simply deducts the salvage value from the initial investment before applying the factor.

ACCELERATED VS. STRAIGHT LINE DEPRECIATION

Under the provisions of ERTA, the taxpayer may choose one of three straight line options rather than accelerated depreciation. For 5 year property, the straight line options are 5, 12, and 25 year straight line. The five year option will reduce the present value of depreciation tax savings slightly. A more likely option for a taxpayer who doesn't want to depreciate the asset in a period as short as 5 years would be to choose 12 year straight line. We will illustrate the effect of this option on the present value of cash inflows in comparison to the 5 year accelerated option using the component method. To be consistent with the half-year convention built into the rapid ACRS percentages, we should use a half year's depreciation in year 1 and the remaining half in year 13 but for simplicity we will use 1/12 of the total depreciation in each of the first 12 years.

After-tax cash inflow, yrs. 1-15 = $7,000 (1 - .52) (8.5595)	=	$28,760
Plus: Tax savings from depreciation = $30,000 ÷ 12 (.52) (7.5361)*	=	9,797
Equals: Present value of after-tax cash inflow =		$38,557

*Factor for 8%, 12 years from Table III.

The difference in present value of after tax cash inflow from using 12 year straight line rather than 5 year accelerated is $2,550, which is the difference in the present value of the depreciation tax savings between the two methods.

INVESTMENT CREDIT

The federal investment credit currently (1984) in effect allows income tax-paying businesses to deduct from their federal income taxes up to 10 percent of the cost of eligible investments that meet certain qualifications within specific limitations. In addition there are investment credits for specific energy investments and for rehabilitating certified historic structures.

The 10 percent credit is allowed on the entire amount of investment in 5, 10 and 15 year ACRS property if such property is eligible for investment credit. Three year property receives a 60 percent qualification for investment credit, making the effective investment credit on such property 6 percent. Most three and five year property is eligible for investment credit but many 10 and 15 year items are not eligible. In addition, some states provide investment credits. These should be included in cash flows if a business is located in a state which provides for such credits. If the firm has an income tax liability at least equal to the investment credit that will be earned if the investment is made, the savings in taxes that would be realized from using the investment tax credit should be reflected in the cash flows used in analyzing the investment proposal.

Returning to the example described earlier, let's illustrate how we can bring into consideration the Federal investment credit, assuming the property is eligible for the full 10 percent credit. We did not opt to reduce the basis for depreciation by one-half of the allowable investment credit. Therefore we will need to subtract two percentage points from the 10 percent rate and use eight percent in our analysis.

Investment credit = $30,000 x .08 = $2,400

The investment credit is an after tax cash inflow because it is a reduction in taxes. The investment credit should be included as a cash inflow in the year it is expected to be used to reduce taxes. In most cases, this will be at a time later than the investment is made. A good rule of thumb is to make the investment credit a cash inflow one year after the outflow to acquire the investment. For example, if the outflow occurs at time zero, the investment credit would be an inflow at year 1.

TERMINAL VALUES

Expected terminal values of items included in an investment proposal usually are considered to be cash inflows at the end of the planning period. The usual assumption is that items are sold at the end of the planning period. Any gain, that is the difference between the expected sale price and the book value, will be taxable as either ordinary income or capital gain income. The latter is discussed in the next section. An example of computing the after-tax cash inflow from the terminal value, assuming ordinary gain, is shown below.

Let's assume that the expected terminal value of the $30,000 machine used in the example above is $2,000 at the end of 15 years. Salvage value is ignored when using ACRS depreciation so the machine will be fully depreciated at the end of either five or twelve years and will have a zero book value at the end of the 15 year planning period. Therefore the entire $2,000 selling price will be gain, and in this example it will be ordinary gain. With a tax rate of .52, the after tax cash inflow at the end of 15 will be: $2,000 (1 - .52) = $960. The $960 discounted to the present at 8 percent results in a present value of $960 (.3152) = $303.

THE COMPLETE EXAMPLE

The complete example will compute the net present value, including the outflow, annual after-tax cash inflows, depreciation tax savings with 5 year ACRS, investment credit and salvage value. The component method and an 8 percent after-tax discount rate will be used. A time line will be used to help you visualize the after-tax cash flows.

	0	1	2	3	4	5	6	15
Outlay =	-30,000							
Net inflows =		3,360 .	. .	. .	. .	. .	. . . . . .	3,360
Depr. tax savings =		2,340	3,432	3,276	3,276	3,276		
Investment credit =		2,400						
Terminal value =								960

PRESENT VALUE CALCULATIONS

The calculations will begin with before-tax cash flows. If the relationship between the numbers below and the after tax cash flows above are not obvious to you, make some calculations to convince yourself.

Years		Present Value
1-15	After-tax cash inflow = $7,000 (1 - .52) (8.5595) =	$28,760
1-5	Depreciation tax savings = $30,000 (.52) (0.7915) =	12,347
1	Investment credit = $30,000 (.08) (0.9259) =	2,222
15	Terminal value = $2,000 (1 - .52) (0.3152) =	303
	Present value of after-tax cash inflows =	$43,632
	Less: Present value of outlay	30,000
	Net present value =	$13,632

CAPITAL GAIN INCOME

In some proposed capital investments a substantial part of the cash inflows may be received as income subject to capital gains tax rather than to ordinary income tax. The general provisions of the Federal tax law follow. For detail see IRS publications. Currently (1984) for individuals, 60 percent of income qualifying for capital gains treatment on Federal returns is excluded from taxable income, making the effective tax rate on such income only 40 percent of the rate paid on ordinary income. However, in some cases the taxpayer may be subject to a minimum income tax on the portion of capital gain excluded from taxable income. For corporations, capital gains are taxed at an alternative rate of 28 percent if this rate results in a lower tax than the rate on ordinary income. Many states also have different rates for capital gain income than for ordinary income.

Under some conditions, income from sales of land, buildings and livestock may be treated as income from sales of capital assets rather than as ordinary income. If a proposed investment would result in some of the cash inflow being subject to capital gain rather than ordinary income tax, this fact should be recognized in adjusting cash flows to an after-tax basis.

The two types of investments most likely to result in income subject to capital gains treatment are land and dairy and breeding livestock. Buildings may also result in capital gain income. Although it is possible, equipment will practically never result in capital gain.

For example, suppose that a dairy farmer is considering a business expansion that would result in an additional $3,000 of cattle sales each year that would be eligible for capital gains treatment. Assume he is in the 30 percent tax bracket. In adjusting the annual cash flows to an after-tax basis, this $3,000 should be reduced by $360 rather than $900. The $360 = $3,000 x .40 x .30 and accounts for the fact that only 40 percent of capital gain is included in taxable income.

While investment in breeding livestock is likely to result in annual income that may be eligible for capital gains treatment, land and buildings normally would result in capital gain income only if the entire business (or a substantial segment of it) were sold. Most proposed land and building investments are not made with the idea that they will be sold at some specific future date. But many investments will result in some terminal value at the end of the time period (say five or ten years) that seems legitimate for planning purposes. This terminal value may result in some income that would be capital gain if the items with terminal value actually were sold. For example, the value of a piece of land might logically be expected to be higher at the end of a ten-year planning period than at the beginning and thus result in capital gain (if sold). A building could result in capital gain if sold for more than the depreciated book value. However, there are certain limitations on treatment of the gain from sale of buildings as capital gain.

How do we determine a realistic terminal value of an asset at the end of the planning period? This terminal value should be our best estimate of the sale value of the asset at that time. One might argue that the terminal value should somehow represent the discounted value of the income stream that could be expected beyond the end of the planning period. Thus the terminal value of an asset is determined by assuming the asset will be sold at the end of the planning period even though we may know that the asset will not be sold.

The asset may, in fact, be worth more to the investor at the end of the planning period than the probable sale value. If so (and considering the effects of capital gains treatment of the income if the asset is sold and ordinary tax treatment of the income received if the item is held), it should be held rather than sold. Thus, the probable sale value of the asset at the end of the planning period, assuming it is realistically determined, is a conservative value. It may actually be worth more if held. In no case should it be worth less to the investor because if it is worth less to hold than to sell, it should be sold.

Using land as an example, let's look at the adjustment of terminal values to an after-tax basis. Assume that land which would now cost $50,000 could reasonably be expected to be worth $75,000 at the end of a ten-year planning period. It is reasonable to include $75,000 as a cash inflow (before taxes) at the end of year ten to recognize that the land would be worth that much if sold at the end of year ten. How do we adjust this $75,000 to an after-tax basis? Do we reduce it by the amount of tax on the ordinary income (say 50 percent) of the investor? Or do we apply the capital gains tax rate? In fact, there will be no tax on the first $50,000 because land may not be depreciated so the book value will be $50,000. But should the $25,000 gain be considered as ordinary or as capital gain income? The $25,000 would be considered capital gain under current (1984) tax rules. Capital gain tax rates should be used in adjusting this cash inflow to an after-tax basis.

To summarize, it can be said that some investments logically can be expected to produce income that will be subject to capital gain rather than ordinary income tax and that capital gain rather ordinary tax rates should be used to adjust such income to an after-tax basis. But a prospective investor should be careful not to apply capital gain tax rates to income that in reality will be ordinary income at the time it is received.

8

THE COST OF CAPITAL

We have made frequent reference to the "cost of capital" as being the cutoff rate or minimum rate of return which must be earned by a capital expenditure project to make it acceptable. In both discounted cash flow measures of investment worth (i.e., the net present value and internal rate of return methods) the need for an appropriate discount rate for the firm is explicit. We cannot determine the net present value of a project without using a reasonable discount rate. Similarly, we must compare the internal rate of return of an investment proposal with some standard to determine whether the project is a desirable one.

We will now introduce the term "weighted average cost of capital" or WACC. We have really been using WACC all along when talking about the cost of capital, but didn't want to burden our faithful readers with all those words until we were ready to define the term -- which we will do a couple of pages hence. While we will continue to use the term cost of capital, it will mean WACC unless otherwise stated. Whether the weighted average of cost of capital to the firm provides us with an appropriate discount rate is a question which is currently under debate by academicians and business managers. Before presenting our rationale for using WACC as the discount rate, we will discuss briefly some of the controversy surrounding the choice of an appropriate discount rate.

In Chapter 3 we discussed three components of the time value of money, (1) alternative uses of money or the pure time value of money; (2) risk and uncertainty; and (3) inflation. The cost of capital is closely related to the time value of money and includes the same three components.

Some authors argue that the appropriate discount rate for evaluating investment proposals is the default-free rate rather than the weighted average cost of capital. 1/ Conceptually, the default-free rate is one at which a banker could lend with no significant danger of not being repaid or one at which a business could borrow if the creditor believed that there was no significant danger of default. Presumably, both these descriptions describe the same rate. Those who advocate use of the default-free rate for discounting also adovcate that uncertainty about future cash flows be handled in other ways, such as those we will discuss in Chapter 10.

1/ For example, see Bierman and Smidt, The Capital Budgeting Decision, Macmillan Publishing Co., Inc., 5th ed., 1980.

One might conclude that the default-free rate is one which measures only the pure time value of money. Perhaps the best approximation of the default free rate is the rate on government debt such as treasury bills. Anyone has the opportunity of investing money at these rates with practically no risk of default.

While the interest rate on government debt can be considered the default free rate, this rate is not inflation-free. Buyers of government securities may believe there will be no default, but they probably do not believe there will be no inflation during the period they hold the securities. Therefore, the return on such securities must include some premium for inflation as well as a factor for the pure time value of money. Therefore, the decision makers who uses the default-free rate for discounting must be sure that inflation is appropriately handled in the cash flow projections. Such procedures are discussed in Chapter 11.

Leaving aside the problem of inflation, a basic argument against using the firm's cost of capital as its "hurdle rate" is that this measure consists of two components: 1) the pure time value of money and 2) a factor which adjusts for the risk of the firm as a whole. When each investment is evaluated, it is done both on the basis of the timing of its cash flows, and according to the risk position of the company. The pure time value component of the cost of capital is an acceptable start, but the second factor, the risk component, is in effect saying that the risk of the investment is equivalent to the overall risk of the company. Of course, this does not necessarily hold. A high risk company may choose to invest in some very safe projects. The net present value of these projects would be understated since the cash flows would be discounted with a cost of capital containing a high risk assessment. Conversely, a very stable, low risk corporation may overstate the present value of some very risky projects by discounting them with a cost of capital which does not include enough risk. Chapter 10, Handling Uncertainty, will suggest some methods by which this inherent problem of the cost of capital may be dealt with.

Despite the above discussion, the cost of capital can be a practical estimate of a firm's appropriate discount rate if it is applied with good judgement. The cost of capital is currently a widely used discount rate for discounted cash flow procedures in the business world. The use of the cost of capital as a cut-off rate -- as a yardstick for testing the acceptability of investments -- implies that the economic well-being of the owner(s) will be enhanced by the acceptance of capital expenditure projects that promise a rate of return in excess of the firm's cost of capital.

We now turn to the problem of measuring the cost of capital. In doing so, the reader should recognize that there are some conceptual as well as measurement problems associated with quantifying the cost of capital. Estimating the firm's cost of capital requires considerable managerial judgment -- just as in other phases of decision making. But useful guidelines are available to the investor for arriving at a meaningful estimate of the firm's cost of capital. We will present in an abbreviated non-technical manner the way of looking at the cost of capital which makes the most sense to us. Since no one has yet discovered the correct way of estimating the cost of capital for a firm and since some controversy exists over the best way of measuring the cost of equity sources of capital, the approaches given herein should not be viewed as the final word on the matter. Rather they are presented as a widely accepted way of viewing the cost of capital that can be useful to most business managers in answering the question: "What rate of return shall we establish as a cut-off rate in determining the economic desirability of investment proposals?"

RATIONALE FOR A WEIGHTED AVERAGE COST OF CAPITAL

Most firms use several sources of funds for capital expenditures. Most firms employ both debt and equity capital. Debt capital represents capital funds obtained through loans from banks, from various other credit agencies, and from individuals who are not owners of the business and, in the case of large firms, by issuing bonds. Equity (or ownership) capital is generated by the owners injecting more of their own funds into the business (e.g., by issuing more preferred or common stock in the case of corporations) and by retaining part or all of a firm's earnings.

Since we are discussing capital investments (i.e., projects that have impacts on the business over a reasonably long future period of time), we are not concerned with sources of short-term credit, for example, short-term liabilities such as accounts payable, taxes payable and the like. For investment analysis purposes, we focus on the long-term debt and net worth elements of the balance sheet.

Please note that we have not mentioned depreciation as a source of capital funds. Depreciation is the accountant's method of allocating the original cost of a depreciable capital asset to the business over a period of years. Changing the rate of depreciation will not alter the amount of cash available for investment, except to the extent that it affects the amount of income taxes paid and hence the amount of cash left for the firm. This would affect the owner's equity or retained earnings which is a source of capital for investment. Depreciation, as a source of capital, would not be considered in the computation of the firm's cost of capital.

The cost of obtaining capital from various sources differs widely. As most readers realize, and as will be explained later, equity capital generally is more expensive than dept capital. Some argue that if an investor is considering the purchase of $20,000 worth of equipment this year and if the investor knows that if he buys the equipment, he will borrow the money from a bank at, say, an effective rate of interest of 12 percent, the relevant cost of capital for this investment is 12 percent. On the other hand if the cost of equity capital is 15 percent and the following year's projects would have to involve equity financing -- because the debt limit of a sound capital structure would have been reached -- they would argue that the project in the following year should be subjected to the standard of a 15 percent rate of return.

The above short-run approach to computing a cost of capital can be arbitrary and dangerous. If it were followed consistently, the cost of capital would be an erratic quantity, fluctuating up or down as the firm obtained additional increments of capital from varying sources. More important, this approach involves a basic fallacy. A business does not have unlimited sources of credit. Lenders usually insist that a borrower's total indebtedness bear a reasonable relationship to his net worth. In order to engage in debt financing for a given project, the firm must have an adequate equity base that will permit the use of additional debt. The use of debt financing for any year implies that a firm also is using up some of the equity base which it has already developed. If in subsequent years additional expansion takes place, at some point the firm will find it necessary to use additional equity financing. Otherwise the debt-to-equity ratio would become unbalanced. Thus, when calculating a cost of capital, it is logical to use a weighted-average cost of capital which reflects the costs of all forms of financing that the firm uses. In effect, we argue that the decision as to whether or not a business investment proposal is desirable should be separated from the decision as to how this particular project will be financed.

The cost of capital can be computed either on a before-income-tax basis or on an after-income-tax basis. Since decisions in a tax paying business should consider the effect of taxes, the cost of capital should be a weighted average cost of capital after taxes. The use of an after-tax cost of capital assumes that our cash flows have been adjusted to reflect the impact of income taxes as discussed in Chapter 7.

Before we turn to some widely accepted guidelines available to a manager for estimating the firm's cost of capital, we should remind ourselves that the investor should be interested in estimating what capital will cost in the future. For capital investment decisions -- as for any decision -- managers should be interested in the future, rather than the past or present. But usually we must rely heavily on the present and recent past as a guide for the future. Thus, as a practical matter, an analysis of the cost of capital in the present and recent past is a useful starting point for projecting the future. The investor then modifies the firm's cost of capital to reflect his or her judgment of the future.

COMPUTING A WEIGHTED AVERAGE COST OF CAPITAL

To compute a weighted average cost of capital, we need to determine:

(1) The cost of capital funds from each source employed by the business and

(2) The weights to be given each source of capital in computing a weighted average cost.

Taking the second problem first, the proper set of weights to use is the relative proportion of each type of capital in the firm's capital structure.

The important assumption is that the firm will, in fact, raise capital in the proportions assumed in the weighting system. We want a marginal cost of capital to the firm as a whole. For the weighted average cost of capital to represent a marginal cost, the weights must be marginal; the weights must reflect the proportions of financing that the firm intends to employ in the future.

The raising of capital is "lumpy". Consequently, strict proportions cannot be maintained. For example, a firm would find it difficult to finance each investment project that it undertakes with 25 percent bank loans, 25 percent other long term debt and 50 percent from equity capital. In practice, it may finance with debt in one instance and with equity in another. However, most firms are able to finance in roughly a proportional manner over time.

As we will see subsequently, the costs of the various sources of capital usually are based upon the existing capital structure. We are faced with a problem if the firm wishes to change its capital structure, because the costs of the current methods of financing may differ from those that will prevail once the firm has achieved its desired capital structure. Since the firm cannot measure its costs directly at the desired capital structure, it must estimate the costs of each source.

During a transition period from the present capital structure to a capital structure that is desired in the future, the firm usually will rely on one type of financing. For example, it may finance mostly with debt capital until the desired capital structure is reached. In such an instance, what cost of capital should be used for appraising the worth of investment proposals during the transition period? We think that it is best to use an estimated weighted average cost of capital based on the desired capital structure. In other words, if bank loans represent 25 percent of an individual proprietorship's total desired capital structure, bank loans should be assigned a weight of 0.25. If equity capital represents 50 percent of the total long-term capital of the firm, it would be given a weight of 0.5 and so on. This approach will lead to an average cost of capital that reflects the proportion and cost of each type of capital represented in what management considers to be a sound, balanced capital structure that will be viable for the long pull in the future.

If management thinks that the present capital structure is a sound, viable one for the future - in other words, if it intends to finance over time in the future in approximately the same proportion as the firm is currently financed, it can use its current capital structure to obtain the weights used in arriving at a weighted average cost of capital. If this is done, the market values of the different sources of financing should be used in arriving at the weights, rather than the book values. The proportion of the total capital structure of the firm from equity capital should be the total market value of common stock rather than the book value of common stock plus the retained earnings as shown in the balance sheet.

ESTIMATING THE COSTS OF CAPITAL FROM VARIOUS SOURCES

We now turn to the problem of estimating the cost of capital from various sources. We will present an overview to offer the basic principles and, hopefully, to stimulate the reader to explore the problem further. 2/

COST OF DEBT

Debt capital may be in the form of loans from commercial banks, life insurance companies, and other lending institutions; lease agreements; or, in the case of large corporations, the flotation of a bond issue. We will use a loan as our illustration for determining the cost of debt capital, since it is a typical form of debt and the cost of other forms of debt will follow similar logic.

The problem of calculating the cost of a loan for purposes of ultimately arriving at an estimate of the firm's cost of capital centers around two considerations: (1) determining the "effective rate" of interest — what is actually being paid — as opposed to the quoted or reported rate and (2) consideration of income taxes. The problem of determining the effective rate of interest after allowing for service or finance charges, flotation costs, and the like, is considered in detail in other publications. 3/ The requirements of the "truth in lending" law also facilitate the calculation of the effective rate. For our present purposes, let us assume that we have determined that the effective rate of interest on loans is 11 percent. Individual proprietors, partners and firms subject to income taxes must consider taxes since capital expenditure proposals should be evaluated on an after-tax basis. Interest expense is deductible in computing income taxes. If the individual or firm is in the 40 percent tax bracket, \$1.00 of interest will reduce taxes by \$0.40, and the effective interest rate after taxes will be 60 percent of the effective interest rate before taxes. Obviously, universities, churches, and other tax free institutions should not make these tax adjustments.

To summarize, we suggest the following procedure for placing a meaningful cost on term loans:

After-tax interest cost = Effective rate of interest paid before taxes X (1 - marginal income tax rate)

For our illustration:

After-tax interest cost = 11.0 percent x (1.00 - 0.40)

= 11.0 percent x 0.60

= 6.6 percent

COST OF EQUITY CAPITAL IN PROPRIETORSHIPS AND PARTNERSHIPS

Placing a meaningful cost on equity capital is much more difficult than placing a cost on debt sources of capital since equity capital (as opposed to debt capital) has no

2/Recommended reference is Ezra Solomon, The Theory of Financial Management, New York and London, Columbia University Press, 1963.

3/The interested reader is referred to Frank J. Smith, Jr., and Ken Cooper, The Financial Management of Agribusiness Firms, University of Minnesota Extension Service Special Report 26, September 1967, Chapter 5.

contractually binding cost -- no interest is paid. But despite the fact that many managers would seem to view equity capital as "costless", it certainly does have a cost, and to the extent the business finances capital expenditures from ownership capital, the cost of this source of capital should be reflected in the yardstick that is used in judging the desirability of investments.

When a proprietor or partner puts more capital into his or her business -- perhaps by the route of plowing back earnings -- or leaves capital in the business, the use of these funds for other purposes is denied. In short, there is an opportunity cost to leaving funds in the business. The true cost of equity capital is the return on these funds that could be earned by investing them elsewhere in an investment of comparable risk. If, by investing in his or her own business, the owner foregoes making an investment that would return, say 14 percent, equity capital should be viewed as costing the business 14 percent. The assumption implicit in this viewpoint is that the individual owner would employ his or her resources elsewhere if a greater personal profit could be obtained elsewhere. In reality, of course, many proprietors and partners receive an intrinsic reward from operating their own businesses over and above the money profits related thereto. Nevertheless, we argue that they should consciously and objectively analyze what it is really costing them to provide capital to their own businesses.

If we agree that the cost of equity capital in a proprietorship or partnership is the return that this capital would earn the owners if they invested it elsewhere in an investment of comparable risk, how can the investor go about measuring this opportunity cost? The problem of measuring this cost is a difficult one. No one has yet discovered a method for arriving at a precisely correct way of determining the cost of equity capital -- nor are they likely to do so in the future. Determining the cost of equity capital in large part must remain a matter of judgment. But certain definite things can be said that should be helpful to the investor in placing a cost on equity capital:

(1) The cost of equity capital should be viewed as being significantly higher than the cost of borrowed capital. This stems from the fact that the suppliers of debt capital assume a lot less risk than the suppliers of equity capital. Creditors of the firm have first claim on earnings and first claim on assets. They receive maximum protection from loss. On the other hand, the owners get what is left. If no earnings are left, they get nothing. Conversely, the owners of a business receive all of the rewards above the fixed commitments -- if the firm should strike a bonanza. Thus, the argument that equity capital should be viewed as being a more expensive source of capital than borrowed capital. 4/ For example, if we determine that the rate of interest on terms loans is 12 percent, as a starting point we know that the cost of equity capital is higher than 12 percent.

4/From the point of view of the owners, the use of more debt -- at least up to a point -- frequently is considered to be an advantage because it provides what is called "leverage." The amount paid as interest per dollar received from creditors generally is considerably less than that required by an owner per dollar of his or her investment. Consequently, within limits, the higher the proportion of the funds financing an investment project obtained from debt sources, the greater the share of each inflow from the investment that accrues to the owners. If the firm earns more than it pays for the use of debt funds, the returns to the owner(s) will be magnified because all "excess" returns accrue to the owner(s). However, the blade cuts both ways. The creditors absorb less than their share of the firm's risk. The more debt outstanding, the greater the danger of bankruptcy to the owners. In short, the leverage provided by the incurrence of more debt represents both an increase in expected earnings of the owner(s) and an increase in owner's risk. This suggests that the average cost of capital for a firm declines as debt funds are substituted for equity sources of capital - up to a point. But beyond this point, which represents the ideal proportion of debt to equity and the firm's lowest cost of capital, the average cost of capital will increase as a result of the introduction of more debt funds.

(2) The cost of equity capital should be viewed as differing from one business to another. The opportunity costs of owners' capital differs among owners even in the same industry since the individual owners: (1) differ in their abilities to find alternative investment possibilities for their capital; (2) differ in their abilities to manage capital in other places; and (3) have businesses that differ in their riskiness.

Very little additional can be said regarding placing a cost on equity capital in a proprietorship or partnership. With the viewpoints outlined above in mind, the individual must use judgement in placing a cost on capital used in his or her own business. Usually the best that a manager can do is to end up by concluding that equity capital should be viewed as costing approximately X percent — which will probably be a round number of say 12, 14, or 16 percent.

The important thing is for the proprietor or partner to recognize that equity capital is not "costless" -- as a matter of fact it should be viewed as being a relatively expensive source of capital -- and to think in the terms that have been outlined. After all, it is not too serious if an estimate of 14 percent is used as the cost of capital when the "actual" cost of capital -- established by some yet undiscovered way -- is 15, or even 16, percent. The "error" in estimating the firm's cost of capital will make "mistakes" in judging the desirability only of marginal investments -- which will probably be accepted or rejected on the basis of intangible considerations anyway. As unsatisfactory and as frustrating as this approach may be for estimating the cost of equity capital, the viewpoint is sound and can steer us away from major errors — for example, assuming that equity capital in a partnership or proprietorship or retained earnings in a corporation are costless to the firm.

Adjustment for Taxes

As stated earlier, the cost of equity capital should be based on opportunity cost -- that is, the return that this capital could earn if put into another investment with risk comparable to that of investing in the proprietor's own business. The owners of a noncorporate business receive their compensation out of profits before taxes. The return from alternative investments is also received on a before-tax basis. The investor must then pay personal income taxes which makes the after-tax rate of return less than the before-tax rate.

Let's assume that a return of 14 percent could be earned in the alternative investment (e.g., a mutual fund). If the investor is in the 30 percent tax bracket, the after-tax return would be 9.8 percent (ignore for now the fact that part of the return would be capital gain taxed at a lower rate). Now let's compare this with a prospective investment in the proprietor's own business where a 9.8 percent cost of equity capital (14 percent adjusted for the 30 percent tax bracket) has been used in evaluating the investment. Assume that this is a marginal investment (i.e., the net present value equals zero). The owner would be earning exactly 9.8 percent on equity capital to the extent equity capital was being used. Since the cash flows used in evaluating the investment are after-tax cash flows, the after-tax rate of return would be 9.8 percent, the same as the after-tax return from the alternative investment (again, assuming no part of the income is capital gain). If the 14 percent cost of equity capital had not been adjusted to an after-tax return rate in evaluating the proposed investment, the owner would make an after-tax return of 14 percent which would be greater than the after-tax rate of return from the alternative investment in this comparison.

An additional comment should be made with respect to capital gains. Investment in a proprietor's own business usually provides the opportunity to earn part of his or her income as capital gain which is taxed at a lower rate. But in most cases the alternative investment also will result in part of the income being earned as capital gain. The proportion of the income from the two alternatives received as capital gain may be quite different depending on the investor and the alternative being considered. In general, the opportunity to earn income as capital gain is probably about the same in the proprietor's own business as in alternative investments of comparable risk. If a particular investor knows that this is not the case in the investments being considered, the cost of equity capital should be adjusted accordingly.

COST OF EQUITY CAPITAL IN CORPORATIONS

Corporations generate equity capital by selling preferred and/or common stock and by retaining part or all of the firm's earnings.

Cost of Preferred Stock

Preferred stock is considered to be a form of equity capital, since the holders of it receive dividends from after-tax income, and inability to pay these dividends does not bankrupt the company. However, preferred stock also carries some characteristics of debt because its dividends, like interest payments, are contractually fixed over time and it has a claim prior to that of common stock for the firm's assets. Also, preferred stock generally has a perpetual life. This allows us to approximate its market value as a perpetuity (i.e., an annuity payable forever), according to the following formula:

$$\text{Market price per share after flotation costs} = \frac{\text{Annual dividend per share}}{\text{Effective cost of preferred stock capital}}$$

This is true since, as in any other investment, the buyer will be willing to pay a price for the stock which amounts to the present value of all future expected benefits. In the case of preferred stock, the future expected cash inflows will be a stream of dividends. Since these dividends are anticipated to continue forever, or at least for a long period of time, the value of the stock may be estimated with the above perpetuity formula.

By mathematically converting our formula into an equivalent form, we can approximate the cost of preferred stock to the firm. Management should use an average market price per share after flotation costs over a period which it feels to be meaningful.

$$\text{Effective cost of preferred stock capital} = \frac{\text{Annual dividend per share}}{\text{Market price per share after flotation costs}}$$

For example, if the net amount realized by the firm after flotation costs is \$50 per share and the dividend payment is \$7.00 per year, the effective cost can be calculated as follows:

$$\frac{\$7.00}{\$50.00} = 14 \text{ percent}$$

Since the dividends are paid out of profits after taxes (i.e., they are not deductible in computing the firm's taxable income), the above is an "after-tax cost" or a net cost of preferred stock to the corporation. This is in sharp contrast to the tax benefits associated with debt capital.

Cost of Common Stock

In attempting to make a reasonable estimate of the cost of capital raised by selling common stock, management should think in terms of the returns expected by stockholders. The corporation must satisfy the shareholder's expectation of profits or returns. New shareholders purchase stock expecting to receive a return on their investment, which is the purchase price of the stock. Likewise, once they have purchased the stock, stockholders continue to own it based on the expectation of receiving a return on their investment in the stock -- a return on the price that they could receive for it if they sold the stock. Thus, prospective stockholders and existing stockholders are alike in that both expect a future stream of income as a return on their investment which is represented by the present market value of the stock. Therefore, the corporation's investment program should promise earnings from which the stockholders' expectations can be satisfied. In short, management should think in terms of answering the following question: "What returns are required by common stockholders in order to induce them to part with their money and let the corporation use it?" 5/

The basic viewpoint outlined above is sound and not subject to controversy. The only problem and the only area about which there is controversy is the matter of how best to go about measuring owners' expectations. The most widely accepted guideline for estimating the cost of common stock capital is the dividend-valuation method.

The dividend-valuation approach to estimating the cost of common stock capital is based on the premise that the rate of return expected by stockholders is the rate which makes the series of dividends expected indefinitely in the future equal to the current price of the stock. Thus, the value of a share of stock to a stockholder is the present value of the expected future stream of income to be received. Because dividends are all that stockholders as a whole receive from their investment in stock, this stream of income is the cash dividends to be paid in future periods. Following the argument, the cost of common stock capital is defined as the rate of discount that equates the present value of all expected future dividends per share with the current market price of the stock.

The formula for estimating a cost of common stock capital that comes out of this framework is as follows: 6, 7/

$$\text{Cost of common stock capital} = \frac{\text{Current dividend per share}}{\text{Current market price per share}} + \text{Growth rate expected in dividends}$$

For example, if the present dividends on XYZ Corp. common stock are $4 per share, if the current market price of stock is $40 per share and if dividends per share are expected to grow in keeping with the growth in the economy, say about 4 percent a year, XYZ's cost of common stock, using the dividend valuation method, would be approximately:

$$\frac{\$4}{\$40} + .04 = .14 \text{ or } 14 \text{ percent}$$

The costs calculated using the above formula are "after-tax" costs since dividends paid by a corporation are not tax deductible.

5/ Ideally, we should know the future returns required by stockholders. Obviously we cannot be certain as to the amount of future earnings or returns expected by the stockholders -- both existing and new stockholders. On the other hand, it does not seem unreasonable to assume that the stockholder, in general, is basing his or her expectations of the future on the past.

6/ M. J. Gordon and Eli Shapiro, "Capital Equipment Analysis: The Required Rate of Profit," Management Science, Vol. 3, No. 1, October 1956.

7/ Since this formula is based on dividends to be paid in perpetuity, it does not explicity consider expected capital gains. It is possible to modify the formula to reflect explicitly capital gains. If we do this, the cost of common stock capital is based on the dividends expected during some limited period of time in the future and the expected price of the stock at the end of that period as compared to the current price.

Although the dividend-valuation approach provides a guideline or logical framework for approaching the problem of measuring the cost of common stock capital, its application is difficult, and considerable managerial judgment is required. A thorough treatment of the problems is beyond the scope of this publication. We will suggest two problems. First, the securities of many firms are not actively traded; and consequently management has no market values of common stock to guide it. Thus, the evaluation of shares and, in turn, the measurement of the cost of common stock capital becomes a special problem. In such instances, management may constructively approach the problem through one or both of the following routes: (1) think in terms of the possible opportunity costs as if the firm were a proprietorship or partnership; and (2) use as a guide the dividend price ratios of other firms with comparable risk and stability whose securities are actively traded.

Second, the particular dividend valuation model presented herein presumes that dividends will grow at a constant rate over time. The critical assumption that dividends per share will grow at a constant rate will be a fair approximation of investor expectations in some situations. The important factor is measuring the growth in dividends per share as perceived by investors. Other dividend valuation methods are available if the expected growth in dividends per share is other than a constant rate over time. Unfortunately, these models, although more realistic for some situations, are also more complex.

For all situations, the important thing is to estimate the growth rate in dividends that equates the future dividends expected by investors with the current market price of the stock. Expected growth in dividends must be estimated. The major difficulty involved in estimating the cost of equity capital lies in making that estimate. In situations where there have been reasonably stable patterns of past growth, we might reasonably project this trend into the future. However, we must temper the projection to take account of current market sentiment. Company executives must attempt to think as investors do when they estimate the firm's cost of equity capital.

In short, all we are saying is that the proposed guidelines for estimating the cost of common stock capital must be tempered by considerable managerial judgement. But at least it gives management a useful way to approach the job of measurement. The important thing to remember is that the cost of equity capital is the rate of return required by investors on the equity financed portion of an investment proposal, holding constant the capital structure, business risk and dividend policy of the firm. This cost can be measured by determining the rate of discount that equates the present value of expected future dividends per share with the current market price per share of common stock. This cost should be adjusted for flotation costs and underpricing of stock if the stock is sold externally.

Cost of Retained Earnings 8/

Retained earnings (i.e., earnings or profits which are not paid out to owners but are plowed back into the business) are an important source of capital for many firms. The costs associated with retaining some part of the current earnings are not obvious. But contrary to the view all too commonly taken by some corporate officials, retained earnings are not cost free. By retaining earnings, the firm denies the use of the funds to the stockholders. If we consider the economic interests of stockholders as overriding, the cost associated with these funds should be measured by the opportunities that our stockholders must forego if the firm retains earnings rather than distributing them as dividends. The stockholders have a right to expect earnings on the funds plowed back the same as they have a right to expect earnings on their original investment.

8/ Recommended reference is Harold Bierman, Jr. and Jerome E. Hass, An Introduction to Managerial Finance, New York, W. W. Norton & Company, Inc., 1973, Chapter 12.

One way to deal with this problem is to view the act of retaining earnings as being similar to any other act of investment by the stockholder. The difference is that the company rather than the individual makes the decision to invest. At first glance, under this definition of retained earnings as an investment, it may appear that we can evaluate the cost of retained earnings exactly as we would any other investment of equal risk that might be made by the stockholder. However, two factors reduce the net amount to be invested if dividends are paid out rather than retained. If earnings are paid out to the stockholder rather than being reinvested within the company, the stockholder is obligated to pay income taxes on the dividends before the funds are invested elsewhere. Moreover, when this dividend income is invested, a portion of it will be paid out as brokerage fees. Each of these factors tend to make the cost of retained earnings less than the cost of new equity capital. The first factor is usually much more important than the second.

The following formula can be used as a guide to placing a cost on retained earnings:

$$\text{Cost of retained earnings} = \left(\begin{array}{l}\text{\% return that stockholders} \\ \text{could have obtained by} \\ \text{investing dividends in} \\ \text{alternative investments}\end{array}\right)\left(1 - \begin{array}{l}\text{Marginal} \\ \text{income tax} \\ \text{rate of} \\ \text{stockholder}\end{array}\right)\left(1 - \begin{array}{l}\text{Brokerage fee} \\ \text{as \% of the} \\ \text{dollars} \\ \text{invested}\end{array}\right)$$

The major points to consider in viewing the cost of retained earnings are: (1) retained earnings aren't cost free; (2) their cost is closely related to that of common stock; and (3) their cost is less than that of common stock by the marginal tax rate of stockholders and a small factor for brokerage fees.

In our calculations of a weighted average cost of capital for a corporation, retained earnings are not separated from other sources of equity capital (such as the book value of common stock), nor should they be. The cost of retained earnings cannot be separated from the cost of common stock capital. Our only point in mentioning retained earnings here is to remind the reader that retained earnings are not cost free. Although there are no explicit cost payments that must be met, there should be a cost attached because the firm retains funds which otherwise would have been distributed in dividends. As a consequence, we can view this as a new act of investment by the existing stockholders, differing from the initial investment only in that the decision to reinvest is made by corporate officials rather than by the stockholders themselves.

COST OF EQUITY CAPITAL IN COOPERATIVES 9/

Cooperatives generate equity capital through the use of revolving funds and by selling preferred and/or common stock.

Cost of Revolving Funds

For many years revolving funds have been a major source of equity capital for farmer cooperatives. "Revolving funds," as used in this text, refer to any nonpermanent type of equity capital -- i.e., investment in equity which carries an implied or explicit promise to pay at some future date prior to liquidation of the cooperative. Most revolving funds in cooperatives are obtained either from retention of earnings (profits) from the business or by retaining a portion of returns due members for products delivered to the cooperative for marketing. Considering the economic interests of patrons as overriding, the cost

9/ Taken from material developed by Richard A. Neis, Springfield Bank for Cooperatives, Springfield, Massachusetts and published in a manual entitled Maximizing Return on Investments, used in a workshop for managers of farmer cooperatives, 1969. This manual was based on Aplin and Casler, 1st ed., and co-authored by R. D. Aplin.

associated with these funds should be measured by the opportunities that patrons must forego if the cooperative retains such funds rather than distributes them to patrons. In short, there is an opportunity cost to the patron identical to that of an individual proprietor. (See discussion in section entitled "Cost of Equity Capital in Proprietorships and Partnerships".)

The cost of revolving fund capital is the return on these funds that could be earned by the individual holders by investing them elsewhere in an investment of comparable risk. If by investing in the cooperative, a patron foregoes making an investment that would return 12 percent, the cooperative patron should view investment in revolving funds as costing 12 percent. The assumption implicit in this viewpoint is that the patron would employ his or her resources elsewhere if a greater personal profit could be obtained. In reality, of course, many patrons of cooperatives may place some intrinsic values on such things as being an owner of the business, or having a home for his or her production or a place where quality supplies and services may be obtained at reasonable prices. Nevertheless, patrons of cooperatives should consciously and objectively analyze what it is really costing them to provide this kind of capital for their cooperative.

Continuing on the premise that the cost of revolving fund capital is the return that this capital would earn for the owners if it were invested elsewhere at comparable risk, how can management go about measuring this opportunity cost? No one has yet discovered a precise method of determining opportunity cost. One method is to arrive at a numerical range and then narrow this down, largely through judgment, to what might be an average. For example, on the low end of the scale, a patron could earn approximately 5 percent if he or she did nothing more than invest the money in an ordinary savings account. On the other hand, it would be more logical for the patron to reinvest such funds in his or her own farm operation where earnings might be 10, 15, or 20 percent, depending upon the ability of the owner to generate profit on his or her investment. Then, considering the risk element, it could be safe in some instances to say that the investment in the cooperative carries less risk because of its corporate structure than investment in the patron's own business.

The reasoning behind this statement is that in an incorporated cooperative, a member's liability or risk is limited by law to the amount of capital which he or she had invested in the cooperative. Theoretically, this would also be true in farm operations that are incorporated. However, it is common practice amongst lenders to corporate farm operations to have notes of the corporation endorsed or guaranteed by the principal stockholders and, in fact, at times such indebtedness is secured by liens on personal property of the stockholders. To the extent a stockholder in a corporate farm operation permits this situation to exist, the shelter of the corporate structure is relinquished as it pertains to limits of liability and thereby places him/herself in nearly the same risk category as an unincorporated farm business.

Therefore, after consideration of all the factors, it could then be rationalized that the patrons' "average" opportunity cost could be in the 10 to 15 percent area.

The foregoing is indeed an oversimplification, but it does help bring into focus the thought processes necessary to arrive at an opportunity cost to farmer cooperative patrons for the various investments they make in their cooperatives on which no dividends or interest are paid. It is based largely on judgment, and the preciseness of judgment is always directly related to the accurateness of the information used in making the judgment. The important thing, however, is to recognize that <u>investments</u> made by farmer-patrons in their cooperatives <u>are not costless</u> whether or not interest is paid on certificates. <u>Their cost to the cooperative is the opportunity cost to the investor</u>. Even if the certificates draw interest, the opportunity cost of the patrons rather than the interest should be viewed by management as the cost of revolving fund money. For example, if a cooperative's certificates pay 5 percent interest and management estimates that the patrons, on the average, have an opportunity cost of about 12 percent, the cost of non-permanent capital should be viewed as being 12 percent (i.e., the 5 percent paid patrons plus 7 percent which is the difference between the interest received and the members' opportunity cost).

One additional aspect with regard to revolving funds, which does not have a direct application to computing an average cost of capital, but which has a direct bearing on the willingness of farmers to make additional investments in their cooperatives, is the time period during which these equities must be held by patrons before they are revolved in cash. Based on the theory of the time value of money, such equities with revolving periods of ten years are less valuable in current dollars than those which have shorter revolving periods.

For example, let's assume a farmer received a $100 revolving fund certificate for each of two cooperatives and knows that Cooperative A revolves in three years and Cooperative B revolves in ten years. Referring to the Present Value Table II in this manual, and assuming the farmer's opportunity cost is 12 percent, it is seen that the present value of the $100 certificate in the case of Cooperative A is $71.10, whereas the same investment in Cooperative B is worth only $32 in current dollars. Its present value would be $10 if it were not to be revolved for twenty years.

The fact that many cooperatives find it extremely difficult, if not impossible, to revolve such equities in relatively short time periods seriously affects their ability to use this type of investment in their organizations. This is particularly true since I.R.S. now requires that such allocations be included in patrons' gross income in the year received. Some cooperatives are now looking at other forms of equity (risk) capital for their capital base. An example would be the requirement of a permanent investment of equity by the patron in the cooperative.

Cost of Permanent Capital

Determination of the cost of permanent capital in cooperatives is less elusive than nonpermanent capital, since in most cooperatives a dividend cost is either explicit or at least established through practice. Therefore, the term "permanent capital," as used in this text, is any equity capital investment for which a cost has been established. Usually these are labeled as common stock or preferred stock. If a cooperative does have stock, or some other form of equity, on which no dividend is paid, then its cost could be determined to be the opportunity cost to the holder in the same manner as described in the previous section.

Capital stock investments in cooperatives will never appreciate in value since all profits are shared with users. Therefore, for all practical purposes, its value can be considered to be equivalent to its par value, and its cost is simply the annual dividend rate.

A FINAL COMMENT ON THE COST OF EQUITY CAPITAL

In summary, management should recognize that dividend-free equity capital is not "costless" and, as a matter of fact, it should be viewed as a relatively expensive source of capital. While an attempt has been made here to provide a format for calculating the opportunity costs of owners' capital, it can differ among owners even in the same industry, since the individual owners (1) differ in their abilities to manage capital in other places; and (2) have businesses which differ in their riskiness.

OVERALL COST OF CAPITAL

We have explained the weights that should be used in determining a weighted average cost of capital. We have also discussed ways in which the cost of debt and equity capital can be estimated. When the investor has applied the suggested guidelines, the calculation of the estimated overall cost of capital for the firm is merely a matter of arithmetic. We compute the weighted average cost of the several sources of capital employed by the firm as illustrated below:

Source	(1) Amount Used	(2) Proportion from Each Source*	(3) After-tax Cost	(4) (2) x (3) Weighted Cost
Bank loan	$125,000	25%	7.2%	1.8%
Other long term debt	125,000	25	6.0	1.5
Equity capital	250,000	50	16.0	8.0
	$500,000	100%		11.3%

*This should reflect the financing proportions the firm intends to employ over time in the future. If management thinks the firm's present capital structure represents a sound, viable capital structure for the future and consequently chooses to use historial weights based on balance sheet figures, it should use market value weights - not book value weights.

The weighted average cost of capital is about 11 or 12 percent in the example. It reflects the proportion and cost of each type of capital used. The manager now has a benchmark which should help prescribe the use of capital funds. Investment proposals promising an internal rate of return of less than 11 or 12 percent (i.e., projects with a negative net present value using 11 or 12 percent) would appear undesirable. On the other hand, projects promising an internal rate of return of something over 11 or 12 percent would appear to be beneficial to the owners. But managerial judgment must enter the decision because, among other things, the cost of capital is not a figure that may be determined with certainty -- although the guidelines and framework discussed above enable management to establish limits and determine a useful approximation of the firm's cost of capital.

COST OF UNUSUALLY LARGE AMOUNTS OF CAPITAL IN A GIVEN PERIOD

The reader should be aware that thus far we have assumed implicitly that the firm is able to procure capital funds without limit at its cost of capital. In practice, it isn't possible for firms to obtain unlimited amounts of capital at one time at the same cost. Logically, we would expect that even firms of excellent reputation would encounter increasing costs when they attempt to obtain unusually large amounts of funds in the market in a given period. We can visualize an upward sloping supply curve for capital. In other words, the weighted average cost of capital increases in the short run, as the total amount of capital raised in a given period increases. Such an upward sloping supply curve for capital is visualized for a hypothetical firm in Figure 2.

An upward sloping supply curve suggests that the firm cannot raise an unlimited amount of capital at any given time at a given rate. Rather it suggests that a digestion period is needed during which the firm makes investments and demonstrates to creditors and owners the firm's ability to generate profits on those investments. For example, the hypothetical firm whose supply curve for capital is portrayed in Figure 2 can raise capital in amounts up to X dollars at one time at a cost of about 9 percent. The average cost of capital increases if more than X dollars of capital are raised in a given time period. After a sufficient digestion and demonstration period, however, the firm will again be able to raise capital at a cost of about 9 percent.

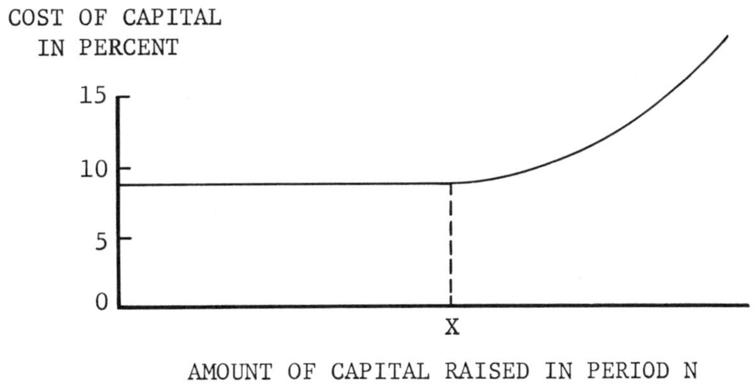

Figure 2. Supply Curve for Capital

However, if the amount of financing in a particular period does not differ significantly from the amounts invested in previous periods, the firm will be raising capital in about the same area of its supply curve. There is no reason to believe that the cost of capital will fluctuate significantly from period to period unless inflation fluctuates widely. Thus, the approach for estimating the firm's cost of capital that has been described will provide an appropriate approximation of the firm's cost of capital. However, if the firm does undertake substantially more financing in a particular period than it has in previous periods, the firm's cost of capital may be higher than would be estimated with the approach previously discussed. Such a circumstance would probably lead to the rejection or postponement of some projects providing returns close to an estimated cost of capital that would have been accepted during a period when more normal amounts of investment and financing were being made.

COST OF CAPITAL NOT A PROFIT GOAL

The reader should keep in mind that we have not used the cost of capital as a "profit goal." Management hopes to have many investment opportunities that promise to return considerably more than the firm's cost of capital. The cost of capital, as we are suggesting it be used, sets a cut-off rate, a minimum test, to which management can subject investment possibilities.

Some firms use an arbitrary discount rate in their calculations of net present values that is higher than the cost of capital (e.g., a minimum rate of return that is a profit goal). A profit goal -- rather than the firm's cost of capital -- can be used as the discount rate in applying the present value techniques for evaluating investment opportunities. If management does so, the discounted cash flow methods still will be useful and provide guidelines superior to the payback period method as well as others that don't reflect the time value of money. But management in so doing should recognize two things: (1) Some of the rationale that underlies the net present value method breaks down, and (2) it is arbitrarily rationing capital or limiting the amounts of funds that it invests, thus foregoing profits that it could have made.

9

SOME SPECIAL PROBLEMS IN PROJECTING CASH FLOWS AND IN ANALYZING INVESTMENTS

EXPECTED TERMINAL OR SALVAGE VALUES

Disposal values (sometimes called terminal or salvage values) should be reflected in investment decisions. No special problem is posed if we remember that in analyzing investment alternatives, we are interested in flows of cash -- either into or out of the business.

There can be three terminal values that are relevant to an investment analysis:

1) estimated terminal value of new asset at the end of its expected useful life (or the end of the planning period being used in the analysis);

2) present salvage value of an old asset that would be replaced if the investment is made;

3) expected salvage value of the old asset at the time of normal retirement.

The last two types of terminal values are relevant only when an asset presently owned by the business will be replaced if the particular investment under consideration is made. Let us briefly examine the manner in which each type of terminal value should be handled for investment analysis purposes.

ESTIMATED TERMINAL VALUE OF NEW ASSET

Any funds that management forecasts the business could obtain from selling the new asset at the end of its useful life (or that it could obtain at the end of the planning period) will increase the flow of funds in that year.

For example, if a machine is expected to have a salvage value of approximately $1,000 (after taxes and after removal costs, if any) at the time of its expected retirement in ten years, the cash flows for year ten should include, in addition to any other benefits in the tenth year, $1,000 to reflect the expected inflow of funds.

SALVAGE VALUES OF OLD ASSET BEING RETIRED

As indicated above, if an existing asset will be replaced by the new investment, one, or possibly two, other terminal values should be considered. The present salvage value of the old asset should be viewed as increasing the cash inflows for this year (or decreasing the cash outlay and thus reducing the net investment required by the new asset). But if the asset is replaced now, the salvage value that would have been realized at the end of its useful life will not be obtained. This has the effect of reducing the cash inflow of that later year.

ILLUSTRATION

Assume the present equipment has a salvage value now of $2,000 and an expected salvage value in five years of $400 (at which time the equipment would be physically unusable). The new equipment will have a salvage value at the time of its expected retirement (i.e., end of ten years) of $1,000. All figures are on an after-tax basis. The cash flows arising from the salvage values would be:

	Year 0	Year 5	Year 10
Cash flows of			
Retaining the old		$400	
Purchasing the new	$2,000		$1,000
or			
Net cash flows of			
Replacing now	$2,000	-$400 ↑ an opportunity cost if replace now	$1,000

The alert reader (and that is the only kind that we have) will note in the above example that we are ignoring the problem of having two alternatives with unequal lives (i.e., the above cash flows provide equipment for only five years if we keep the old but for ten if we invest in the new). We'll address this problem later in this chapter.

WORKING CAPITAL

Many investment proposals (e.g., expansion projects), if instituted in a business, will result in an increase in working capital requirements -- such as increased payroll, increased funds invested in raw materials and increased accounts receivable. (We are referring to working capital in the net sense -- increase in current assets minus increase in current liabilities.) Some investments may reduce the working capital requirements. If the investment under consideration will change the working capital requirements, this fact should be reflected in the analysis of the economic worth of the investment.

The appropriate way to reflect an increase in working capital requirements associated with a particular investment is to include management's estimate of increased working capital required as an outflow of funds in calculating the cash flow stream that will ultimately be discounted. At the same time management's estimate of the amount of the increased working capital that would be recoverable at the end of the project's life -- or at the end of the planning period being used in the decision-making process -- should be viewed as part of the net terminal value of the investment (i.e., a cash inflow in the last year).

It should be stressed that even if management expected that 100 percent of the increase in working capital requirements associated with a particular investment would be recoverable at the end of the project's life, it would be incorrect to ignore the change in working capital requirements. The business will have that much more capital tied up during the period of use and should expect a return on funds tied up in working capital at least equal to the firm's cost of capital. If an increase in working capital requirements is ignored, the value of the investment under consideration will tend to be overstated.

Similarly, any expected decrease in working capital requirements associated with an investment should be considered in estimating cash flows.

ANALYZING INVESTMENT ALTERNATIVES WITH UNEQUAL LIVES

Management frequently encounters the problem of choosing among investment alternatives from which the benefits extend over unequal time periods. We will refer to such alternatives as investments with "unequal lives." Unequal lives of investment projects pose a problem only when the investments are "mutually exclusive." By "mutually exclusive" we mean that only one of two or more investments can be made -- not all of them can be adopted. For example, equipment replacement problems are often complicated by unequal lives of competing equipment. In this section, we will briefly describe three basic approaches to the problem of unequal lives. To illustrate the three approaches, we will use the following hypothetical problem:

Let us assume that a manager must decide which of two machines to purchase. Both machines will perform the same task, but they have different capital requirements, operating characteristics and expected useful life spans. Machine A requires an initial investment of $1,500 and has an expected useful life of three years. The projected annual cash operating expenses (before depreciation but after taxes) of Machine A are $400 in year one, $700 in year two, and $1,000 in year three. Machine B, which has an expected useful life of five years, would require a capital outlay of $2,000 but would have annual cash operating costs of $600 per year. Neither machine would have any terminal value. Assume that the firm's cost of capital is 10 percent. We are searching for the alternative with the lowest present value of costs.

A straight net present value evaluation of the alternatives follows:

Machine A:

Year	Cash outflow	Present value factor	Present value of cash outflow
0	$1,500	1.0	$1,500
1	400	0.9091	364
2	700	0.8264	578
3	1,000	0.7513	751
	Present value of costs of Machine A =		$3,193

Machine B:

Year	Cash outflow	Present value factor	Present value of cash outflow
0	$2,000	1.0	$2,000
1-5	600	3.7908	2,275
	Present value of costs of Machine B =		$4,275

The present value of costs is $3,193 for Machine A and $4,275 for Machine B. This evaluation would be incorrect because it reflects the provision of equipment to perform the task (whatever it is) for five years with Machine B but for only three years with Machine A. This might suggest that we should divide each present value by the number of years involved (i.e., $3,193 / 3 = $1,064 and $4,275 / 5 = $855). But this procedure can lead to a misleading result because it ignores the compounding of earnings over time -- the timing of the cash flows.

ANALYZING USING COMMON TERMINAL DATES

One correct way of approaching the problem is to establish a common terminal date for each investment alternative and to assume an appropriate salvage value as of that date for the investment that would still have some useful life. Using this approach, we can analyze our sample investments by either (1) using a three-year planning period and assuming a terminal value for Machine B as of the end of year three or (2) using a five-year planning period, assuming that Machine A would be replaced at end of year three, and a terminal value for the second Machine A as of the end of its second year of life (i.e., year five). With either approach, a conventional net present value approach can be applied once the comparable cash flows have been estimated. It should be noted that a very important factor influencing the result in this approach is the estimate of the terminal value used.

To illustrate this approach:

1) Assume salvage value of Machine B at year three was estimated to be $640. The present value calculations would be:

		Machine A		Machine B	
Year	Present value factor	Cash outflow	Present value of cash outflow	Cash outflow	Present Value of cash outflow
0	1.0000	$1,500	$1,500	$2,000	$2,000
1	0.9091	400	364	600	545
2	0.8264	700	578	600	496
3	0.7513	1,000	751	600-640	-30
Total present value of costs			$3,193		$3,041

2) Assume that Machine A is replaced by an identical machine at the end of year three and that second Machine A has an estimated salvage value at the end of year five of $400. The present value calculations would be:

		Machine A		Machine B	
Year	Present value factor	Cash outflow	Present value of cash outflow	Cash outflow	Present value of cash outflow
0	1.0000	$1,500	$1,500	$2,000	$2,000
1	0.9091	400	364	600	545
2	0.8264	700	578	600	496
3	0.7513	1,000 + 1,500	1,878	600	451
4	0.6830	400	273	600	410
5	0.6209	700 - 400	186	600	373
Total present value of costs			$4,779		$4,275

With either set of calculations, Machine B is the preferred alternative. Keep in mind that the result is influenced by the estimates of the salvage values.

VIEW AS A CONTINUOUS REPLACEMENT CYCLE

Another approach to the problem of investment alternatives with unequal lives is to determine the net present value of each alternative viewed as a continuous replacement cycle until a common total life period is achieved. In other words, we compare the alternatives on the basis of what would result if each of the investment alternatives was duplicated every time its useful life ended until a common total span of time was achieved for each alternative. In our example, we would use a total time span of 15 years because 15 is the least common multiple of three and five. We would assume that Machine A would be repurchased four times (i.e., in years 3, 6, 9 and 12) and that the original Machine B would be replaced by identical machines twice during the 15-year period (i.e., in years 5 and 10). An analysis of our two alternatives assuming a continuous replacement cycle until a common total life period of 15 years is achieved would be as follows:

	Present	Machine A		Machine B	
	value	Cash	Present value	Cash	Present value
Year	factor	outflow	of cash outflow	outflow	of cash outflow
0	1.0000	$1,500	$1,500	$2,000	$2,000
1	0.9091	400	364	600	545
2	0.8264	700	578	600	496
3	0.7513	1,000 + 1,500	1,878	600	451
4	0.6830	400	273	600	410
5	0.6209	700	435	600 + 2,000	1,614
6	0.5645	1,000 + 1,500	1,411	600	339
7	0.5132	400	205	600	308
8	0.4665	700	327	600	280
9	0.4241	1,000 + 1,500	1,060	600	254
10	0.3855	400	154	600 + 2,000	1,002
11	0.3505	700	245	600	210
12	0.3186	1,000 + 1,500	797	600	191
13	0.2897	400	116	600	174
14	0.2633	700	184	600	158
15	0.2394	1,000	239	600	144
	Total present value of costs		$9,766		$8,576

ANNUAL EQUIVALENT CASH FLOWS

Still a third approach to the problem of analyzing investment alternatives with unequal lives is to compare the investments on the basis of their equivalent average annual cash flows. Before we explain and illustrate this approach, we should point out that the annual equivalent flow approach involves the same assumption implicit in the previous approach (i.e., using a continuous replacement cycle until a common total life period is achieved) and will lead us to the same conclusion.

The annual equivalent cash flow approach involves two steps:

1) Determining the net present value of each investment alternative over its respective useful life.

2) Converting the net present value of each investment into equivalent annual cash flows. The annual equivalent cash flow represents the annual amount for n years which has a present value equal to the net present value of the particular investment.

The decision criterion in the case of alternatives that will affect revenues as well as costs is to select the investment which provides the highest annual equivalent net inflow. In decisions, such as our hypothetical investment, where we are trying to determine which alternative will minimize costs, the investment that has the lowest annual net cash outflow is the most desirable alternative.

Applying the equivalent annual cash flow approach to our two hypothetical investments will help us understand the approach. First we compute the net present value of the cash flows of each alternative for its respective useful life as follows:

Year	Present value factor	Machine A Cash flow	Machine A Present value	Machine B Cash flow	Machine B Present value
0	1.0000	$1,500	$1,500	$2,000	$2,000
1	0.9091	400	364	600	545
2	0.8264	700	578	600	496
3	0.7513	1,000	751	600	451
4	0.6830			600	410
5	0.6209			600	373
	Present value of costs		$3,193		$4,275

From the above, we know the present value of costs associated with using Machine A for three years is $3,193 and for using Machine B for five years is $4,275.

The next step is to convert each of these present values into equivalent annual cash flows. In the case of Machine A, this involves finding the annual payment beginning one year from now and continuing through year three that is equivalent to a payment today of $3,193, assuming that earnings accumulate at 10 percent, the firm's cost of capital. We really answer the question: "What annual cost incurred each year for three years is equivalent to incurring a cost of $3,193 today, if our time value of money is 10 percent?" For Machine B, it involves finding the annual payment for five years that is equivalent to payment $4,275 today.

To determine the annual equivalent cash flows we use the following formula:

$$\frac{\text{Net present value of cash flows}}{\text{The present value of \$1 per year for the appropriate number of years discounted at the firm's minimum acceptable rate of return}} = \text{annual equivalent cash flow}$$

Machine A:

$$\frac{\$3{,}193}{2.4869} = \$1{,}284$$

Machine B:

$$\frac{\$4{,}275}{3.7908} = \$1{,}128$$

At 10 percent, the annual equivalent cost of Machine A is $1,284 and of Machine B is $1,128. Since revenue will be unaffected by our choice of machines in this instance, we conclude that Machine B is superior to Machine A, since it has lower equivalent average annual cash outflow.

SUMMARY

To correctly evaluate and choose from among investments that have different expected life spans, management should use some method to place the alternatives on a comparable basis from the viewpoint of life span. We have discussed and illustrated three basic approaches for properly handling the problem of alternative investments with unequal lives.

The reader should realize the last two methods considered (i.e., continuous replacement cycle until common total life period is realized and annual equivalent cash flow) implicitly assume that the investments will be reproduced precisely. If management has some good reason for believing that some factor, such as new and significantly different technology, would result in the replacement of the shorter-lived investments with an investment that has significantly different cash flows, it should use the other approach -- assuming a common terminal date and appropriate terminal values.

OTHER USES OF ANNUAL EQUIVALENT CASH FLOWS

The concept of equivalent average annual cash flows has been introduced as a technique for properly handling, in many instances, the problem of evaluating alternative investments with unequal lives. It should be pointed out that the equivalent annual cash flow technique can be useful in analyzing capital expenditures where problems of unequal lives are not involved. For example, as explained in the next section, it may be helpful, because of the uncertainty of actual benefits that will materialize from an investment, to determine how much the annual net income of the business would have to increase in order to justify the additional capital outlay required. The annual equivalent cash flow approach will give us such an estimate. With this figure in mind, management may be able to see that the investment is clearly justified (i.e., although it is unable to forecast the exact level of benefits, it feels certain that benefits will far exceed the additional annual net benefits needed) or that it is clearly not justified.

10

HANDLING UNCERTAINITY

In making decisions on capital expenditure projects, the manager is basically concerned with three estimates. First, estimates must be made of additional cash outflows or reductions of cash inflows that will be associated with a proposed alternative. Second, estimates must be made of the additional cash inflows, or reductions in outflows, that will result from it. These first two estimates indicate changes in the net cash pattern. Third, the manager must determine the discount rate that should be used to compute present values of the cash flows.

We now turn to the real world situation of dealing with the problem of uncertainty.1/ We will discuss briefly some basic and practical approaches to handling uncertainty in the decision process. Other approaches, although perhaps theoretically sounder, are still in the developmental stages. In what follows, we will examine ways in which estimates of the economic worth of investments can be made in an environment of uncertainty. For reasons of simplicity, most of our discussion will center on the net present value approach.

BREAK-EVEN APPROACH

One practical -- but theoretically weak -- way of wrestling with the problem of uncertainty is the so-called "break-even approach." This approach is particularly useful when the amount of the capital outlay required by an investment can be estimated with considerable certainty but the benefits -- the net cash inflows -- are highly uncertain.

In such circumstances, the break-even approach involves using the annual equivalent cash flow approach explained earlier to determine how much the annual net income of the business, in cash flow terms, would have to increase to justify the additional capital

1/ "Risk" and "uncertainty" have often been distinguished based on the knowledge of the probability distribution of the outcomes. In the case of risk, the distribution of the outcome in a group of instances is known. In the case of uncertainty, the distribution in not known. This definition of risk and uncertainty has been used by economists for a long time, possibly too long. The definitions actually represent special cases at each end of a continuum of imperfect knowledge. With the increased acceptance of subjective knowledge, the distinction between risk and uncertainty is weaker and the terms are often used interchangeably.

outlay required. With this figure in mind, management may be able to see that the investment clearly is justified or that it clearly is not justified.

Let us illustrate with a simple example. A farmer is attempting to decide between investing in a conventional silo or a sealed storage silo. The former requires an investment of $24,000 and the latter, $50,000. Both silos have an expected useful life of 15 years. The sealed storage will have a terminal value of $5,000 but the conventional silo will have no value at the end of 15 years. The farmer's cost of capital is 12 percent. Further assume that the farmer, because of unknowns, feels unable to quantify the superiority of the sealed storage over the conventional silo. Our farmer wants to use the "breakeven" approach to determine the additional annual return necessary to justify the additional outlay required by the sealed storage. For simplicity, the income tax implications will be ignored.

First, the additional outlay required by sealed storage must be put in present value terms:

Outlay for sealed storage =	$50,000
Less present value of terminal value = $5,000 x 0.1827 =	- 914
Less outlay for conventional silo =	-24,000
Equals net additional outlay required by sealed storage in present value terms =	$25,086

Secondly, the following question must be answered: "How much more net cash inflow is needed annually over 15 years to equal a $25,086 difference in capital outlay?" This question can be answered by determining the annual equivalent cash flow equal to $25,086 when 12 percent is the appropriate discount factor:

$$\frac{\$25,086}{6.8109} = \$3,683$$

The farmer now knows that the sealed storage must increase net cash inflows by about $3,683 a year (ignoring income taxes) more than the conventional silo to justify the additional capital outlay required by sealed storage. The break-even approach to handling uncertainty is based on the presumption that the farmer will have a sound basis for judging the likelihood of sealed storage generating this much additional benefits over the other alternative even though the exact level of benefits that will materialize from the additional investment cannot be forecast with certainty.

If in the farmer's judgment, the probability of exceeding the break-even benefits is extremely high, the decision to purchase the sealed silo can be made without knowing anything more about the benefits and their probabilities. If, however, the chances of falling below the break-even benefit level are too high in the manager's opinion, the sealed storage should be rejected.

Break-even analysis using annual equivalent cash flow thinking is useful for problems such as determining the amount of use that must be made of a machine each year for it to be a break-even investment. Let's illustrate by using a problem which includes income tax adjustments.

The example is the one used in Chapter 7 to illustrate adjusting cash flows for income taxes. Suppose that the before-tax benefits of $7,000 per year are the result of producing 1000 units of output, each of which has a margin of $7. Using the example with 5 year rapid ACRS depreciation, a $2000 salvage value, an 8% discount rate, and including 8% Federal investment credit, the net present value of investment in this machine is $13,632, as calculated below:

Years		Present value
1-15	After-tax cash inflow = \$7,000 (1-.52) (8.5595) =	\$28,760
1-5	Depreciation tax savings = \$30,000 (.52) (0.7915) =	12,347
1	Investment credit = \$30,000 (.08) (0.9259) =	2,222
15	Terminal value = \$2,000 (1-.52) (0.3152) =	303
	Present value of after-tax cash inflows =	\$43,632
	Less: Present value of outlay	30,000
	Net present value =	\$13,632

Because the net present value is positive, we know that the machine could break even at less than 1000 units of output, assuming \$7 margin per unit. To find the breakeven number of units we could use either of the following methods:

1. Find the annual equivalent cash flow (AECF) of \$13,632 -- which is the net present value if 1000 units are produced.

$$\frac{\$13,632}{8.5595} = \$1,593 = \text{AECF, after tax}$$

The after-tax cash flow could be reduced \$1,593 per year and still break even. With a 52% tax bracket, this is equal to \$1593 ÷ 0.48 = \$3,318 in terms of before-tax cash flow. At \$7 per unit, output could be reduced 474 units and still break even. Therefore the breakeven number of units is 1000 - 474 = 526.

Alternatively we could find the after-tax cash flow per unit = \$7 x 0.48 = \$3.36, divide this into \$1,593 and obtain 474 units as the reduction in units of output and still break even.

2. The breakeven output level can be calculated directly without first calculating the net present value for a particular level of output. This method involves finding the present value of all flows related to the investment except those directly related to output. For our example:

P.V. of investment credit =	\$ 2,222
P.V. of terminal value =	303
P.V. of depreciation tax savings =	12,347
P.V. of initial outflow =	-30,000
P.V. of all "fixed" flows, after tax =	-\$15,128

This present value is converted to an annual equivalent cash flow:
\$-15,128 ÷ 8.5595 = \$-1,767

Dividing this AECF, after tax (and for convenience, dispensing with the minus sign) by the after-tax cash flow per unit of output results in the breakeven level of output:

\$1,767 ÷ 3.36 = 526 units.

Suppose that instead of the breakeven output level we would like to know the breakeven cash inflow per unit, assuming 1000 units. One method would be to convert the after-tax AECF to a before-tax AECF:

\$1,767 ÷ 0.48 = \$3,681 AECF, before tax.

\$3,681 ÷ 1000 units = \$3.68 minimum before-tax cash inflow per unit needed to breakeven.

Keep in mind that all the above breakeven calculations assume that the cash flows such as depreciation tax savings and salvage value remain constant regardless of the level of output produced.

The break-even approach can be applied usefully to more complex investment decisions where the length of life of an investment is uncertain and where variables external to firm (e.g., market share and selling prices) lead to highly uncertain benefits from an investment alternative. Under such circumstances, management may want to construct a number of alternative situations that could develop, changing one or a few variables at a time. This would help management understand, for example, the market share or selling price required to yield annual benefits sufficient to more than justify the investment.

Although the authors have found the break-even approach useful in working with managers, they recognize that it has limitations. It places a proposal which may provide a 50 percent expected return on the same level as one with a 10 percent expected return, if both have about the same chance of being above the break-even point. Stating it another way, this approach ignores the desirability of risking losses if the chances for large gains are great. We recognize that it is a conservative approach to shedding light on uncertainty that avoids a full analysis of uncertainty.

ADJUSTING THE DISCOUNT RATE

Up to this point, we have been using the firm's cost of capital as the cutoff criterion in judging the desirability of investment proposals. However, as elucidated in Chapter 8, The Cost of Capital, there are difficulties encountered concerning the variation in risk between investment alternatives when this approach is utilized. Another method of choosing a discount rate that provides a practical -- although theoretically weak in many instances -- way for managers to deal with uncertainty involves requiring higher rates of return on projects with greater uncertainty than for projects involving less uncertainty. Thus, instead of using the firm's cost of capital as the yardstick to measure the desirability of all investments, projects are classified by the degree of uncertainty. Then different minimum rates of return are used for different classes of projects depending upon their uncertainty.

To illustrate this approach, let us assume that our firm's cost of capital is 11 percent. On investments which are of the same degree of uncertainty as the average or typical project in which the company is currently investing, we would use an 11 percent discount factor -- the same rate as the cost of capital to the company. On slightly more certain investments, we might use a rate of 9 or 10 percent -- granting a bonus of 1 or 2 percent for this lesser degree of uncertainty. On very speculative investments, we might add a very severe penalty -- say 5 percent -- and discount with a factor of 16 percent. When using the net present value approach for evaluating investment alternatives, the effect of using higher discount rates is to lower the present value of the benefits -- and in turn, to lower the net present value of a project. If the internal rate of return method is used, the IRR for a proposal would be compared with the rate of return adjusted for uncertainty. Thus, the greater the uncertainty of the project, the higher the "hurdle rate" it will have to leap to be acceptable.

The principal difficulty with varying the discount rate to adjust for uncertainty is in determining the appropriate discount rate for a particular investment.2/ This determination is likely to be subjective and rather arbitrary. Management knows that invest-

2/In some cases The Capital Asset Pricing Model (CAPM) may provide assistance in determining the appropriate discount rate. For example, when a firm is considering entry into a new industry or when it is evaluating a corporate acquisition the CAPM could be useful. For a discussion of the capital asset pricing model see Weston and Brigham, Managerial Finance, 7th edition.

ment in a new product requires a higher discount rate than the investment in an item of labor-saving equipment in its plant. But the real and difficult question is how much of a penalty -- how much higher a discount rate -- is appropriate? This is a vital question because the present value of a sum to be received in the remote future may be dramatically different with the change of just a few percentage points in the discount rate. The question of what minimum rate of return to use is likely to be resolved in a subjective manner based on managerial judgement and intuition. There is no easily used formula for guiding management in determining what discount factors should be used for investments with various degrees of uncertainty.

Another problem with using this approach rests with the assumption that uncertainty with respect to the projected cash flows increases, in a compounding fashion, over time (i.e., the probability of a dollar of estimated cash flow actually occurring decreases each year by a fixed percentage of the probability in the preceding year.) In some investments, this may be a good assumption, but in others the major uncertainty regarding cash flows that will be generated occurs in early periods rather than in the later years of the planning period. For example, take the case of an oil wildcatter. There is ready market for all the oil the prospective well will produce. The uncertainty is in the cost of drilling the well and whether oil will be found. Adjusting the discount rate for uncertainty would not accurately portray the circumstances of this case.

USING A RANGE OF POSSIBLE OUTCOMES

Up to this point we have used "single-valued" estimates of cash flows in our illustrations. In a world of perfect certainty, year-to-year cash flows would be predictable without serious error. In practice, managers are seldom, if ever, certain of the cash flows likely to result from a particular investment. Management does not know and cannot know all the future events that will affect the outcome of each investment alternative. Usually in the real world of uncertainty, there are several possible outcomes of an investment -- not a single set of cash flows. A useful and practical approach to gaining insight about, and handling, the uncertainty associated with investment alternatives is to recognize that many investments have more than one possible outcome by working with a range of possible cash flows that reflect different possible payoffs.

Recognizing the impracticability of determining cash flows for all possible outcomes, we suggest the following procedure as being a practical method of handling uncertainty in many situations. First, determine the net present values of an investment alternative under a series of different assumptions ranging from a pessimistic to an optimistic set of circumstances together with estimates within this spectrum one of which represents the most likely series of events. Once this pessimistic-optimistic range of estimated cash flows has been determined (which in itself will provide management with valuable insights), management has, as will be suggested, several alternatives available to it for handling the two complications associated with uncertainty:

1) The likelihood that each of the projected possible outcomes will materialize, and

2) The attitude of management toward risk which reflects, in part, how undesirable the unfavorable possible outcomes would be.

Approaches are available for rather quantitatively and "scientifically" handling these two dimensions of uncertainty or, more accurately, for thinking about them. We merely will introduce these approaches in hopes that some readers will investigate them in other sources. But first an example.

EXAMPLE

The Big Red Company has the opportunity to acquire a widget business for $30,000. The management of Big Red, which is considering the acquisition strictly for monetary reasons, recognizes that many factors, some of which are external to their control, could affect the incremental cash flows during the planning period that it is using to evaluate the desirability of this investment. Two major factors that create uncertainty regarding future cash flows (and consequently the worth of the widget business to Big Red) are levels of widget sales and widget prices in the future.

After considerable investigation, management was able to determine to its satisfaction a reasonably pessimistic set of developments, as well as a reasonably optimistic series of events, regarding both future sales volumes and prices. It also rendered a judgement as to the most probable circumstances regarding these two variables. It then proceeded to project annual cash flows under these three sets of circumstances and to compute the net present value (using the firm's weighted average cost of capital) of the widget business for each possibility:

Alternative outcome	Net present value of widget business
Pessimistic (low volume and prices)	$-20,000
Most likely	+20,000
Optimistic (high volume and prices)	+100,000

When management reached this stage of its analysis, it already had considerable insight into the desirability of the investment. Under the most probable conditions, the acquisition of the widget business by Big Red seems desirable (i.e., a positive net present value of $20,000). Moreover, if all goes well, the investment seems very desirable. However, under adverse conditions, it would be an undesirable investment to the tune of decreasing the value of their business up to $20,000 in present worth terms. In view of this, what should be Big Red's decision? To answer this, management must consider the two elements of uncertainty: (1) the probability of each possible outcome and (2) management's reaction to risk which would depend, among other things, on the firm's capacity to assume loss and the willingness of the suppliers of capital to gamble. At this stage, management might decide to handle these two implications in a highly qualitative way, and, without further formal analysis, either start formal negotiations for the purchase of the business or forget the acquisition. If so, thinking in terms of a range of possible outcomes, rather than just one possible payoff, has given management valuable insights. However, in many situations, further formal analysis to cope with uncertainty may be justified.

PROBABILITY DISTRIBUTION APPROACH

In connection with the willingness and capacity to assume risk, formal evaluation of the probability of possible outcomes frequently will be useful. For example, the acquisition of the widget business by the Big RedCompany could lead to a sizable loss (i.e., a negative net present value of $20,000), but what is the likelihood -- probability -- of this happening? If it is only one chance in fifty, most managers would take the gamble. However, if it is one chance in three, fewer managers would. In other words, not only is the range of possible outcomes important but the probability of occurrence should also be considered.

Estimates of the probability of occurrence of some particular outcome range from careful studies to simple guesses. Whether the estimates are formalized or not, the manager uses them every time a decision is made . He or she has a "feeling" that one outcome is more likely than another. These subjective estimates of probability arise out of experience. They can be made even more useful when they are put into a formal probability framework.

The sum of probabilities of all possible outcomes is 1.0. Let's assume that after using all available information, experience, and judgement, Big Red management comes up with the following subjective probabilities for the three outcomes being considered:

Pessimistic outcome	0.4
Most likely	0.5
Optimistic outcome	0.1

The Big Red management can now compute the expected monetary value of acquiring the widget business by multiplying the probability of each outcome considered by its expected net present value as follows:

Alternative outcome	(1) Net Present Value of outcome	(2) Probability	(3) (1) x (2) = Monetary expectation
Pessimistic	$-20,000	0.4	$- 8,000
Most likely	+20,000	0.5	+10,000
Optimistic	+100,000	0.1	+10,000
	Expected net present value =		$+12,000

The expected net present value of cash flows is $12,000, which suggests that the acquisition of the widget business would be a desirable investment. The expected net present value does not tell the investor what the return of the project actually will be since it is very unlikely that the present value of this project, ex post, will turn out to be exactly $12,000. This measure simply says that if this or similar investments were made numerous times by Big Red, the average net present value of these investments would be close to $12,000. The expected value criterion does not give a perfect decision rule. It simply provides more information to which managerial judgement must be applied.

Further information about an investment may be obtained by computing standard deviation around the expected values. The process by which this is done is considered in other texts and won't be presented in this one. 3/ Once the standard deviations of expected cash flows are calculated, they give us a measure of variability in our expected return. For example, each of two mutually exclusive investments shows an expected value of $1,000. The first investment has a standard deviation of $500 while the second has a standard deviation of $1,500. All other things being equal, the risk averse investor would choose the first alternative, since it has lower variability in returns. Investment number one has an equal probability of obtaining a present value between $+500 and $+1500 as investment two has of returning $-500 to $2,500. Again, in most cases these data will not be enough to make the best action for the manager clear, but will aid in making the final decision.

DECISION TREES

A decision tree is another way to evaluate uncertain cash flows as well as other information. Moreover, it is a technique for analyzing sequential decisions.

Up to this point we have been considering a single investment decision. The alternatives have been relatively straight forward and the decision has been merely to accept or reject the investment under analysis. In reality, most capital budgeting decisions are more complex and many involve sequential decisions.

A sequential decision means that we face different but related decisions at different points in time. In addition, it implies that a decision at one point in time will have an

3/ One reference is: J. Fred Weston and Eugene F. Brigham, Managerial Finance, 7th edition, Hinsdale, Illinois, The Dryden Press, 1981, Chapter 14.

effect on a decision at another point in time. It is quite obvious that the decisions we make today will have an impact on the decisions we make in the future. For example, suppose a student is considering whether to take a job directly after graduation or to go on to graduate school. The decisions he or she will be making a year from now will be very different depending on the alternative the student selects now. But the interrelated nature of sequential decisions flows both ways. That is, the decisions we may make one year from now will have an impact on the decisions we make today. This is much less obvious, but will be illustrated as we discuss the concept of decision trees.

Before we go any further we must outline the structure of a decision tree. A decision tree consists of five components:

1) Decision points. Each decision point represents the opportunity to select one of several courses of action (i.e., alternatives). We will use boxes to represent decision points.

2) Decision alternatives. Emanating from each box will be two or more lines which represent the different courses of action the manager has to select from. These are the investment alternatives, of which only one can be selected.

3) Chance events. These indicate there is uncertainty associated with some or possibly all the decision alternatives. A circle is used to symbolize a chance event.

4) Alternative outcomes. These are the different results that may arise from a chance event. Each line emanating from a chance event indicates a different alternative outcome. In addition, there is a probability associated with each alternative outcome representing its approximate chance of occurrence. The probabilities of all alternative outcomes from a single chance event must add up to 1.0.

5) Time line. The time line indicates the useful life and annual inflows and/or outflows of the investments under consideration as well as the timing of decisions (i.e., decision points) and chance events.4/

Decision trees are just an orderly way to present and evaluate data and information. Like the estimation of cash flows, a manager may find the mere construction of a decision tree useful in evaluating complex investment decisions. However, once a decision tree is constructed, it is relatively easy to evaluate the cash flows using the net present value method.

EXAMPLE: HEREIN LIES THE RUB (SKAKESPEARE)

The Adam and Eve Corporation builds and operates (legitimate) massage parlors. The firm has decided to open an outlet in town, but is uncertain of the size of operation to establish. The problem is that management is uncertain of demand. It estimates a 60% probability of low demand and a 40% chance of high demand. Adam and Eve are considering two sizes: a large (4 room) parlor and a small (2 room) parlor. The expected cash flows associated with each alternative are:

4/Chance events are normally assumed to occur when a decision is selected (i.e., at a decision point) but this is not necessary. They should be positioned at the point in time they are most likely to occur.

Size	Initial Cost	Amount Net Cash Inflows with: High Demand	Low Demand
Large	-$50,000	$30,000	$12,000
Small	- 25,000	15,000	10,000

If the company intially builds a small facility, management will evaluate its performance after one year. If demand is high Adam and Eve may expand the massage parlor. It costs $26,000 to convert a small facility into a large one. Experience with other expansion projects indicates there is a 90 percent chance net proceeds will increase to $30,000 and a 10 percent probability that they will remain at approximately $15,000. The time horizon for these investments is five years and they will have no salvage value. Assume all cash flows are expressed on an after tax basis. Should Adam and Eve initially build a large or a small facility?

The Procedure

Application of decision tree with net present value analysis involves an eight step process. We will discuss each step.

Step one: describe the problem verbally. This is what we have already done in presenting the example.

Step two: illustrate the problem using a decision tree. Start with the initial decision point and identify the decision alternatives--in our example to build large or small. Locate the chance events and the alternative outcomes. In this case, we are assuming each chance event would occur immediately after the decision alternative is selected. The procedure should be followed for all decision points.

The step includes adding the time line to indicate the timing of decision points, the duration of alternative outcomes, and the position of chance events.

Figure 3 illustrates the results of Step One.

Step three: insert the data. After a manager has described the situation verbally and graphically, it is time to insert the data. There are two types of data to be included.

The first type is cash flows. Whenever possible it is simplest if annual cash inflows and cash outflows are reduced to net cash flows. Other cash flows also incorporated are capital outlays, and salvage values, if any.

The second type of data is the probabilities associated with the different alternative outcomes at each chance event. They must always add to 1.0 at each chance event.

Figure 4 illustrates a decision tree with the data added. There are a few subtleties that should be noted. First, if the firm builds small there is a $15,000 net cash inflow in the first year if demand is high. Second, with decision point 2 there is no chance event associated with continuing small. If the outcome of initially building small was $15,000 and management decides to continue small, then it knows with more or less certainty it will continue to receive $15,000 per year for the remaining four years. Finally, if the company does build small it will incur a $26,000 capital outlay at the end of the first year only if it expands.

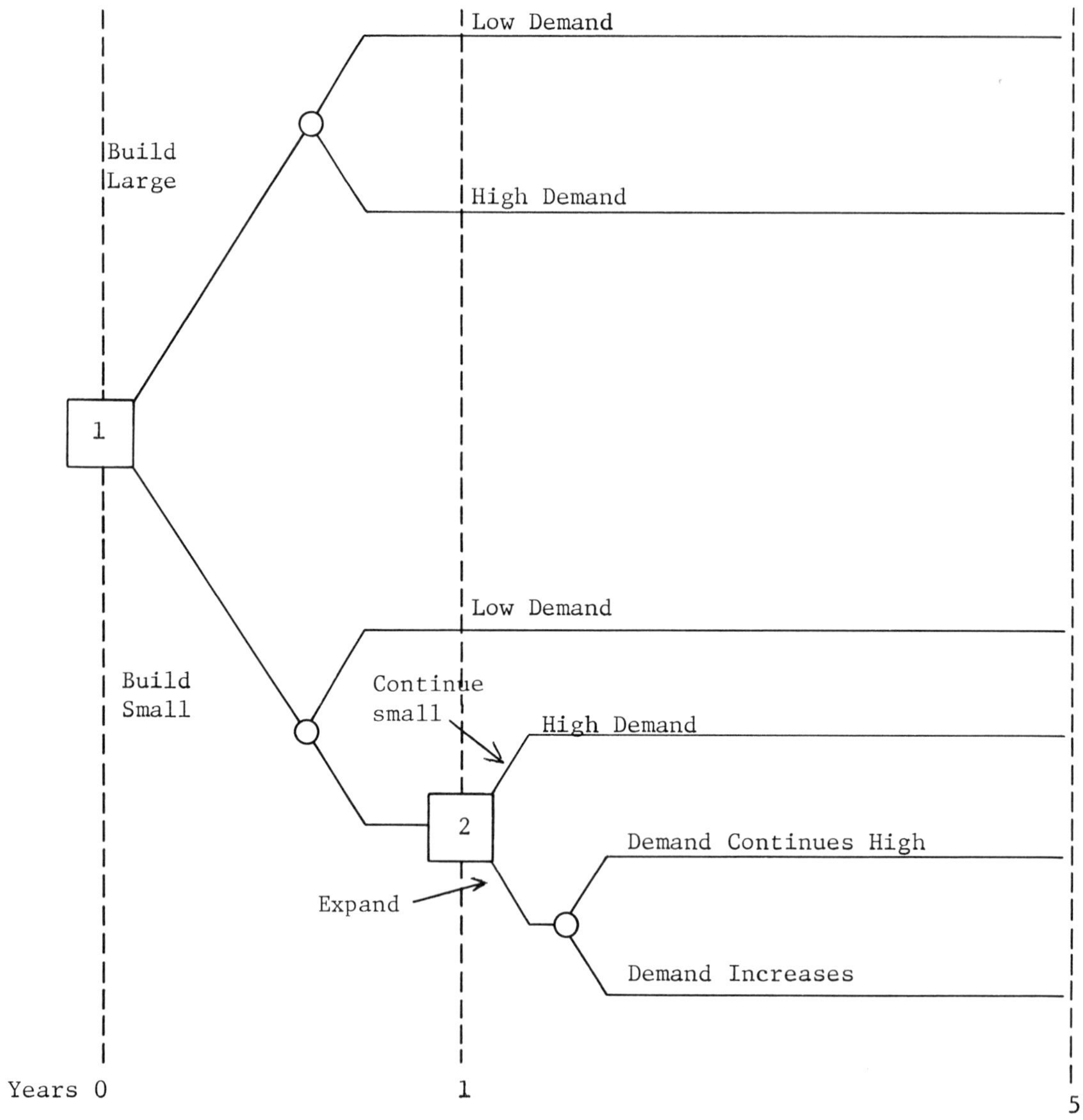

Figure 3. Decision Tree for Adam and Eve

Step four: select the appropriate discount rate. Just like in the case of the probability distribution approach the appropriate discount rate is the firm's risk adjusted discount rate. Since this investment is similar to the firm's investment in other parlors, a reasonable estimate of the firm's discount rate is its current weighted average cost of capital. We will assume the firm's WACC is 14 percent.

If the new parlor represented higher risk than its other investments, a higher discount rate (one with a higher premium for risk) would be appropriate. The opposite is true if this investment represented less risk to the firm.

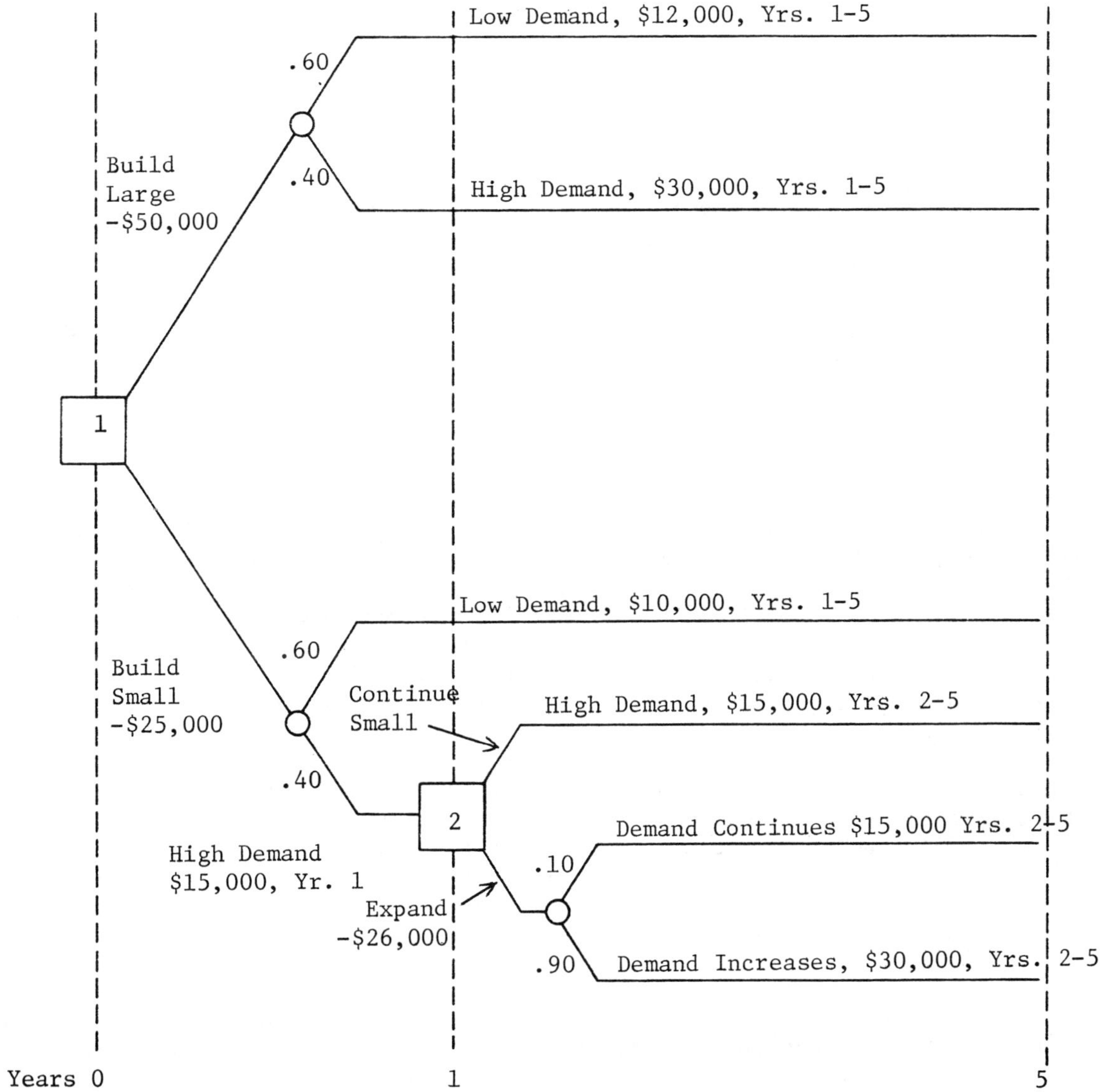

Figure 4. Decision Tree for Adam and Eve with Data Added

Step five: compute the net present value of each decision alternative starting at the most distant decision point. In our example there are two decision alternatives at decision point 2: continue small and expand. Let us analyze each separately, starting at the bottom of the decision tree.

Expansion

Since there is a chance event associated with expansion, each outcome must be multiplied by its respective probability. Often the most difficult issue to resolve is: what annuity factor to use? The correct annuity factor is a_{1-4}, 14%. Each decision point is initially treated as if it were at time point zero, and subsequent cash flows are generated for the following four years. As will be illustrated below, the present value derived by using the annuity factor $a_{1-4,14}$ will later be multiplied by the present value factor $a_{1,14}$. The end result is the same as initially using the annuity factor $a_{2-5,14}$.

Demand Continues Unchanged	
$15,000 (2.9137) (.10) =	$ 4,371
Demand Increases	
$30,000 (2.9137) (.90) =	78,670
Present Value of Inflows	$83,041
Capital Outlay	-26,000
Expected Net Present Value	$57,041

Continue Small

In our example, no capital outlays or uncertainty are associated with continuing with the small parlor.

Expected Net Present Value	
$15,000 (2.9137) =	$43,706

Step Six: select the best alternative at the most distant decision point. Naturally, management would want to consider all the qualitative factors involved, but for our purpose we assume the best alternative is the one with the highest net present value. It is the one that maximizes the value of the firm and the wealth of its owners. Management would then elect to expand the facility if it were ever presented with the situation just analyzed--management initially built the small parlor and demand turned out to be high. It is possible management may never face this situation. It may initially build the large facility. Let us examine the situation in more detail.

Today, the firm must decide whether to initially build a large or small establishment. It does not need to decide which alternative (expand or continue small) it will select at decision point 2. It can wait a year for that if it constructs the two room parlor and will never need to worry about it if the four room facility is built now. Why then do we start by analyzing the second decision first? The reason is because the decision we may make a year from now will effect the decision we make today.

In evaluating the alternative of building small, management must realize that it will face a future decision if demand is high. Analysis of the initial decision should include the alternative management would select at decision point 2 and only that alternative because it will have an impact on the net present value of the "build small" alternative at decision point 1. This is why when we deal with sequential decisions we say the decision we would make a year from now may effect the decision we make today.

The net present value of the preferred alternative at a decision point is referred to as a position value. At decision point 2 the position value is $57,041--the net present value of expansion. Hereafter, we neglect the present value of all alternatives except the preferred one.

We have completed one iteration in the "Rollback Procedure." The rollback procedure involves starting at the furthest decision point, discounting the cash flows, applying the probabilities and determining the preferred decision alternative.

Step seven: continue the rollback procedure for each furthest decision point. This involves using the position value of the preceeding decision point, discounting, adjusting for uncertainty, and computing the net present value for each decision alternative. In our example the next decision point is decision point 1 with two alternatives--build a small facility or construct a large one. The preceeding decision point is decision point 2.

Build Small

High Demand	
($57,041 + 15,000) (.8772) (.40) =	$25,778
Low Demand	
$10,000 (3.4331) (.60) =	20,599
Present Value of Net Inflows	$46,377
Capital Outlay	-25,000
Expected Net Present Value	$21,377

Note that both the position value of $57,041 and the cash flow of $15,000 for the first year are discounted by the present value factor for one year. Consequently, the cash flows received in years two through five are now expressed in terms of discounted dollars for years two through five. Also, it should be noted that the appropriate annuity factor for the cash flows in the case of low demand is $a_{1-5,14}$.

Build Large

High Demand	
$30,000 (3.4331) (.40) =	$41,197
Low Demand	
$12,000 (3.4331) (.60) =	24,718
Present Value of Inflows	$65,915
Capital Outlay	-50,000
Expected Net Present Value	$15,915

Step eight: finally select the best alternative at decision point 1. In our example, management would probably decide to construct the small parlor because its net present value is $21,377 compared to $15,915 for the large facility. We say "probably" because we do not know management's aversion to risk.

A FEW COMMENTS ABOUT DECISION TREES

Decision trees are another technique to assist managers in evaluating risk and uncertainty in complex investments. Specifically, they are designed to organize and evaluate sequential decisions--decisions that are interdependent rather than independent. As our example suggests, decision trees are merely an extension of the probability distribution approach. Both techniques are tools that managers should find to be very useful.

INVESTOR'S AVERSION TO UNCERTAINTY

Thus far in discussing the handling of uncertainty, we have avoided a problem that managers cannot ignore -- the investor's attitudes toward uncertainty. A very important fact of life is that different people and different firms have different attitudes toward uncertainty. The possibility of a very large gain may outweigh in importance to the investor the possibility of a very large loss. However, just the opposite may be true (i.e., the possibility of a rather small loss may outweigh the importance of a possible large gain). Clearly the investor's attitudes toward uncertainty must be considered in decision making. The investor must decide whether he or she desires a relatively safe position and small profits, or whether he or she is willing to make more drastic changes and assume the uncertainty and possible losses that accompany them.

People who are continuing to push back the frontiers of capital budgeting are working on methods that enable us to at least think more constructively about how to handle uncertainty including the investor's attitude toward uncertainty.5/ These approaches are beyond the scope of this publication. We merely will suggest the nature of two of them. One approach involves the investor rather objectively describing his risk preferences in the form of a utility function. The utility function provides an index of the relative satisfaction that would be derived if a particular outcome actually occurred. Once the utility function has been determined, we merely substitute measures of utility for the dollar outcomes and compute the expected utility of the investment. Using the Big Red example, the expected utility is calculated as follows:

Alternative outcome	(1) Utility	(2) Probability	(3) (1) x (2) = Utility expectation
Pessimistic	-200	0.4	-80
Most likely	+120	0.5	+60
Optimistic	+300	0.1	+30
		Expected Utility =	+10

If the utility function accurately describes the relative satisfactions (or dissatisfactions) that the firm would derive from various outcomes, it would appear that Big Red should acquire the widget business because the expected utility is positive -- although apparently the grief from a relatively small loss is nearly as great as the pleasure from a large profit.

Another approach to handling the problem of uncertainty is the certainty equivalent approach. For a discussion of this approach, see Weston and Brigham, Managerial Finance, 7th edition, Chapter 14.

A PARTING REMINDER

An important thing to keep in mind is that the consideration of uncertainty in no way invalidates the basic concepts and approaches that we have discussed -- rather it just complicates their application. We should appreciate that uncertainty means that we must supplement the simple decision rules that we have discussed -- not throw them away.

5/ Bierman and Smidt, The Capital Budgeting Decision, Macmillan Publishing Co., 5th edition, Parts II and III.

11

HANDLING INFLATION

Inflation 1/ may affect both the cash flows of an investment proposal and the cost of capital to the investing firm. 2/ Ignoring inflation or pretending that it does not exist can lead to incorrect investment decisions. When inflation rates were relatively low (such as one or two percent per year) ignoring inflation when analyzing proposed investments had much less serious consequences than it does with the inflation rates of the last decade.

Briefly, inflation means that the purchasing power of the dollar declines. The idea of the purchasing power of a dollar gives us a start towards developing a methodology to handle inflation. If we can express the cash flows of an investment in terms of real purchasing power, we can determine if the investment is desirable under the inflation conditions which we expect to exist.

On the other hand, if we can express all the flows in terms of physical dollars, we can also determine the desirability of the investment. We shall return to this later, but it suffices to say at this time, that the general method for handling inflation is to express the cash flows of an investment in terms of a common unit of measure -- whether that unit of measure is real purchasing power or physical dollars is irrelevant, as long as we are consistent. After getting all of the flows into a common frame of reference with respect to inflation we can then use our present value thinking to put the flows into a common time frame of reference.

REAL FLOWS AND MONEY FLOWS

At this point, a discussion about the meaning of money and real flows should be helpful. "Money flows", sometimes called nominal flows, are the actual physical dollar bills that change hands in the period of time under consideration. For example, consider an

1/ For a discussion of "What is Inflation?", see Bierman and Smidt, The Capital Budgeting Decision, Macmillan Publishing Co., 5th ed., pp. 426-427.

2/ This chapter is based partly on an unpublished paper entitled "Inflation and Capital Budgeting", by Joseph C. Taber, former student, Graduate School of Business and Public Administration, Cornell University, written at the time he was a teaching assistant in one of our courses.

entreprenuer who enters into a five year lease with annual payments of \$100. Every year, for the next five years our entrepreneur will have to pay out 100 dollar bills to honor the lease arrangement. However, these money flows or actual physical dollars that change hands in the future periods will have different purchasing power due to inflation. Thus, to determine the "real flow" in a future period we must first decide on a base period or year. The purchasing power of a dollar at one instant in time is arbitrarily set as the real value of a dollar. Thus a "money" or physical dollar paid one year after the base year is not as valuable because of inflation. The dollar we pay out at the end of the year one cannot buy as much as a dollar we pay out today because prices have increased. Thus, in investment analysis it is logical to set the base or purchasing power of a dollar at time period zero, the point at which we make our decision. Then the net present value of an investment alternative expressed in "real" dollar terms will represent the value of the investment to us in today's purchasing power.

The "real" value or flow in any future time period is the purchasing power in today's terms of the money or physical dollars at that point in time. Although capital budgeting decisions may be made using either money or real flows, there may be differences in our ability to estimate the costs and benefits of an investment project. Generally, if revenues or costs are mainly determined by market forces in the period in which the outlays are made or the revenues received, then estimates in terms of real cash flows are likely to be more accurate than estimates of money flows. But, if future costs and revenues are determined by immediate decisions, by income tax considerations, or by long-term contractual relationships -- then estimates in terms of money flows are likely to be more accurate. For example, it is very easy for the entreprenuer mentioned above to determine the money flow associated with the lease arrangement, since it is with certainty that there will be an outflow of 100 physical dollars each year for the next five years.

Now suppose the same entreprenuer is looking at the revenues from the company's sale of goods. Suppose further that the price of the goods sold is expected to follow the general inflation level. It may be easier to project future sales revenue in terms of today's prices than to project the actual money flows (which will be partially determined in any given year by inflation). This would be a "real flow." The future prices of the goods sold would be increasing (thereby increasing the physical dollars received in future periods) at the same rate as the general level of inflation. Hence, the purchasing power of the sales revenue would remain the same, assuming the same number of units are sold each year, even though sales dollars are increasing. So, expressing future sales in terms of today's prices would be a real cash flow since the flow is expressed in terms of today's purchasing power.

Converting a real flow to a money flow and vice versa, is basically a simple matter. To illustrate the procedure, let's return to our hypothetical entreprenuer. Further assume that the level of inflation is expected to be 5% per year over the next five years. First we will convert the lease payment flow (which is a money flow) into a real flow, a flow which will express the future lease payments in terms of today's purchasing power.

Year:	0	1	2	3	4	5
Lease payment:		-\$100	-\$100	\$-100	-\$100	-\$100

Consider the \$100 payment at the end of year one. Over the first year, inflation of 5% has occurred so that the purchasing power of \$100 received by the lessor at the end of year one is somewhat less than it is today (time zero). To convert this \$100 money flow into today's purchasing power we must deflate it. Since inflation of 5% has taken place over the year, the purchasing power of the \$100 in today's terms is:

$$\frac{\$100}{1.05} \quad \text{or} \quad \$95.23$$

Now, consider the $100 lease payment at the end of year two. With annual inflation of 5%, the purchasing power of this payment has been eroded by two rounds of inflation, one in year one and one in year two. In order to show that inflation acts in a compounding manner (such as compound interest) consider an item which sells for $1.00 today. If the price of this item inflates at 5%, at the end of year one the item will sell for $1.00 x 1.05 = $1.05. If inflation is again 5% over year two, the price of our item will be $1.05 x 1.05 = $1.1025 at the end of year two. In essence, inflation on previous inflation occurs, just as compound interest gives us interest on previous interest.

Thus, the effect of inflation on our year two lease payment has compounded over two time periods and hence the purchasing power in today's terms is:

$$\frac{\$100}{(1.05)^2} \quad \text{or } \$90.70$$

The same result may be obtained by using the present value factor for two years and 5%: $100 x .9070 = $90.70. The purchasing power of the $100 payments in years 3, 4 and 5 is calculated similarly.

Summarizing the lease payments we have:

Year:	0	1	2	3	4	5
Money Flow:		-$100	-$100	-$100	-$100	-$100
Real Flow:		-95.23	-90.70	-86.38	-82.27	-78.35

Note that the fixed lease payment becomes smaller in real terms each year. The lessee tends to gain at the expense of the lessor.

Now turn to the flows associated with sales revenue. Assume sales are 100 units per year for the next five years and that sales take place at the end of the year. Today's price is $10.00 per unit and it is expected to follow the overall 5% per year inflation rate. Therefore, the real flow will be the same each year.

Year:	0	1	2	3	4	5
Real Flow (today's purchasing power)		+$1,000	+$1,000	+$1,000	+$1,000	+$1,000

To convert this real flow into a money flow, we must inflate the real flows to signify the increase in physical dollars which will occur due to price increases. Inflating real flows is just the opposite of the deflating process which we used before. If the price is $10 today, it will be $10.50 at the end of year one, $11.025 at the end of year two, etc. Hence, our money flows from sales will be:

Year:	0	1	2	3	4	5
Money Flow:		+$1,050	+$1,102.50	+$1,157.63	+$1,215.51	+$1,276.28

Before we move on to consider the relation between inflation and the discount rate, let's consider a different but not rare case -- that is, when an item has a different inflation rate than the general level of inflation. In this case the same methodology applies, but in a slightly more complex fashion.

To illustrate, assume our entrepreneur is now concerned with the future labor expense. Suppose that there is a labor contract which calls for a 2% increase in wages each year. In addition to this 2% increase, the contract has a cost of living clause which is tied to the consumer price index which we will assume represents the general level of inflation. If inflation is expected to be 5% per year for the next five years, the workers will get an annual wage increase of 7%.

Assume our entreprenuer has a constant labor force which works 5,000 hours per year and gets paid at the end of each year. The current wage rate paid is $6.00 per hour. Projecting the labor usage at today's wage for the next five years we have:

Year:	0	1	2	3	4	5
Flow:		-$30,000	-$30,000	-$30,000	-$30,000	-$30,000

Unfortunately, this "flow" is neither a real flow nor a money flow. It's not a real flow -- because of the 2% automatic increase in the contract there is no way $30,000 in future periods can buy us the same amount of labor as it does today. Even in the absence of general inflation, we must pay 2% more each year to have equal purchasing power with respect to labor hours.

It's not a money flow either, since our wage bill, in physical dollars, will also be higher than $30,000 in the upcoming years.

To project the money flow associated with our labor usage, we must determine what our actual wage bill will be in each of the next five years. Again let's assume 5% annual inflation, giving us a 7% annual wage increase.

Year	Wage Bill in Previous Period	times	1 plus Rate of Increase	=	Wage Paid
1	$30,000	x	1.07	=	$32,100
2	32,100	x	1.07	=	34,347
3	34,347	x	1.07	=	36,751
4	36,751	x	1.07	=	39,324
5	39,324	x	1.07	=	42,077

So, our money flow (physical dollars) will be:

Year	0	1	2	3	4	5
Money Flow:		-$32,100	-$34,347	-$36,751	-$39,324	-$42,077

Note that we simply inflate the $30,000 by 7% each year in a compound fashion.

In order to express our wage expense in real flow terms, we must now deflate the money flows by the 5% annual inflation rate.3/ The resultant flow will tell us how many "year zero" dollars would be needed to purchase the 5,000 hours of labor each year. Remember that a real flow is in terms of constant purchasing power expressed in today's terms. The real flows for wages will be:

3/Another, less accurate, way to compute real cash flows would be to multiply the original $30,000 by a factor of 1.02 for each of the five years. The two methods give slightly different results. When any cash flow is multiplied by two or more compound interest or present value factors a cross product should also be included in the computation. Since the error is slight at low inflation rate one may ignore this inconsistency, but when inflation rates are high, for example as in some less developed countries, the cross product should be included.

Year (n)	Money Flow (Physical Dollars)	divided by	1 plus Inflation Rate^n	=	Real Flow
1	\$32,100		1.05		\$30,571
2	34,347		1.05^2		31,154
3	36,751		1.05^3		31,747
4	39,324		1.05^4		32,352
5	42,077		1.05^5		32,968

Here we deflated the money flows by our 5% inflation in a compound fashion. Summarizing our labor expense flows, we have:

Year:	0	1	2	3	4	5
Money Flow:		-\$32,100	-\$34,347	-\$36,751	-\$39,324	-\$42,077
Real Flow:		- 30,571	- 31,154	- 31,747	- 32,352	- 32,968

One last detail before we move on. Those of you who understand the compounding phenomenon have probably already discovered an easier way to deflate and inflate cash flows. As you know, the present value factors given in Table II are the reciprocal of the compound interest factors given in Table I. Therefore, to deflate a flow in period n for a given annual rate of inflation, we can simply multiply by the present value factor for period n (Table II) for the percent of inflation desired. For example, to deflate the \$32,100 money flow for labor in period one we simply multiply \$32,100 by .9524 = \$30,572. To inflate a flow for a given year we simply divide by the present value factor for the period and rate in question.

INFLATION AND THE DISCOUNT RATE

As discussed earlier, the weighted average cost of capital includes three components as shown in the following equation:

$$WACC = A + R + I$$

where WACC = weighted average cost of capital,

A = alternative uses of money or the pure time value of money,

R = an allowance or premium for risk or uncertainty,

I = an allowance or premium for inflation.

For the purpose of correctly handling inflation in evaluating proposed capital investments, the important consideration is whether I, the premium for inflation, is or is not included in the cost of capital used to discount the cash flows. The rules for handling "I" are simple:

1. If the projected cash flows are "real" flows (i.e., inflation has been removed) the cost of capital used for discounting the flows must be an inflation free rate -- it must not include "I".

2. If the projected cash flows are "money" flows, the discount rate must include "I", the premium for inflation.

Correct results can be obtained with either formulation. The important point is that inflation be handled consistently in the cost of capital and in the projected cash flows.

Either method -- using real flows discounted with a cost of capital which excludes the inflation premium or money (nominal) flows discounted with a rate which includes a premium for inflation -- will yield satisfactory results. Hence, a manager may project the flows in the simplest way possible and by using the proper discount rate on either type of flow, will be able to determine the net present value in terms which will represent purchasing power.

COMPUTING THE AFTER-TAX REAL DISCOUNT RATE

The weighted average cost of capital as normally computed is in nominal rather than in real terms. (By nominal, we mean that inflation is included.) Therefore it is usually easier to start from a nominal discount rate than from a real rate even when the goal is a real rate with which to discount real flows. Ignoring income taxes, the formula for computing the real rate is:

$$1 + r = \frac{1 + n}{1 + f}$$

where: r = real discount rate
n = nominal discount rate
f = inflation rate

Example: n = .16, f = .10

$$1 + r = \frac{1.16}{1.10} = 1.0545;\ \text{therefore } r = .0545$$

An approximation frequently used is to compute nominal and real rates from each other by simple addition or subtraction. In our example, if the inflation rate is subtracted from the nominal rate, the result is .16 - .10 = .06 rather than .0545. For many purposes, the simple subtraction does no great harm but the analyst should remember that it is an approximation.

Computation of the real, after-tax discount rate from the nominal, before tax discount rate (or WACC) may be done with the formula:

$$1 + r = \frac{1 + n\,(1-t)}{1 + f}$$

where: r = real, after tax discount rate
n = nominal before tax discount rate
t = marginal tax rate
f = inflation rate

Example: n = .16, t = .25; and f = .10

$$1 + r = \frac{1 + .16\,(1-.25)}{1.10} = \frac{1.12}{1.10} = 1.01818 \text{ or } r = .01818$$

This formula is satisfactory for computing a real, after-tax discount rate based on a nominal weighted average before tax cost of debt and equity capital for a business which is not a publicly held corporation. For example, an individual proprietor is in the same marginal tax bracket when considering the taxes to be paid on earnings from equity capital as when considering the taxes saved as a result of interest paid on debt.

Computation of a real, after tax discount rate for a publicly held corporation employs the formula:

$$1 + r = \frac{E\,(1 + e) + D\,[1 + d\,(1 - t)]}{1 + f}$$

where: r = real, after tax discount rate
E = proportion of equity
e = nominal cost of equity, after tax
D = proportion of debt
d = nominal cost of debt, before tax
t = marginal tax rate

The reason for using this formula is that the cost of equity capital in corporations typically is stated as an after tax cost.

AN EXAMPLE

We would like to find the present value of a lease payment of $100 per year for two years, the first payment one year from now. The lease payment is a money flow. We will ignore income taxes and use the simple subtraction of the inflation rate from the weighted average cost of capital to obtain the real discount rate.

The WACC is 9 percent and the inflation rate is expected to be 5 percent per year for the foreseeable future. (Note: I = 5% = inflation rate, this implies that investors have perfect knowledge concerning inflation for future periods and are willing to invest if they are compensated for the inflation as well as for their time value of money.) Therefore A + R = WACC − I = .09 − .05 = .04 which will be used as the real discount rate.

Finding the present value of a lease payment of $100 for the next two years (paid at the end of each year) can be done two ways:

METHOD ONE: USING REAL FLOWS

Year:	0	1	2
Money Flow		−$100	−$100
Real Flow (deflated for 5% inflation)		$-\frac{\$100}{1.05} = -\$95.24$	$-\frac{\$100}{(1.05)^2} = -\$90.70$

Discounting for the time value of money, using an <u>inflation-free</u> rate on <u>real</u> flows:

Present value of year 1 flow: $\frac{-\$95.24}{1.04} = -\$91.58$

Present value of year 2 flow: $\frac{-\$90.70}{(1.04)^2} = -\$83.86$

Present value of lease payments = −$175.44

METHOD TWO: USING MONEY FLOWS

Year:	0	1	2
Money Flow		−$100	−$100

Discounting simultaneously to take care of inflation and the time value of money, using a rate which includes a premium for inflation:

	Year 1		Year 2		
Present value of payments:	$\frac{-\$100}{1.09}$	+	$\frac{-\$100}{(1.09)^2}$	=	-\$175.91

The answers are not quite the same because of the approximation we used in computing the real rate. However, they are close enough for practical purposes and therefore, we can label the two methods as equivalent.

The following section of this chapter is a more complex example which will help you to understand the problem of inflation and how to approach it in capital budgeting situations. We urge you to solve the problem, even though a solution is provided.

THE BALLOON MANUFACTURING COMPANY

The Balloon Manufacturing Company is considering the acquistion of a machine to inflate its custom "parade" balloons with helium. Mr. I. N. Flate, president of the company, believes there will be a profitable market for pre-inflated balloons, stating, "Everyone loves a parade." Mr. I. N. Flate has been approached by Ms. Lotta Gass, a representative of Hot Air Products Company, with a proposition to provide the machine for $4,000 per year for three years with an operating lease.

Mr. Flate has projected the expected cash flows for the investment for the first year as follows:

Revenues	$20,000
Labor	- 9,000
Materials	- 5,000
Lease payment	- 4,000
Before tax net income	$ 2,000

These flows are in "money" terms as of the end of year 1. Assume the following:

1. Since the new machine will not require any additional office staff or factory space, the above expenses are the only relevant expenses.

2. Expected demand (physical volume of sales) and efficiency in the use of materials and labor will stay the same over the next three years.

3. The expenses and revenues occur at the end of each year.

Mr. Flate expects that average price levels will rise by 10% annually over the next three years and this price level change will be reflected in strictly proportional changes in the product and material prices. In other words, he expects product selling prices and material costs to inflate in the future at about the same rate as the general economy. However, his labor expense is expected to rise at a rate two percentage points above the projected inflation rate.

The following is information about the Balloon Manufacturing Company:

Marginal tax rate = 40%
After-tax inflation-free minimum required rate of return = 6%
Before-tax weighted average cost of capital = 20%

Answer the following questions:

a. Determine the after-tax net "money" cash flow for each year.

b. Determine the "real" flow for each item for each year. Then determine the after-tax net "real" cash flow for each year.

c. Determine the after-tax present value of leasing this equipment. Remember that this is an operating lease, not a financial lease.

d. Which flows did you use to answer part c, "real" or "money"? Explain and illustrate another sound approach to arrive at essentially the same answer.

e. Why should management concern itself about inflation in making capital investment decisions?

f. Consider that Mr. Flate has an opportunity to buy the same machine for $10,000, instead of leasing the needed machine from the Hot Air Products Company. The purchased machine is expected to have a useful life of three years and no salvage value at the end of that time. It will be 60 percent qualified for Federal investment credit because it is three-year property. Assuming the Balloon Company uses straight-line depreciation, generate the real after-tax cash flows in each year.

g. Determine whether Mr. Flate should lease or buy the machine. Use the net present value approach and deal with the problem of inflation in an appropriate manner.

SOLUTION TO BALLOON MANUFACTURING COMPANY

As discussed earlier in this chapter, the cost of capital or minimum desired rate of return includes three components: the pure time value of money, an adjustment for inflation and an adjustment for risk. Mr. Flate believes this investment has the same amount of risk as the average of his business. Therefore, the discount rate should include the risk adjustment. Also, we are considering the after-tax cash flows, so we want an after-tax discount rate. For real flows we want an after-tax, inflation-free rate, which is 6%. For money flows we want an after-tax rate including the adjustment for inflation. With 10% inflation, this rate is equal to 10% + 6% = 16%. Note that we are using the simple addition or subtraction of inflation when going from one rate to the other. The before-tax cost of capital is irrelevant because we are dealing with after-tax cash flows regardless of whether we are discounting money flows or real flows.

<u>Part a</u>: "Money Flows" -- 10% inflation, plus an additional 2% increase in labor cost.

Money flows for revenue and materials inflate at 10% per year, therefore:

<u>Revenues</u>:	in year 1,	$20,000 (given)
	in year 2, $20,000 x 1.1	22,000
	in year 3, $22,000 x 1.1	24,200
<u>Materials</u>:	in year 1,	$ 5,000 (given)
	in year 2, $5,000 x 1.1	5,500
	in year 3, $5,500 x 1.1	6,050

<u>Labor</u>: Money flows for labor inflate at 12% per year so:

in year 1,	$ 9,000 (given)
in year 2, $9,000 x 1.12	10,080
in year 3, $10,080 x 1.12	11,290

The lease payment of \$4,000 per year is fixed by contractual agreement and therefore does not inflate. You may think it's a real flow but in fact it's a money flow.

Year:	1	2	3
Revenue	\$20,000	\$22,000	\$24,200
Materials	- 5,000	- 5,500	- 6,050
Labor	- 9,000	-10,080	-11,290
Lease	- 4,000	- 4,000	- 4,000
Before-tax money flows	\$ 2,000	\$ 2,420	\$ 2,860
After-tax net money flows =	\$ 1,200	\$ 1,452	\$ 1,716

Part b: "Real Flows":

Real flows can be determined by adjusting the money flows for inflation. We have chosen to express the real purchasing power in period 0 dollars. Therefore, the year 1 money flows as well as the flows in future periods must be deflated to obtain real flows:

		10% PV Factor	Real flows
Revenues:	in year 1, \$20,000 x	.9091 =	\$18,182
	in year 2, \$22,000 x	.8264 =	18,182
	in year 3, \$24,200 x	.7513 =	18,182
Materials:	in year 1, \$ 5,000 x	.9091 =	\$ 4,545
	in year 2, \$ 5,500 x	.8264 =	4,545
	in year 3, \$ 6,050 x	.7513 =	4,545
Labor:	in year 1, \$ 9,000 x	.9091 =	\$ 8,182
	in year 2, \$10,080 x	.8264 =	8,330
	in year 3, \$11,290 x	.7513 =	8,482

Lease: Lease payments are money flows, so they must be adjusted.

in year 1, \$ 4,000 x	.9091 =	\$ 3,636
in year 2, \$ 4,000 x	.8264 =	3,306
in year 3, \$ 4,000 x	.7513 =	3,005

Year:	1	2	3
Revenue	\$18,182	\$18,182	\$18,182
Materials	- 4,545	- 4,545	- 4,545
Labor	- 8,182	- 8,330	- 8,482
Lease	- 3,636	- 3,306	- 3,005
Before-tax real flows	\$ 1,819	\$ 2,001	\$ 2,150
After-tax real flows = before-tax x (1-t) =	\$ 1,091	\$ 1,201	\$ 1,290

Part c:

To find the after-tax net present value, use the "real" flows and discount with the after-tax, inflation-free rate of 6%, using the appropriate factors from Table II.

1,091(.9434) + 1,201(.8900) + 1,290(.8396) = \$3,181 = after-tax NPV

Part d:

Another sound approach is to use "money" cash flows and discount with the after-tax, inflation-free rate of 6% plus the adjustment for inflation of 10% = 16%.

1,200(.8621) + 1,452(.7432) + 1,716(.6407) = $3,213 = after-tax NPV

This answer is not exactly the same as in part c because of the approximation we used in computing the discount rate, including inflation.

Part e:

Future cash flows may differ not only in timing but also in purchasing power. Management should be concerned with inflation because: 1) costs and revenues may inflate at different rates and thus must be adjusted to have an accurate comparison; and 2) management should be concerned with an accurate estimate of the purchasing power of the returns of the investment and not just money comparisons.

Part f: Using Real Flows

Year:	1	2	3
Revenue	$18,182	$18,182	$18,182
Labor	- 8,182	- 8,330	- 8,482
Materials	- 4,545	- 4,545	- 4,545
Before-tax real flows	$ 5,455	$ 5,307	$ 5,155
After-tax, before depreciation real flows	$ 3,273	$ 3,184	$ 3,093
Plus, real depreciation tax savings*	$ 1,212	$ 1,102	$ 1,001
Plus: investment credit**	436		
After-tax real flows	$ 4,921	$ 4,286	$ 4,094

*Annual straight-line depreciation = $\frac{\$10,000 - 0}{3 \text{ years}}$ = $3,333/year, "money" flow.

Annual tax savings in money terms = $3,333(t) = $1,333/year; this must be converted to real flows as follows:

	PV Factor @ 10%		Real Flow
in year 1, $1,333 x	.9091	=	$1,212
in year 2, $1,333 x	.8264	=	1,102
in year 3, $1,333 x	.7513	=	1,001

**$10,000 x .60 x .08 = $480 money flow. Real flow = $480 x .9091 = $436. We have chosen the two point reduction in federal investment credit rather than the basis reduction.

Part g:

In "real" terms, buying the machine has a net present value of:

NPV = -$10,000 + 4,921(.9434) + 4,286(.8900) + 4,094(.8396)

NPV = $1,894

If we compare this to the net present value calculated for leasing in part c, the answer is that in this situation Mr. Flate should lease the machine rather than buy it.

NPV if lease = $3,181
NPV if buy = $1,894

Both NPV's are positive, but the operating lease is the preferred alternative in net present value terms.

SUMMARY

To summarize our discussion of handling inflation for capital budgeting decisions, we offer the following list of important things to remember:

1. Flows which measure the amount of physical dollars that are changing hands in a series of time periods are called "money flows."

2. Flows which measure cash flows in terms of constant purchasing power are called "real flows."

3. Satisfactory results can be obtained using either money flows or real flows, as long as the analyst is careful in consistently applying the appropriate discount rate for the type of flows that have been generated, when adjusting for the time value of money.

4. When finding the net present value of a money flow use a discount rate which includes an allowance for inflation.

5. When finding the net present value of a real flow, use a discount rate which is inflation-free, because the cash flows are already in terms of constant purchasing power (i.e., they already have been adjusted for the effects of inflation) and need only be adjusted to reflect the time value of money.

12

ACQUISITION OF ASSETS WITH A FINANCIAL LEASE VS. PURCHASE AND LOAN

This chapter illustrates the use of present value calculations to compare a purchase and loan with a financial lease as alternative methods of acquiring the same asset. A financial lease usually is described as a contract for a time period which covers a major portion of the life of the asset and is non-cancelable. We are not considering an operating lease. Operating leases typically cover shorter periods of time such as a month or a year and are cancelable. Often the lessor provides for maintenance of the leased item.

The emphasis here is on the method of comparing a financial lease with a purchase and loan, not on whether a lease is a superior or inferior method of financing. You should be aware that there are methods other than present value which can be used to analyze a lease vs. a purchase and loan. We believe that present value is the most accurate method of comparing the quantitative aspects of a lease with a purchase and loan.

There is considerable disagreement over the correct formulation of the lease vs. buy present value model. However, the differences in results among models are small. The method presented here is one of the easiest to perform. We will be computing the present value of the after tax costs of the purchase-loan and lease alternatives. The decision criterion is to choose the alternative with the lowest after tax present value of costs.

The type of financial lease analyzed here really is just an alternative method of financing. The lessee will be responsible for the maintenance of the leased item, the same as if it were purchased with either cash or a loan. If the lease provides for the lessor to pay some of the expenses which the lessee would be obligated to pay if the item were purchased rather than leased, such expenses can be included in the present value analysis.

In the case of a lease, the entire lease payment qualifies as an expense for tax purposes, assuming that IRS agrees that it truly is a financial lease and not a disguised loan. The lessee may claim the investment tax credit if the lessor agrees. However, many leases provide that the lessor retains the right to the ITC. The Economic Recovery Tax Act of 1981 and the Tax Equity and Fiscal Responsibility Act of 1982 contain many provisions relative to leases with which a manager should be familiar before analyzing the lease-purchase decision.

In the case of a purchase and loan, the owner may claim depreciation and interest as expenses for tax purposes and also may claim the investment credit on eligible items.

One of the controversies in present value analysis of the lease vs. purchase option is the choice of the discount rate. Several alternatives exist. Two of the most commonly used are (1) the weighted average cost of capital, after-tax, the same as used by the firm for other net present value calculations and (2) the after-tax interest rate on the loan that would be required if the asset were purchased. One argument for the latter is that we are interested in effects of the two methods of financing and that the loan is the alternative to the financial lease. Another reason for using the after tax interest rate on the loan is that it simplifies the calculations. If the after-tax loan payments are discounted to the present with the after-tax interest rate on the loan, the result is the initial loan balance. Therefore, the cost of the asset may be used as an outflow at time zero in computing the present value of the cost of the purchase and loan alternative. A third reason is that most of the cash flows associated with the two financing alternatives are known with certainty: the lease payment and the loan payment and depreciation. There is little risk associated with these flows, so the discount rate should be one that reflects little risk. To the extent that the cost of equity is higher than the cost of debt, choosing the cost of debt rather than the weighted average cost of capital as the discount rate should result in a rate with a lower amount of built-in risk.

If there are likely to be flows associated with either the lease or purchase that can be expected to be uncertain, those who recommend using the after-tax loan rate also recommend that the weighted average cost of capital, after tax or some other risk adjusted rate be used to discount such flows. An example of such a flow is the expected terminal value of the purchased asset.

We will adopt the practice of using the after tax loan interest rate as the discount rate for flows known with certainty and the weighted average cost of capital for flows not known with certainty.

The reader should be aware that if the WACC, after tax, rather than the after tax loan rate were used as the discount rate, the results of the lease-purchase comparison in terms of the lower cost alternative would rarely change. Only if the alternatives were close in present value terms, the patterns of cash flows were quite different for the two alternatives or the WACC were quite different from the loan rate would one expect the lower cost alternative to change if the WACC, after tax rather than the loan rate, after tax is used as the discount rate.

ILLUSTRATION

EXAMPLE A

This example probably is simpler than most leases but is intended to illustrate the present value method of analyzing a lease vs. purchase without being too complicated. We are looking for the lowest cost alternative and our answers will be defined in terms of costs. Therefore our outflows will bear positive signs and inflows will have negative signs.

A food processor has decided to acquire a $50,000 sauerkraut maker and is trying to decide whether to purchase or lease it. If the machine is purchased, the interest rate on the loan will be 16%. The firm is in the 25% tax bracket. The planning period will be 5 years and there will be no salvage value. All after-tax payments will be discounted to the present using the loan interest rate as the discount rate. The discount rate will be .16 (1 - .25) = .12.

Lease

The lease provides for 5 payments of $13,984 each, with the first payment due when the machine is delivered. The tax benefit from each lease payment will be received one year after the payment. This is not necessarily always the case, but frequently the tax savings from a lease payment will be received some time after the payment is made.

Years		12% factor	Present value
0-4	Lease payment $13,984	4.0374	$56,459
1-5	Tax savings from lease payment = $13,984 x .25 = 3,496	3.6048	-12,602
	Present value of after-tax cost to lease	=	$43,857

Purchase and Loan

The purchase and loan provides for 100% financing at 16% interest on a 5 year amortized loan with payments at the end of each year. Payments are $15,270.47 per year. The machine is 5 year ACRS property and fast ACRS recovery will be used. The machine is eligible for investment credit. The two point reduction in the Federal 10 percent investment credit will be used rather than the basis reduction option.

The business is located in New York which has a six percent investment credit so the total investment credit will be .08 + .06 = .14. If you are in a state which has no investment credit, you should use only the Federal credit. If your state has an investment credit, you should use the appropriate rate in your calculations. The interest payments are tax deductible. The loan is amortized over 5 years so the interest payment changes each year. Therefore, year-by-year calculations must be made to find the after-tax payments and the present value of the after-tax payments.

Year	Payment	Interest	25% tax Savings	Payment, after-tax	12% factor	Present value
1	$15,270.47	$8,000.00	$2,000.00	$13,270.47	.8929	$11,849
2	15,270.47	6,836.72	1,709.18	13,561.29	.7972	10,811
3	15,270.47	5,487.33	1,371.83	13,898.64	.7118	9,893
4	15,270.47	3,922.02	980.50	14,298.97	.6355	9,081
5	15,270.47	2,106.27	526.57	14,743.90	.5674	8,366
		Present value of payments, after-tax			=	$50,000
1	Investment credit: 50,000 x .14 = 7,000				.8929	-6,250
1-5	Depreciation tax savings: 50,000 x .25 = 12,500				.7114	-8,892
	Present value of after-tax cost of purchase and loan					$34,858

In our example, the present value of the cost of the purchase-loan alternative is less than the present value of the cost to lease by $8,999. This suggests that the lease is an inferior method of financing in this situation. This does not illustrate that leases are always inferior to loans.

Note that the present value of the loan payments, after tax, is equal to the original loan. This will always be true, within rounding error, when the discount rate is equal to the after tax interest rate on the loan. In future examples when the after-tax interest rate on the loan is used as the discount rate, we will simplify the calculations by entering the original loan balance as the present value of the loan.

ADDITIONAL CONSIDERATIONS

The comparison of a lease versus loan can be affected by changes in several of the items used in the calculations. Some examples are the tax rate, method of depreciation, terminal values, and number of years over which lease payments are spread relative to years over which depreciation and loan payments are spread. Some illustrations follow.

EXAMPLE B: THE TAX RATE

Suppose the marginal tax rate of the investor is 50%, rather than 25%. All other items in the previous example remain the same, except that the discount rate, after tax and the after-tax interest rate are changed by the tax rate. The discount rate, after tax, is now 8%.

Lease

Years		8% factor	Present value
0-4	Lease payment $13,984	4.3121	$60,300
1-5	Tax savings from lease payment = $13,984 x .5 = 6,992	3.9927	-27,917
	Present value of after-tax cost of lease =		$32,383

Purchase and Loan

The present value of the loan payments, after tax will be $50,000.

Years		8% factor	Present value
1-5	Loan payments		$50,000
1	Investment credit, $7,000	.9259	- 6,481
1-5	Depr. tax savings: $50,000 x .50 = 25,000	.7915	-19,787
	Present value of after-tax cost of purchase and loan		$23,732

In this example the present value of the cost of the purchase and loan is $8,651 less than the present value of the cost of the lease. Although the lease is still inferior to the loan, it is better relative to the loan than with a lower tax rate.

LESSEE PAYS NO TAXES

If the lessee pays no income taxes currently, has paid no taxes for the last three years and expects to pay no taxes in the future, the lease vs. purchase analysis should ignore income taxes. Using Example A and the 16 percent loan rate as the discount rate, the calculations are:

Lease

Years		16% factor	Present value
0-4	Lease payment $13,984	3.7982	$53,114

Purchase and Loan

The present value of the loan payments is equal to the original loan, or $50,000. The lease is $3,114 more expensive than the loan in present value terms.

A NOTE ON TERMINAL VALUES

The examples so far assume a zero terminal value. If the purchased machine can be expected to have a terminal value, the present value of the terminal value, after tax should be included in the purchase and loan calculations. In some cases, the leased machine could also have a terminal value. For example, some leases provide that the lessee may purchase the leased asset at the end of the lease for a nominal fee which may be less than the actual terminal value.

EXAMPLE C: A MORE REALISTIC CASE

Frequently leases are written for a shorter period than a machine or structure would be used if the item were purchased. An accurate present value analysis must account for this unequal life situation. Two logical methods consistent with likely situations may be used:

1. Assume the leased item will be purchased at the end of the lease and held long enough so that the life of the lease/purchase option is the same as the life of the purchase option. (ERTA rules allow the purchase price at the end of the lease to be specified in the lease).

2. Assume that the leased machine will be replaced by another leased machine. In this case, the repair bill may be lower on the second leased machine than on the old purchased machine. In addition, there may still be unequal life problems. These might be handled by using annual equivalent cash flows.

Method 1 will be used to illustrate a comparison of a $50,000 machine which would be held 8 years if purchased. The lease provides for 4 annual payments of $16,600 each with the first payment due when the machine is delivered. At the end of 4 years, the machine will be purchased for $10,000 (borrowed at 16%) and depreciated with 5 year ACRS. The purchased machine will be financed with a 5 year loan at 16%. The machine will be assumed to have a $5,000 terminal value at the end of 8 years regardless of whether it is initially leased or purchased. The potential lessee is in the 25% tax bracket and has a WACC, after tax of 14%. All flows except terminal values will be discounted at the after-tax loan interest rate which is 12%.

Lease

Years		12% factor	Present value
0-3	Lease payment $16,600	3.4018	$56,470
1-4	Tax savings from lease payment $16,600 x .25 = 4,150	3.0374	-12,605
4	Purchase, $10,000	.6355	6,355
5	Investment credit, $1,400	.5674	- 794
5	Depr. tax savings $1,500 x .25 = 375	.5674	- 231
6	Depr. tax savings $2,200 x .25 = 550	.5066	- 279
7	Depr. tax savings $2,100 x .25 = 525	.4523	- 237
8	Terminal value, after tax * = $4,800	.3506**	- 1,683
	Present value of cost to lease, after tax =		$47,014

*No depreciation is allowed in the year of disposal on ACRS property. If the machine is sold for $5,000, there will be $800 ordinary gain because the book value will be $4,200. Terminal value, after-tax = $5,000 - $200 tax on gain = $4,800.

**Discounted with 14 percent WACC, after tax.

Purchase and Loan

Years		12% factor	Present value
1-5	Present value of loan payments, after-tax		$50,000
1	Investment credit, $50,000 x .14 = 7,000	.8929	-6,250
1-5	Depreciation tax savings, $50,000 x .25 = 12,500	.7114	-8,893
8	Salvage value, after-tax $5,000 x .75 = 3,750	.3506***	-1,315
	Present value of after-tax cost to buy		$33,542

***Discounted with 14 percent WACC, after tax.

Comparison

The present value of the purchase and loan option is $13,472 less than the present value of the cost to lease. In this case the purchase and loan is the superior alternative.

QUALITATIVE FACTORS INFLUENCING THE LEASE VS. PURCHASE DECISION

A number of factors other than the lowest present value of after tax costs could affect the lease vs. purchase and loan decision. Some of these so-called "qualitative" factors could be included in the present value analysis by making estimates of the monetary value of the factors but some will remain qualitative. A discussion of some of these factors is provided in Chapter VII of Bierman, Harold, The Lease vs. Buy Decision, Prentice Hall, 1982.

13

CAPITAL RATIONING

Thus far we have assumed that the firm has a cost of capital that can be estimated and that it could, and would, raise capital funds in amounts sufficient for it to make all capital investments that have a positive net present value at this discount rate. This assumption does not hold in all cases in the business world. One type of situation where it does not hold is the case where management decides to arbitrarily limit the total amount invested in a given period to a certain budgeted amount (e.g., an amount equal to depreciation plus retained earnings) or to establish an acceptance criterion that is higher than the firm's cost of capital (e.g., insist on a percentage return that is a profit goal). In so doing, management is arbitrarily limiting the amount of funds that it invests or "rationing capital." The other type of capital rationing situation is one imposed by the market rather than by the firm itself: Management would like to raise more capital at the firm's cost of capital than it can. In other words, market "imperfections" limit the firm's ability to raise sufficient capital to make all investments that are profitable in a present value sense when analyzed using the firm's estimated cost of capital.

When capital rationing is present, there is no simple solution to the firm's investment decisions. Analytical techniques are available to management to guide it toward solutions. But these approaches are complex and often require knowledge of future investment possibilities that is not available in sufficient detail in practice. Rather than attempt to even suggest the nature of these quantitative techniques, we'll leave it to the interested reader to explore them in other sources. We will merely mention some approaches to the capital rationing situation that may help the investor to a practical, but in some cases approximate, resolution of the problem.

Let's take the situation where management arbitrarily establishes a cut off rate for investments that is higher than the firm's cost of capital. For example, suppose a firm establishes a profit goal of 15 percent as the acceptance criterion on investments when it estimates its cost of capital to be 10 percent. It can use this profit goal as the discount rate in evaluating capital investments. If management does so, the net present value method still will be useful and will avoid some errors in ranking investments that could be made by other measures of investment worth. But in so doing, management should recognize two things: (1) Some of the rationale that underlies the net present value method breaks down, and (2) it is arbitrarily rationing capital or limiting the amount of funds that it invests.

In the other internally imposed capital rationing situation, management decides for some reason to place an overall limit on capital spending in a given period. When the authors have faced this situation, they have found that each of two approaches offer a practical guide to deciding how to allocate the limited total budget among competing profitable projects. One approach involves the use of the internal rate of return method; the other, the net present value method.

If management desires to use the internal rate of return method, it can compute the IRR of each investment alternative and then array the projects in descending order of their internal rates of return. Then it selects the projects by working down the list of projects until the capital funds required by the most profitable projects will have used up an amount of capital equal to the total capital budget that has been established. This approach is illustrated in Figure 5 where the x-axis represents total dollars of investment and the y-axis represents the internal rate of return. A point in the figure labeled with a letter (e.g., C) represents the IRR of a particular investment (rate on y-axis) and the total amount of capital required to make the investment as well as the investment(s) which will yield rates of return higher than this particular investment (dollars on x-axis). In other words, the x-axis represents the aggregate investment. The amount of investment in any particular project is the difference between the dollar amount on the scale corresponding to a particular investment and the dollar amount for the investment with the next highest internal rate of return. For example, the amount of capital required by project D is about $30,000 (i.e., $90,000 - 60,000). The dashed line represents the firm's estimated cost of capital (i.e., 10 percent). We will assume that the firm has arbitrarily established a total budget restraint of $100,000 for this year.

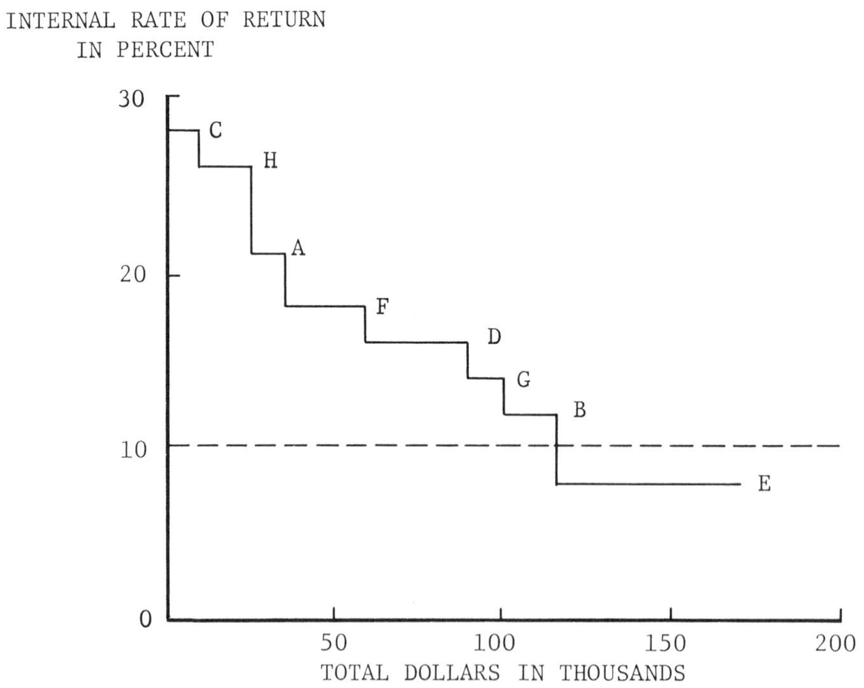

Figure 5. Graph of Projects in Descending Order of Internal Rate of Return

In the hypothetical case portrayed, if the firm used this approach to handle capital rationing, it would make investments C, H, A, F, D, and G. This combination of investments would use up the total budget constraint of $100,000. Actually investment B is an economically desirable one since the internal rate of return is greater than the firm's 10 percent cost of capital, but the limit established on the total capital budget will not permit the firm to invest in project B and still invest in the more profitable projects. It will be noted that the IRR of investment B (about 12 percent) can be viewed as an opportunity cost of capital to the firm.

The other practical, but approximate in some cases, approach to allocating a fixed overall budget among competing and desirable investment projects involves using the net present value method. With this approach, the net present value of each investment is determined using the firm's cost of capital as the discount rate. Then by repetitive trials, that combination of investments (with positive net present values) that will produce the largest total net present value for the limited budget is determined. The reader may note that this approach may not lead to the selection of the project that yields the largest net present value because the net present value of an investment per se does not take into account the size of the investment needed by a particular project to generate it.

The reader should remember that we have presented only simplified approaches for dealing with capital rationing. However, except in bizarre or perverse investment situations, they should provide management with practical and meaningful guides to dealing with capital rationing situations.

14

SUMMARY AND CONCLUSIONS

Capital investment decisions are important because they are frequently large, permanent commitments of capital that influence the long-run flexibility and earning power of the business. It is imperative that management develop carefully laid plans based on reliable forecasting and evaluation procedures.

Although common sense action in some instances is too obvious to warrant formal pro- and con-analysis, many investments are large and far-reaching enough in their effects to make urgency, necessity and subjectivity unsound and dangerous approaches. Since the overriding criterion in most investment decisions should be the maximization of long-run earnings, guesses, hunches and intuition should be secondary to economic considerations and formal analysis in evaluating most capital expenditure projects.

We have focused on measures available to managers for evaluating the economic worth of investments and for ranking proposals in order of their relative profitability.

The two widely used measures of investment worth, the payback and simple rate of return methods, are simple and easily understood approaches. These two measures may provide adequate guidelines to management where the expected returns far exceed the cost or where there are limited alternative investments. But both of these measures suffer from major weaknesses that can result in suggesting incorrect decisions to management. A weakness common to both the payback and simple rate of return methods is that they fail to reflect the time value of money -- that a dollar in hand today is more valuable than a dollar to be received or spent in the future.

The publication focuses on two measures of investment worth that allow the investor to reflect the time value of money: The net present value method and the internal rate of return method. These two approaches, correctly applied, can provide management an excellent basis for applying its judgement in making capital investment decisions.

The two so-called present value or discounted cash flow measures supplement -- but they do not replace -- the other important ingredients (i.e., imagination, hard work, and good judgment) of sound capital expenditure decision making. The complete consideration of alternatives and the reliable forecasting of the magnitude and deviations of benefits that are likely to result from an investment remain as key and imposing steps in the whole capital budgeting process.

Although judgment and work are important ingredients of the capital investment decision-making process, the discounted cash flow techniques stressed in this publication provide managers with powerful tools for analyzing routine investments as well as for analyzing complicated investment problems such as decisions to lease or buy, make or buy and various types of business expansion decisions. These approaches help crystallize the factors relevant to a decision and should help the investor toward more intelligent decision making on capital investments.

APPENDIX A
GUIDELINES FOR DETERMINING THE INTERNAL RATE OF RETURN OF AN INVESTMENT

As explained earlier, we must determine the internal rate of return of an investment essentially by a trial and error process. Use of the following formula, however, can facilitate the trial and error search for the IRR of an investment.

$$Aa_{n,i} + A'a_{n,i} + A''a_{n,i} + Sa_{n,i} = C$$

where A, A', ... A'' = estimated cash inflows (or benefits) after taxes of A, A', ... A'' amounts, respectively,

n = number of years that inflows (or benefits) of A, A', etc. amounts are expected to be received,

a = the present value factor for the appropriate n and i, thus:

$a_{n,i}$ = the present value of $1 received per period at i rate of interest for n years <u>or</u> the present value of $1 received in year n at i rate of discount, whichever is appropriate,

S = expected terminal salvage value in year n,

and C = the capital outlay required or the amount of the investment.

In this formula, i is the unknown and equals the IRR of the investment.

EXAMPLE 1

First, let us illustrate the use of this formula in determining the IRR of the simple investment described on pages 31 and 32 for which we already have determined the IRR to be approximately 13 or 14 percent (page 33). To repeat the problem: Find the IRR on $6,000 invested immediately (i.e. time 0), when the estimated net cash inflows are $1,500 the first four years and $3,000 in the fifth year. Remember that to find the yield we must answer the following question: "What rate of discount will make the present value of $1,500 received each year for four years beginning one year from now plus the present value of $3,000 received five years from now equal to $6,000?"

Using the formula as a guideline, two alternative formulations are possible for our sample investment:

(1) $\$1,500\ a_{1,i} + \$1,500\ a_{2,i} + \$1,500\ a_{3,i} + \$1,500\ a_{4,i}$

$+ \$3,000\ a_{5,i} = \$6,000$

in which case all present value factors (i.e. $a_{1,i}$, $a_{2,i}$, etc.) are present value of \$1 received once (i.e., Table II).

(2) $\$1{,}500\ a_{1-4,i} + \$3{,}000\ a_{5,i} = \$6{,}000$

in which case the present value factor $a_{1-4,i}$ is the present value of \$1 received per year for years 1 through 4 (Table III) and $a_{5,i}$ is the present value of \$1 received in year 5 (Table II).

For illustration, we will estimate the IRR using the second formulation. For convenience, we reduce the coefficient of one term to unity. Here we divide all coefficients (i.e., the net cash inflows and the capital outlay) by \$1,500 and thereby reduce the formulation to:

$$1\ a_{1-4,i} + 2\ a_{5,i} = 4$$

The next step is to scan the present value tables and estimate in which column (i.e., for which rate of discount) of Table III -- the present value of \$1 received per period for 4 years -- the figure opposite n = 4 --, plus two times the figure opposite n = 5 in Table II -- the present value of \$1 received in year 5 -- equal 4.

Let us try i = 10 percent:

	One times figure opposite n = 4 in table of present value of \$1 received per period (Table III)	=	3.1699
plus	Two times figure opposite n = 5 in table of present value of \$1 (Table II) = 2 x 0.6209	=	1.2418
	Total	=	4.4117,

which is more than 4. Therefore, we need to try a higher discount rate.

Let us try i = 15 percent:

	One times figure opposite n = 4 in Table III		=	2.8550
plus	Two times figure opposite n = 5 in Table II	= 2 x 0.4972	=	0.9944
	Total		=	3.8494,

which is less than 4.

Therefore, we know that the IRR of this particular investment is between 10 and 15 percent, and much closer to 15 than 10. Consequently let us try 13 percent on our next trial:

	One times figure opposite n = 4 in Table III		=	2.9745
plus	Two times figure opposite n = 5 in Table II	= 2 x 0.5428	=	1.0856
	Total		=	4.0601,

which is slightly greater than 4, but not much.

Consequently, we know the IRR is between 13 and 15 percent -- and closer to 13. If we wanted a more precise estimate, we'd next try 14 percent:

	One times figure opposite n = 4 in Table III		=	2.9137
plus	Two times figure opposite n = 5 in Table II	= 2 x 0.5194	=	1.0388
	Total		=	3.9525,

which is slightly less than 4.

Thus we conclude that the IRR of this investment is between 13 and 14 percent. If we wished and if the degree of precision in the forecasts of cash flows warranted -- and it usually will not --, we could interpolate to find that the IRR is 13.6 percent.1/

EXAMPLE 2

Some readers may find it worthwhile to work through the determination of the IRR of another investment: Find the IRR on $10,000 invested immediately (i.e. time 0), when the estimated cash inflows are $2,000 the first year, $4,000 the second year and $12,000 in the third year.

To find the IRR of this particular investment, we have to answer the following question: "What rate of interest will make the present value of $2,000 received in year one, $4,000 received two years from now and $12,000 received three years from now equal to $10,000?"

Using the formula given on page __ as a guideline, several alternative formulations are possible for our sample investment. These alternative formulations include:

$$\$2{,}000\ a_{1,i} + \$4{,}000\ a_{2,i} + \$12{,}000\ a_{3,i} = \$10{,}000$$

or $$\$2{,}000\ a_{1-3,i} + \$2{,}000\ a_{2,i} + \$10{,}000\ a_{3,i} = \$10{,}000$$

or $$\$2{,}000\ a_{1-3,i} + \$2{,}000\ a_{2-3,i} + \$8{,}000\ a_{3,i} = \$10{,}000$$

Which formulation should we use? We should choose the easiest. Which is the easiest in this case? The first one. Why? Because we can stick to one present value table (Table II) while the other two formulations would require the use of both present value tables.

So let us use:

$$\$2{,}000\ a_{1,i} + \$4{,}000\ a_{2,i} + \$12{,}000\ a_{3,i} = \$10{,}000$$

For convenience, we reduce coefficient of one term to unity. In this case, we divide all coefficients by $2,000.

$$1\ a_{1,i} + 2\ a_{2,i} + 6\ _{3,i} = 5$$

The next step is to scan the table for the present value of $1 (Table II) and estimate in which column (i.e., which rate of discount) the figure opposite n = 1, plus two times the figure opposite n = 2 for the same rate of discount plus 6 times the figure opposite n = 3 for the same rate of discount equal 5.

1/Interpolation can be done as follows:

Difference in yield = 14% - 13% = 1%

Coefficient at 13%	=	4.0601	Coefficient at 13%	=	4.0601
Coefficient at 14%	=	3.9525	Desired coefficient	=	4.0000
Difference	=	0.1076	Difference	=	0.0601

Then: $$\frac{0.0601}{0.1076} \times 1\% = 0.56\%$$

Thus the IRR is 13% + 0.56% = 13.6%. It should be recognized that a slight bias is introduced by this method of interpolation since the values in the present value tables do not change in linear fashion as the rate of discount is increased. But the degree of precision in the forecasts of cash flows probably rarely justifies interpolation anyway and certainly does not justify concern about such bias.

First let's try a nice round figure - say 10 percent, and do it roughly:

One times figure opposite n = 1	= 1 x .90	=	0.9
Two times figure opposite n = 2	= 2 x .83	=	1.6
Six times figure opposite n = 3	= 6 x .75	=	4.5
Total		=	7.0

which is much more than 5, so we need a much higher discount rate.

Let's try i = 30 percent:

One times figure opposite n = 1	= 1 x .76	=	0.76
Two times figure opposite n = 2	= 2 x .59	=	1.18
Six times figure opposite n = 3	= 6 x .45	=	2.70
Total		=	4.64

which is too low, so the IRR is somewhat less than 30%.

We know from above that the IRR is between 10 and 30% but much closer to 30% than 10%.

So we might try 25 percent next:

One times figure opposite n = 1	= 1 x .8000	=	0.8000
Two times figure opposite n = 2	= 2 x .6400	=	1.2800
Six times figure opposite n = 3	= 6 x .5120	=	3.0720
Total		=	5.1520

which means present value of cash proceeds at 25% is a little too high, so we try a slightly higher discount factor.

Try 27 percent:

One times figure opposite n = 1	= 1 x .7874	=	0.7874
Two times figure opposite n = 2	= 2 x .6200	=	1.2400
Six times figure opposite n = 3	= 6 x .4882	=	2.9292
Total		=	4.9566

which is very close to 5.0 so we know the IRR is approximately 27%.

In actual practice, when we reduce one term to unity, the other terms usually will not be whole numbers. Nevertheless, the procedure for determining the IRR is the same.

Computer programs are available that will calculate the internal rate of return of an investment. These programs employ a trial and error process.2/

2/For example, see LaDue, E.L. Yield: A computer program to calculate yield of an investment with uneven cash flows and/or uneven periods. A.E. Ext. 75-16, Dept. of Agricultural Economics, New York College of Agriculture and Life Sciences, Cornell University, 1975.

APPENDIX B
PROBLEMS INVOLVING THE APPLICATION OF DISCOUNTED CASH FLOW MEASURES OF INVESTMENT WORTH

NOTES

(1) The first few problems are not directly related to capital expenditure decisions but are included to help you build your skill and understanding of the time value of money concept and the use of the present value tables.

(2) The capital outlays are assumed to be made at the beginning of the year, and the benefits are assumed to accrue to the investor at the end of the year. We recognize that in actual practice the benefits of many of these investments would accrue to the investor throughout the year -- rather than at the end of the year. Consequently, our solutions represent slight approximations -- actually this assumption tends to understate the desirability of the example investments. However, since the benefits represent forecasts of an uncertain future, this simplifying assumption seems reasonable. Going to the trouble to avoid such an assumption might well imply a degree of precision that the data do not justify.

(3) In each problem, the figures given as the assumed benefits of each investment (i.e., the added net income or decrease in expenses) are expressed in terms of cash flows. Depreciation has not been included as an expense -- although depreciation is assumed to have been considered in adjusting cash flows from a before-tax basis to an after-tax basis because depreciation provides a tax shield. Other non-cash expenses are not reflected in the figures given in each problem. Moreover, interest expense, if any, was not considered in forecasting cash flows, since this expense constitutes part of the cost of capital or the minimum acceptable rate of return.

(4) Ignore the effects of income taxes unless the question indicates the tax bracket of the investor.

(5) Due to tax laws currently (1984) in effect, any question in which the tax savings from depreciation and investment credit must be considered may have several answers. This is because the taxpayer has the option of claiming the Section 179 expense election and also must choose between reducing the basis or reducing the investment credit as explained in Chapter 7. Unless otherwise stated, the problems assume that the investor does not take the Section 179 election and that the two point reduction in investment credit is taken rather than the reduction in basis.

(6) Problems are listed under the heading of the chapter to which each is most closely related. Problems dependent on several chapters are listed under "Multichapter."

PROBLEMS

CHAPTER 4

1. If you deposit $3,000 in the bank today at 10% interest compounded annually, how much will be in the account at the end of 10 years, assuming no withdrawals?

2. Gary wishes to have $10,000 for his second honeymoon in 10 years. How much would he need to deposit in Citizens Savings Bank at 10% interest (compounded annually) now in order to have the $10,000 in 10 years?

3. Terry's father loaned her $15,000 for college expenses. Terry agreed to repay the $15,000 in a lump sum 5 years after graduation. No interest was to be charged. Terry, who is now a senior, has the prospects of marrying a rather wealthy man and wishes to repay the loan on graduation day. Assuming that father can invest the money at 12% interest, how much should he be willing to accept on graduation day rather than waiting 5 years for his money?

4. Cindy's dead-beat brother-in-law owes her $5,000 which he has promised to pay today. He was not able to pay it and the best she has been able to get out of him is a promise to pay $1,000 per year for the next 5 years, with no interest. The first payment will be made 1 year from now.

   a) What is the present value to Cindy of the 5 payments, assuming that she could invest the money at 10% if she had it now?

   b) What would be the present value of the payments if dead-beat would make each payment 1 year earlier?

5. Andy has made an investment that will pay him a return of $1,000 at the end of each of the next 5 years and $2,000 at the end of each of the following 5 years. What is the present value of the income from this investment, assuming that he could earn 11% in an alternative investment.

6. Gary doesn't have enough money to invest now to provide the $10,000 honeymoon in 10 years. Now he wants to know how much he would need to deposit each year for the next 10 years to accumulate the $10,000, assuming he makes the first deposit one year from now and interest at 10% is compounded annually.

7. Dave has just graduated from Cornell and is tired of living in a cramped apartment. However, by cutting housing costs while at college he managed to save enough for an $8,000 down payment on a new house he is planning to purchase now that costs $45,000. Unfortunately, Dave didn't major in business management and wants you to calculate what the payments will be, assuming that annual payments start 1 year from now and the mortgage carries a 14% stated rate with a 25 year term.

8. George is thinking about early retirement. Suppose he deposits $100,000 now at 11% interest. How much could he withdraw each year for the next 10 years if the first withdrawal was made one year from now, the account continues to earn interest at 11% compounded annually, and the account is to be entirely depleted at the end of 10 years.

9. You have just purchased on the market for $1,000 a newly issued bond of the Dot Company. The bond pays $80 interest annually at the end of each year. The face value of this bond is $1,000. It has a maturity date five years from now. Call this Bond A. You are also considering the purchase of another five-year Dot Company bond which has a face value of $1,000 and returns $50 in annual interest payments. The price of this bond, call it Bond B, is unknown to you. Bond B has two years remaining before it matures. The interest on Bond B is also paid only once a year at the end of the year. Assume Bond A and Bond B carry the same amount of risk.

a) What is the "going rate of return" or "current market yield" on bonds of equal risk and maturity to the Dot Company's bonds?

b) What is the highest price you should be willing to pay today for Bond B?

10. The Honest Abe Pension Company offers a retirement program for workers of all ages. John L. Simpo had decided to inquire into a retirement program. He is now 45 and he will work for 20 more years, until he is 65 years old. He feels that he will only live to be 75 years old and wants a steady pension income of $20,000 per year for those last 10 years. The Honest Abe Company wants to sell John a pension program which will pay him $20,000 a year for those last 10 years of his life. If John buys the program, he will receive the first payment at the end of his 65th year. (This means he will receive his last payment from the pension fund at the end of his 74th year, so he has a year to spend it before he dies.) In return, the Pension Company requires that he make 20 equal annual payments of $4,000 each, the first one due immediately, if he accepts the retirement plan.

a) Assuming John's time value of money is 8%, should he accept the retirement plan? Show organized calculations. Ignore income taxes.

b) John has just learned from his Aunt Esther that he has been bequeathed a large sum in the will of his Uncle Max. The will itself will be tied up in court for three years. However, three years from today he will receive a very large sum of money. What lump sum amount would he have to put in the bank at 8% annual compound interest immediately upon receiving his inheritance in order to have the same benefits as provided by the pension program (i.e., the $20,000 annual income as considered in part a)?

11. A college senior has these alternatives following graduation:

1) Attend graduate school for 2 years and earn an M.S. degree
2) Accept a salaried position immediately.

He estimates that 2 years of graduate study will cost $20,000 in lost income (after taxes) and increased expenses for the 24 month period.

He estimates further that following that 2 year period he will have 33 productive or working years. How much would the M.S. have to add to his annual net income (salary after taxes) to make investment in an M.S. program a "good" investment under these assumptions? Assume a time value of money of 9 percent and that the $20,000 is paid immediately.

12. Three years ago you purchased a farm from your father with a 15 year $140,000 contract at 8% interest which requires annual payments of $16,356.10. Your father died and now you are obligated to make the payments to his widow who is your stepmother. She would like the balance due on the principal ($123,261.24 after three payments) immediately. There is no way she can force you to pay up immediately but you would like to pay and get her off your back. Your friendly credit man, Mr. Wickwick, is happy to loan you the money at 13% interest and 12 annual payments, the first due one year from now. You still owe 12 payments to stepmother, the first due one year from now.

a) Using the present value tables, satisfy yourself that $16,356.10 is the correct annual payment. Check to see that $123,261.24 is the correct balance.

b) How much should stepmother accept as a lump sum payment now if <u>you</u> are to be made no worse off with a 13%, 12 year loan than with the 12 payments remaining on the contract? Ignore income tax implications. This is a relatively easy question. Don't make it harder than it is. The intent is to make you think a little. Hint: Think about the size of the payment that you would now make to Wickwick rather than to Stepma.

CHAPTER 5

13. We have argued that depreciation expense should not be considered in determining our estimates of cash flows to be used in a present value investment analysis. Assume that in working with a manager (who has not studied present value analysis as much as you have) you point this out to him and explain that to reflect depreciation per se in our cash flows would result in "double counting." Further assume the manager replies, "What do you mean double counting? I do not see that." Write an explanation that will clarify these points in the manager's mind. Ignore income taxes in answering.

CHAPTER 6

14. The Smith Company is considering making an investment which has the following cash flows:

Year	Cash flow
0	-$ 9,120
1	1,000
2	5,000
3	10,000

Using the net present value method, is the investment a desirable one assuming that the Smith Company's cost of capital is 10 percent? How much in excess of the indicated cost of the investment (i.e., $9,120) could the Company afford to pay for the investment and be no worse off financially?

15. The Alpine Co. is contemplating an investment in a $45,000 Sno-Cat which will be used to transport skiers to the high slopes. Operator Alpine estimates that the machine will generate annual net cash inflows of $8,000 per year for seven years and be worth $5,000 at the end of seven years.

a) Compute the NPV of this investment if Alpine's cost of capital is 14%. Should the investment be accepted?

b) What is the maximum that Alpine could afford to invest in the Sno-Cat?

16. Wheat Straw produces about 200 hectares of small grains and 300 hectares of corn which he has been hiring custom harvested. He is considering purchase of a combine for $85,000 which he believes would handle his harvest for the next 10 years and have a salvage value of $10,000 at the end of 10 years. He believes that the average custom rate per hectare for the next 10 years will be $50 for small grains and $65 for corn. Cash cost of operating the purchased combine (fuel, repairs, labor, etc.) is esimated to average $18 per hectare on small grains and $23 per hectare on corn over the next 10 years.

Wheat's cost of capital is 12%. Using the net present value method, determine whether the combine would be a good investment for Mr. Straw and explain why.

17. Compute, to the nearest 1%, the internal rate of return of the investments in problems 15 and 16.

18. Jeanie's Pizza Company makes and sells frozen pizzas to local retail outlets. Jeanie's cold chest (i.e., a 30° below zero room where the pizzas are frozen) is too small and outdated. Jeanie is trying to decide among three different ways of enlarging and updating her cold chest. Each way involves a different capital expenditure as well as different benefits. She has estimated the capital expenditure as well as the benefits associated with each of the three alternative investments.

She has also applied certain measures of investment worth and obtained the following results.

Investments	Payback Period	ROI	Net Present Value
A	2 years	10%	+$2,000
B	4 years	18%	+ 3,500
C	3 years	15%	+ 4,500

Given the above information, which investment should Jeanie make? Indicate the basis for your recommendation and explain why you relied on the investment measure that you chose rather than the other two measures.

19. Two mutally exclusive investments have projected cash flows as follows:

	Cash Flows in Period				
Investment	0	1	2	3	4
A	-10,000	+$5,000	+$5,000	+$5,000	+$5,000
B	-10,000	0	0	0	+30,000

The appropriate discount rate for the company is 10%. Both A and B have positive net present values when discounted at a rate of 10%. Determine which of the two investments is the more desirable using the internal rate of return method and make sure to clearly indicate the reason for your conclusion by completing this statement.

Investment _______ is superior to Investment _______ because __________.

Plot a net present value graph for investments A and B. Clearly label your graph. Also indicate over what range (if any) of discount rates A is the better investment and for what range (if any) of discount rates B is the preferred investment.

Note: Investment A has an IRR of 35% and Investment B has an IRR of 32%.

20. The Merling Company is currently leasing (on a lease cancellable upon 30 days notice) one of its buildings to another company for $10,000 per year. The estimated current sales value of the building is $15,000. This price is likely to remain unchanged indefinitely -- even if a contemplated redevelopment project results in the building's condemnation. The building originally cost $25,000 and is being depreciated at $500 annually. Its net book value is $10,000.

The Merling Company is seriously considering converting the building into a retail outlet. Such an endeavor would entail remodeling. The costs to open and sustain the retail outlet would be as follows:

Remodeling costs	$10,000
Increase in inventory	30,000
Increase in cash	20,000

Assume these costs are fully recoverable whenever operations terminate.

Management, who paid a redevelopment official $2,000 to discover when and where the redevelopment would be built, is virtually certain that the building will be available for no more than five years.

The management has asked you to give them an analysis of whether the company should continue to lease the building or convert it into a retail outlet, assuming that the minimum annual rate of return desired is 12% over a five year planning horizon. Estimated annual operating data for the proposed retail outlet, exclusive of depreciation, are:

Sales	$150,000
Cash operating expenses	125,000
Initial non-recurring sales promotion costs	15,000
Non-recurring termination costs at the end of year 5	10,000

Management has definitely decided not to sell the building until forced to by condemnation proceedings.

Do an orderly analysis, using the net present value approach, which will indicate whether the Merling Company should discontinue leasing the building and convert it into a retail outlet. Clearly label all figures and indicate the basis for your decision.

CHAPTER 7

To answer the breakeven parts of the following questions, students will need to read the breakeven section of Chapter 10. The instructor may wish to delay the breakeven parts of the questions until later in the course.

21. Make or Buy Decision: A company is currently buying from an outside supplier a part for assembly in a finished product at a cost of $18,000 per year (3,000 units at $6.00 each). A capital expenditure of $40,000 for new equipment would enable the company to manufacture this part. The expected increase in annual cash operating expenses of producing 3,000 units is $8,000 (exclusive of deprecation and interest costs, but before taxes). The machine is 5 year property and is eligible for federal investment credit.

    Terminal value: 0 for equipment at end of expected useful life of 10 years.

    Firm's income tax bracket: 40 percent,

    Minimum desired rate of return, after tax: 8 percent,

    a) Should the company make or buy the part?

    b) How much lower would the purchase price of this part have to be before it would become cheaper for the company to continue purchasing?

22. Cabbage Head can purchase a mechanical cabbage harvestor for $46,000. He has been producing 1500 tons of cabbage per year.

    Cabbage has made the following projections of changes in costs if he purchases the harvester rather than continuing to harvest by hand.

    a. Labor savings of $6.50 per ton harvested.

    b. Operating (fuel, repair, etc.) costs of $1.50 per ton harvested.

    c. Expected reconditioning costs at the end of year 4 regardless of tonnage harvested: $5,000.

    Head estimates that the machine will be useful for 8 years and have a salvage value of $4,000 at the end of 8 years. The machine is 5 year ACRS property and eligible for federal investment credit. In answering the questions below, use the reduction in basis rather than the reduction in investment credit option. Do not use the Section 179 election.

Head's cost of capital (after-tax) is 12 percent. He is in the 25 percent tax bracket.

a) Using the net present value method, recommend to Mr. Head whether he should purchase the cabbage harvester if he plans to continue to produce 1500 tons of cabbage per year.

b) Would the harvester be a good investment if Head were to increase production to 2500 tons per year?

c) What tonnage of cabbage would be needed to make the harvester a breakeven investment?

d) If Head continues to produce 1500 tons per year, what labor savings per ton would be needed to make the harvester a breakeven investment if all other costs remain constant?

23. Cabbage Head, from problem 22, would like to know whether he should, if he buys the harvester:

a) Use the Section 179 election.

b) Choose the reduction in basis or the reduction in investment credit option.

Prepare an analysis that will help Head made each of these decisions. His after tax cost of capital is 12% and his marginal tax bracket is 25%.

24. Investment in a Dairy Cooperative: A dairy farmer delivers one million pounds of milk to his cooperative during the year. The Coop deducts 12 cents per cwt. and gives the dairyman a non-interest bearing certificate with a maturity date ten years hence and a face value of $1,200. What is the cost to the farmer of this investment in his Cooperative Revolving Fund?

He must pay income tax on the full face value when a certificate is received. He is in the 30 percent income tax bracket.

Selected rate reflecting farmers cost of capital: 9 percent.

25. Finance Problem: Disposition of Cooperative Revolving Fund Certificates. A grape grower delivers 100 tons of grapes to his cooperative. He receives $200 per ton in cash, and certificates of $40 per ton. The certificate is non-interest bearing, is transferable, and bears a maturity date of 10 years hence. However, the cooperative has a history of paying off these certificates in 7 years, and he assumes they will continue to do so.

A local broker is buying the certificates from farmers at 50 cents on the dollar in the year of issue.

Income tax regulations state that if the farmer retains the certificate he must include the face amount in his taxable income in the year of receipt. If he sells the certificate in the year of receipt, he reports as income only the amount received for the sale of the certificate. The farmer is in the 30 percent income tax bracket.

Should he sell the certificate, or hold it to maturity?

Farmer's cost of capital, after tax: 10 percent.

26. To Sell or Hold Land: Mr. Green owns 150 acres of land which he uses to grow evergreen trees and shrubs. His after-tax cash flow is $200 per acre and he expects it to stay at that level for at least the next 10 years. He has recently been offered $2500 per acre for the entire 150 acres by a developer. Mr. Green believes the land will double in value in 10 years. Assume that whether he sells now or later, he will pay a capital gain tax of 25 percent on the entire sale price.

    Cost of Capital: 10 percent.

    a) Should Mr. Green hold or sell?

    b) Assuming that the cash flow data above accurately represents the next ten years, compute the minimum selling price 10 years hence to justify holding.

    c) If the land could reasonably be expected to double in value in the next 10 years, calculate the minimum annual after-tax cash flow per acre to justify holding.

27. Mr. Sweet Corn is interested in purchasing a fresh market sweet corn harvester for $60,000. He estimates that the harvester will be good for five years before becoming worn out or obsolete and that its salvage at that time will be $3,000.

    Sweet would use the machine to harvest 250 acres of sweet corn. Currently it costs him $120.00 per acre to hand harvest sweet corn.

    He estimates that the cash costs of owning and operating the machine will be as follows: Insurance, $420 per year. Operating costs per hour are fuel, $5.40; repairs, $12.00 and labor $11.00. The harvesting rate is one acre per hour.

    a) Assuming an after-tax cost of capital of 10 percent, 5 year rapid ACRS depreciation, federal investment credit and a 30 percent income tax rate, should Sweet buy the harvester?

    b) What is the minimum number of acres of sweet corn needed to justify purchase of the machine?

CHAPTER 8

28. Explain why a firm should use a weighted average cost of capital as the discount rate in evaluating a capital investment proposal even though the company might plan to raise the capital required by the particular project entirely through debt financing.

29. The Apalino Company has a problem that they have called you in to solve. Mr. Apalino, president of the company, has just heard about the concept of time value of money and wants to take it into account in judging the desirability of future investment alternatives, but does not know how to go about it. He has called in his staff and they think he should develop an appropriate discount rate (i.e., cost of capital). His secretary said she heard the president mumble, "What I really need is a way to 'discount' my staff."

    The capital structure of the company at the present time is as follows:

Short-term loan (average interest rate of 10%)	$ 75,000
Current liabilities (non-interest bearing)	225,000
Bank loans and other long-term debt funds	350,000
Common stock (4,000 shares)	400,000
8% Preferred stock (par value, $80 per share)	250,000

    The president considers the present capital structure to be "well-balanced" (as opposed to his staff) and intends to continue to use it in the future. Management estimates that long-term debt capital can be borrowed in the foreseeable future at an interest rate of about 9%. The average price of the Company's preferred stock has been $60 per share during the past year. The average price of common stock recently has been $100 per share on which the company has been paying a dividend of $10. Management expects dividends on common stock to grow at a 3% annual rate in the future. The Apalino Company is in the 55% income tax bracket.

Compute a weighted average cost of capital that the management of the Apalino Company can use in judging the desirability of investment alternatives.

30. The following facts apply to the ABC Company:

Cost of long-term loans is 12%.
6,000 shares of common stock. The Company is paying dividends of $14 per share.
The expected growth rate in dividends in the future is 3% per year.
The Company is in the 60% income tax bracket.
The capital structure is as follows:

	Book Value	Market Value
Current liabilities (non-interest bearing)	$100,000	$100,000
Accumulated depreciation	500,000	not applicable
Long-term debt	400,000	400,000
Common stock	200,000	600,000
Retained earnings	200,000	not applicable

Management considers its present capital structure to be a sound one for the future.

Compute for the ABC Company, a weighted average after-tax cost of capital that can be used by management in investment analysis. Show and label your work.

31. The owner of a relatively small business (total assets = $700,000; annual sales are $1.5 million) is interested in determining his cost of capital. He has learned of the net present value method of evaluating capital investments, but he is unable to decide on an appropriate discount rate (i.e., cost of capital). You have been called in as a consultant on this matter.

a) Develop a series of questions you would ask this person in helping him determine his cost of capital. These questions must show more thought than just: "What is your cost of debt?" and "What is your cost of equity?"

b) Suppose this owner-manager is financing his business 40% from debt capital sources and 60% from equity capital. Suppose further that he is in the 40% tax bracket and that he thinks that he can raise debt capital at 12% in the foreseeable future. Further assume that (using the viewpoints and concepts that you have discussed with him) he estimates that the cost of equity capital for his business is 15%. Now assume the actual, true, correct cost of equity capital (estabished by some not yet, and never to be, discovered formula) is 18% (not the 15% he has estimated). What will be the magnitude of his error (using 15% cost of equity capital rather than 18%)? How "far off" will his estimated weighted average, after-tax cost of capital be? How serious is this error? Why?

CHAPTER 9

32. Having given the matter some thought, you decide that you (and your honey) would be equally happy buying:

a) An Imperial and trading every sixth year.
b) An Oldsmobile and trading every third year.
c) A Mustang and trading every year.

You have decided to base your decision on the present value of the alternative investments. You have estimated your costs as follows:

	Imperial	Oldsmobile	Mustang
Original cost	$15,000	$11,000	$7,000
Market value at end of car's life	3,000	5,000	5,000
Annual operating costs, excluding depreciation	1,500	1,600	1,200
Major repairs, fourth year	800		
Major repairs, second year		300	

Your time value of money is 9 percent.

Select the alternative that promises the greatest financial advantage using the net present value approach. Rank the car alternatives in order of financial desirability.

To simplify, assume repairs are made at the end of the year in which incurred. Also assume that replacements, when made, are made at the end of the year. Personal income taxes are not a consideration.

33. The primary purpose of this question is to give you practice in analyzing mutually exclusive investments with unequal lives. It will also give you some practice with breakeven analysis.

Progressive Dairyman has decided to expand his dairy herd and believes he needs a new silo. The two alternatives under consideration are:

Concrete stave, 30' x 60'	$36,000	Sealed, 25' x 90'	$77,000
Unloader	8,000	Unloader	15,000
Total	$44,000	Total	$92,000

Each silo will store 350 tons of silage dry matter which is equivalent to 875 tons of hay crop silage at 60% moisture or 1,095 tons of corn silage at 68% moisture.

In analyzing the problem, Pro has written down the following information and assumptions:

1. After tax cost of capital = 11%
2. Average marginal tax rate, State plus Federal = 25%
3. Silos and unloaders are eligible for Federal and NYS investment credit.
4. The effects of inflation will be ignored.
5. The sealed silo will last longer than the concrete silo. Therefore, he will give sealed a 20 year life and concrete a 16 year life with no salvage value on either.
6. Each silo unloader will need to be replaced halfway through the life of the silo which it serves. Assume he capitalizes these replacements.
7. Annual maintenance and operating costs will be about equal for the unloaders regardless of the silo served.
8. Pro wants to depreciate the silos and unloaders to get the maximum tax savings. All items are 5 year property.
9. Pro will elect the 2 point reduction in Federal investment credit but not the Section 179 election.

Questions

a) Using annual equivalent cash flows, compute the added average annual before-tax cash flow that the sealed storage would need to generate to be as good an investment as the concrete stave silo. Hint: First compute the PV of the after-tax cost of owning each silo if it stands empty.

b) Added information:

(1) Either silo can be filled and emptied twice each year, once with haylage and once with corn silage.

(2) Dry matter in either corn silage or haylage is worth $70 per ton.

(3) The only difference between sealed and concrete silos is the difference in spoilage losses. Spoiled silage has no value.

Compute the difference in spoilage losses (in tons of dry matter) that would be necessary to generate the before-tax cash flow from your answer to (a) to make the sealed silo as good an investment as the concrete silo. What percentage is this spoilage of the total tons of dry matter stored in the silo?

Researchers at MOO U, in whom Pro has confidence, say that in concrete stave silos, 92 percent of the dry matter stored is available for feeding while in sealed silos, 96 percent of the dry matter stored is available for feeding. In other words, there is four percentage points difference in visible plus invisible spoilage losses.

Would the sealed silo be a good investment, in comparison to the concrete stave silo, if Pro believes the MOO U researchers and also believes that the only difference between the two silos is the difference in spoilage losses? Explain briefly in terms of NPV analysis.

c) Some knowledgeable people believe that there are differences (convenience, lower repairs, etc.) between concrete stave and sealed silos in addition to differences in spoilage losses.

Using information (1) and (2) from Question b, and assuming 4 percentage points less spoilage in the sealed silo, compute the added average annual benefits (before tax) in addition to spoilage difference that the sealed silo would need to generate to make it as good an investment as the concrete stave silo.

34. One of the hottest rock groups in the East has its home in Ithaca. That's right its the "Hot Rocks" - with Aplin on lead guitar, Casler on bass and Anderson on drums. (You should see Aplin in his leather pants and red florescent shirt.)

Well, the Hot Rocks are trying to spruce up their act. They would really like to play in swinging college night spots rather than merely grange halls and nursing homes. But the competition is tough and they realize it may require an additional investment.

Unfortunately their banker does not share their taste for music. Consequently, the Hot Rocks will be allowed to make only one of the following two investments.

<u>A Laser Light System</u>

The group can purchase a laser light system for $50,000. It will have a useful life of six years and a salvage value of $10,000 at that time. (Note: This system is classified as a 5 year Property for income tax purposes). With this system, annual revenues are expected to increase $22,000 per year. However, the group must pay for electrical costs, estimated at $1,000 per year. Moreover, their agent with the firm Dewey, Cheatem & Howe, has informed the Hot Rocks that with the system they will be required to carry "Burned Retina Insurance" for an annual cost of $2500 per year.

<u>A Swinging Van</u>

The Hot Rock's other alternative is a van. It would be used to transport their equipment, provide overnight accommodations and hold swinging parties, after their performances. The lead guitarist plans to paint the van psychedelic colors as a means of advertising the Hot Rocks. A fully equipped van costs $30,000. With this group, the van is expected to have a useful life of only 3 years and no salvage value. (Note: For tax purposes it is classified as a 3 year property.) The van is expected to increase revenues by $25,000 from "public relations" alone. Operating costs will be $4,000 per year for gasoline, $1,500 per year for license, insurance and repairs and $1,000 per year to keep if fully equipped for the swinging parties.

The group is in the 25% marginal tax bracket. Their capital structure is composed of one third debt and two thirds equity. Their banker with his unsophisticated taste for music charges them an annual interest rate of 16%. Their after tax cost of equity is estimated to be 21%.

a) Using net present value analysis, indicate which investment the Hot Rocks should select.

CHAPTER 10

35. An ice cream manufacturer follows a policy of providing ice cream cabinets to retailers who sell his product. He is interested in determining the annual sales volume that would be necessary to justify investing in an additional ice cream cabinet.

The following information is available:

Item	Per Half Gallon
Average selling price	$1.65
Less: average manufacturing cost	-1.13
Gross margin at manufacturing plant	$0.52
Distribution costs (depot and delivery, excluding cabinet costs)	
Variable	$ .16
Fixed	.19
Total distribution	$0.35
Net profit before cabinet costs	$0.17
<u>Cabinet Costs (conventional 14 DF)</u>	
Purchase price including installation	$600
Salvage value at end of 10 years	25
Annual maintenance costs	30

Cost of capital 10 percent.

Using the above information, what annual sales volume of ice cream (in half gallons) is needed to make the investment in an ice cream cabinet a "break-even" deal in a present value sense? Ignore income taxes.

36. Decision: Lease Excelsior "QT" or Buy Superior RP-77: The management of the Fancy Fruit, Co. must decide whether to lease an Excelsior "QT" peach sorting machine or purchase a Superior RP-77 peach sorting machine.

The purchase price of the RP-77 is $55,000. The QT machine can be leased (on an operating lease cancellable on 60-days notice) on the following terms:

1) A downpayment of $3,500.
2) A base rental of $5,000 per year for the first 5 years.
3) An annual production rental of $7,500 each year the sorter is used.

Use the following assumptions in making your analysis:

1) The Fancy Fruit Company is in the 55 percent income tax bracket.
2) The firm's after-tax cost of capital is 12 percent.
3) The firm is using a 6-year planning period for this decision.
4) Depreciation is calculated with 5 year rapid ACRS.
5) The Fancy Fruit Company assumes that the exchange value at the end of 6 years if leased and the trade-in value if purchased will be the same.
6) Operating costs of the two machines are equal.

a) Determine, using net present value analysis whether the Fancy Fruit Company should purchase an "RP-77" or lease a "QT".

b) So far, we've implicitly assumed that the firm was indifferent between having a "QT" or "RP-77". Now assume that the management thinks that the sorter that came out as less desirable in question "a" has an operating advantage (e.g. lower maintenance costs, or lower labor requirements because of a slightly higher sorting rate per minute). How much would the annual savings in labor costs and maintenance have to be in order to reverse the decision reached in answering question "a"?

37. One of the approaches that we have considered to handle uncertainty or risk is to vary the discount rate in keeping with the degree of risk (e.g., the greater the risk, the higher the discount rate). Briefly discuss the two principal difficulties with this approach to "risk adjustment."

38. The marketing manager of the McDoogle Fast Food Corporation has recently learned that it is incurring very high maintenance and repair costs on the machine which cuts, folds, and prints the box containers for the McDoogle Super Snack. However, the production people believe that the machine can continue to be used for another ten years if the high level of maintenance and repair is continued. The present machine is fully depreciated on the corporation's books.

The marketing manager has long argued that the container for the Super Snack should be updated. He insists that you cannot market a nutritious, delicious meal-in-itself -- consisting of three beef patties, topped with lettuce, pickles, cheese, onions, and a special sauce all nestled on a seasame seed bun, in the present drab red and yellow cardboard box. He feels that a change in image is needed and that a new container made of pleasing pink and yellow styrofoam is just the thing.

After a long search, the marketing manager has located a machine which will produce these small ecological disasters. This machine will not only produce the type of containers which the marketing manager wants but it will save the company thousands of dollars in repair costs. A schedule of the comparative costs of manufacturing the the present cardboard boxes with the existing machine and the proposed styrofoam containers with the new machine is found in Table I.

Table 1. Costs Per Thousand Containers

Expense Item	Cardboard	Styrofoam
Materials	$13.80	$21.75
Power	6.40	3.25
Labor	4.50	4.50
Repairs and maintenance	8.90	1.30
	$33.60	$30.80

These costs do not include depreciation, interest or overhead burden. They are before tax expenses.

Assume all of the above expense items (i.e., those included in the $33.60 and $30.80) are variable. In other words, for every one more (or one less) container that is produced, cash operating expenses will increase (or decrease) by $.0336 for the old cardboard container type and $.0308 for the styrofoam type. This assumption is not completely realistic, but it will make our lives simpler.

The McDoogle Corporation presently uses 25,000,000 containers annually. It has projected the container requirements will not change in the predictable future. In other words, despite the marketing manager's enthusiasm for the styrofoam container, the management team of McDoogle thinks that future sales will be the same whichever container they use.

The machine to produce the new styrofoam containers will cost $450,000. The machine is expected to have a $5,000 salvage value at the end of its expected useful life of ten years. McDoogle will use 5 year rapid ACRS depreciation. The cost of installing the machine and making the necessary modifications to the factory will be covered by the scrap value of the present box making machine. Therefore the total capital outlay required to purchase and install the new machine is $450,000.

Assume that switching to the new styrofoam package will have no effect on sales nor will it affect any other expenses other than those mentioned above.

In all parts of the problem, assume that expenses are incurred at the end of the year. Further assume that if the company decides to purchase the new machine to make the styrofoam packages, the capital outlay (i.e., the $450,000) will be incurred immediately (period 0).

Note: In answering parts a, b and c, use the following:

1) An after-tax time value of money of 9%.
2) The machine would be eligible for federal investment tax credit.
3) Assume the McDoogle Corporation is in the 60% income tax bracket.

a) Should the McDoogle Corporation purchase the new machine and switch to the new styrofoam packages?

b) Assuming that all other costs were to remain at the levels given, how much would the cost of materials for the styrofoam containers (i.e., the $21.75 given in Table 1) have to be for it to be more economical for the McDoogle Corporation to purchase the new machine and switch to the styrofoam containers?

c) How much would the annual requirement for the containers have to be to make purchasing the new machine and switching to the styrofoam containers the better alternative? Go back to the information originally given, in other words, ignore any change in the price of styrofoam materials that you dealt with in part b.

39. Carter's Avid Rental

Haven't heard too much about Jimmy Carter lately have you? After a long but unsuccessful safari for "killer rabbits" Jimmy has decided to settle down and open a car rental business in Plaines, Georgia. But Jimmy has a problem -- and this time it's not his brother. He can't decide what size fleet he should operate. Jimmy will buy a franchise from Avid, Inc. and Avid has given him two alternative fleet sizes: 1) a 10 car fleet for an initial outlay of $100,000 and 2) a 50 car fleet for an initial outlay of $400,000. The time horizon for both is 5 years and the fleets will have no salvage value at that time.

If Jimmy selects the small fleet there is an 80% probability of high demand and a 20% probability of low demand. If he opts for the large fleet the probabilities are 40% for high demand and 60% for low demand.

The net cash inflows for the first two years for each alternative are expected to be as follows:

	Net Cash Inflows Per Year	
	Small Fleet	Large Fleet
High Demand	$40,000	$160,000
Low Demand	20,000	80,000

If demand for the large fleet is high during the first two years there is a 50% probability demand will increase to $200,000 per year and a 50% probability it will decrease to $130,000 over the remaining 3 years.

Conversely, if the demand for the small fleet is low during the first two years there is a 50% probability it will remain at $20,000, but also a 50% chance it will increase to $50,000 per year for the last 3 years.

Should the 10 car fleet generate cash flows of $40,000 per year during the first two years, Jimmy will be faced with deciding whether or not to add an additional 10 cars to his fleet. The initial cost of the additional vehicles at that time will be $150,000. If he does expand there is a 90% probability net cash inflows will be $110,000 per year for the next 3 years, and a 10% chance inflows will be $80,000 per year. If he does not expand, net cash inflow will continue to be $40,000 per year for the next 3 years.

If demand for the large fleet is low during the first two years, Jimmy must decide whether or not to sell off 20 vehicles. If he does sell he will receive $50,000 for the used cars. However, he faces some risk with this decision. There is a 30% probability his cash flows will increase to $90,000 because of lower overhead costs. But due to the smaller selection of vehicles and more limited availability, there is a 70% chance inflows will decrease to $40,000 per year for the next 3 years. If he does not sell the cars his inflows will continue to be $80,000 for each of the next 3 years.

Jimmy's WACC, after tax is 9 percent. Assume the above cash flows are expressed on an after-tax basis. In other words, ignore the impact of taxes and the ITC.

a) Using decision tree analysis determine whether Jimmy should initially buy the small fleet or the large fleet.

CHAPTER 11

40. Assume the price level is expected to increase by 5% in the coming year. What return do you have to earn on an investment of $100 to earn 4% on your investment in terms of real purchasing power?

41. A one year $100 debt security is issued to yield 10%. It is expected that there will be 8% inflation during the next year. What return, in real terms, will the security earn if the prediction of price level change actually is fulfilled?

42. "When management anticipates inflation in the future, it must give careful consideration as to how to handle inflation in its analysis of the economic desirability of capital expenditure projects. The appropriate discount rate depends on whether money or real cash flows are being discounted." Explain this statement using an example.

43. Why should tax savings from depreciation be discounted with a discount rate that includes inflation?

44. Answer problem 22 a) again assuming that labor costs will increase 6 percent per year and fuel and other operating costs will increase at 10 percent per year. Reconditioning costs will increase at 8% per year. Assume that all costs given in the

original problem were in year zero dollars. The discount rate of 12% includes inflation. Use money flows in computing your answer.

CHAPTER 12

45. Purchase vs. Financial Lease: A construction firm has the opportunity to either buy or lease a crane with a purchase price of $100,000. The decision to control this machine has already been made; the decision now to be made is whether the firm will purchase the machine for cash or acquire it with a financial lease.

The following assumptions relate to both the lease and purchase alternatives:

1) The firm is in the 50 percent tax bracket.
2) The cost of capital, after tax, is 10 percent.
3) The analysis is based on a 5 year planning period.

Assumptions applying to leasing alternative:

1) Five-year lease with annual payments of $34,350 at the beginning of each year.
2) Lease payments are tax deductible expenses.
3) Investment credit retained by the lessor.

Assumptions applying to purchase alternative:

1) The machine would be financed for five years at an interest rate of 14%.
2) The machine would be 5-year property and eligible for investment credit.
3) Depreciation is a tax deductible expense.
4) The machine will have a salvage value of $15,000 at the end of 5 years.

a) Should the firm lease or purchase the machine?

Note: There can be many variations of this problem if assumptions about tax rates, cost of capital, and depreciation methods and rates are changed.

46. The Booker Chemical Company (BCC) has been ordered by the Environmental Protection Agency to begin reprocessing its toxic wastes. Booker has no choice but to obtain reprocessing equipment. Now it must decide whether to buy the machinery or enter into a financial lease.

If purchased the equipment would cost $500,000, have a useful life of 6 years and have a salvage value of $100,000. The equipment will be depreciated using the accelerated depreciation schedule for five year property and it would be eligible for investment credit. BCC would have the equipment maintained through a maintenance contract with the manufacturer. The contract would cost $15,000 per year. Booker would need to borrow 75% of the money to purchase the reprocessing equipment on a five year loan at 15 percent interest.

Booker is in the 40% tax bracket. Its capital structure is made up of 50% debt and 50% equity. The average before tax cost of debt is 16% and the average after-tax cost of equity is 18%.

a) Using NPV analysis determine the highest annual lease payment Booker would be willing to pay and still enter into a financial lease. Maintenance will be included in the lease payment. The first lease payment would be made at the beginning of the planning period and the last at the end of year five.

CHAPTER 13

47. Simplex Company has $1,000,000 allocated for capital investment purposes. The following proposals and associated net present values have been determined.

Project	Capital Outlay	Net Present Value
1	$500,000	$110,000
2	150,000	7,500
3	350,000	70,000
4	450,000	81,000
5	200,000	40,000
6	400,000	20,000

Required:

Which of the above should be undertaken?

MULTICHAPTER

48. Headline: A businessman, reading through the Wall Street Journal, sees the following ad: "Our B-Pack Air Compressor Costs $8,000. But, if you buy one now you can save $10,000."

Copy: "It sounds incredible, but it's a fact. You see the real cost of operating an air compressor is the cost of power. And our new B-Pack starts saving you big money the second you plug it in. It's a super power saver. Compared to competitive rotary machines, it can save you up to $10,000 on power costs over a five year period. Enough to pay for the cost of our new B-Pack and then some. So, even if you recently installed a new compressor of similar capacity, it may be more profitable to replace it with our B-Pack now, than to keep paying for electricity you don't have to use. And consider this, utility rates are predicted to soar 15% annually for the next five years. Our B-Pack can go to work immediately. All you do is forklift it into place and plug it in..."

Admittedly the advertisement is very enticing. Assume that last year a businessman purchased a competitor's rotary compressor of similar capacity. He has asked you to help him evaluate the claims made in the ad to decide whether he should replace his relatively new machine.

The following information concerning the businessman's company is provided:

1) The company is profitable and has a marginal income tax rate of 40%.
2) Federal investment tax credit is applicable.
3) After-tax cost of capital is 12%.
4) The new machine would be 5-year property.

The following information is available on the two compressors:

Purchase price of new compressor	$8,000
Book value of old compressor	5,000
Market value or salvage value of old compressor	5,000
Annual depreciation (straight-line) on old compressor	1,000
Maintenance and repairs expense on either machine (per year)	1,500
Installation expense of new machine (for tax purposes can be deduted as an expense - does not have to be capitalized and depreciated)	1,000
Allocation of depreciation, interest, insurance and property taxes on portion of building housing the machine (per year)	2,000

Assume the following:

1) Either machine will operate for the next five years and neither is expected to have any salvage value in five years.
2) The businessman thinks the $10,000 total saving in energy costs ($2,000 per year) claimed in the ad is a sound estimate of the energy savings for his operations, if the prospects of inflation are ignored.
3) Energy cost savings, allocated expenses, and maintenance and repair costs will occur at the end of each year.
4) Capital outlay, salvage value of old compressor, and installation costs will occur at the beginning of the year.
5) The new compressor is 5 year ACRS property and eligible for federal investment credit. If use of the old compressor is discontinued, the businessman will have recapture (pay back to the government) $670 of investment credit at the end of year 1.

a) Use the net present value approach to determine whether the businessman should replace his old compressor with the new one. Be sure to label your work clearly and to indicate the basis for your decision.

b) Assuming the businessman could rent the new compressor instead of buying it, what is the maximum amount he would be willing to pay annually to rent the new machine, rather than buying it? Assume rent is paid at the end of each year and that the businessman would incur the $1,000 installation charge on the rented compressor, as well as $1,500 per year for maintenance and repairs (i.e., he would have the same maintenance and repair expense and the same installation charge as if he bought it).

c) So far in this question we have ignored the effects of inflation. Assume for this part only, that a general inflation rate of 5% annually is expected for the next five years and that electric utility rates are expected to increase at 15% annually over the next five years. Recompute the answer to a) so that the effects of inflation are properly accounted for. The 12% WACC includes a premium for inflation.

49. The ECAC Company has been purchasing pucks from the Harvard Company. However, it has become clear that the quality of the Harvard pucks is not satisfactory. Consequently, ECAC is considering the purchase of a machine so that it can make its own pucks. It is evaluating two alternative puck-making machines: the CU machine and the Denver machine. These two machines are the best puck-making machines on the market. If they purchase a puck machine it will be housed in a portion of the ECAC plant which has no alternative use.

A comparison of the two machines follows:

	CU	Denver
Expected useful life	5 years	8 years
Initial cost	$ 8,000	$12,000
Annual operating costs (before taxes) for making a season's supply of pucks:		
Labor	600	500
Raw materials	600	700
Utilities	600	800
Maintenance and repairs	200	300
Allocation of depreciation, interest, insurance and property taxes on portion of building housing machine	2,500	2,500
Interest on machine	240	360
Total annual operating costs of machine exclusive of depreciation on machine	$ 4,740	$ 5,160

The ECAC Company has what management considers to be a well-balanced capital structure which it intends to continue to use in the future. The capital structure is as follows:

	Market Value
Current liabilities (non-interest bearing)	$200,000
Short term loans (average interest rate of 11%)	50,000
Bank loans and other long-term debt funds	300,000
12% Preferred stock (par value $50 per share)	300,000
Common stock (4,000 shares)	400,000

Management estimates that long-term capital can be borrowed in the foreseeable future at an interest rate of about 12%. The average price of the Company's preferred stock has been $50 per share during the past year. The average price of common stock has been $100 per share during the past year. The Company has been paying a dividend of $12 a share on common stock. Management expects dividends on common stock to grow at a rate of 4% per year in the future.

Assume the following:

1) No salvage value on either machine.
2) Either machine is 5 year property and would be eligible for investment credit.
3) The Company is profitable and has a 40% marginal income tax rate.

a) Compute an estimate of the weighted average after-tax cost of capital that the management of ECAC can use to judge the desirability of investment alternatives. Be sure to show your work and label your figures.

b) Determine, by doing an orderly analysis using the net present value approach, which machine is preferable. Be sure to label your work clearly and indicate the basis for your decision.

APPENDIX C
TABLES

Table I - Compound Interest 134
Table II - Present Value of $1 135
Table III - Present Value of $1 Received Annually at the End of Each
Year for n Years 138
Table IV - e^{-rt} Values for Continuous Discounting 141
Table V - Present Value of Depreciation Charges, Sum-of-the-Year's
Digits Method, No Salvage 142
Table VI - Present Value of Depreciation Charges, Double Declining Balance
Method with Switchover to Straight Line, No Salvage 143
Table VII - Present Value of Accellerated Cost Recovery 144

TABLE I

COMPOUND INTEREST

$$A = (1+r)^n$$

Amount at End of Year	1%	4%	5%	6%	7%	8%	9%	10%
1	1.0100	1.0400	1.0500	1.0600	1.0700	1.0800	1.0900	1.1000
2	1.0201	1.0816	1.1025	1.1236	1.1449	1.1664	1.1881	1.2100
3	1.0303	1.1249	1.1576	1.1910	1.2250	1.2597	1.2950	1.3310
4	1.0406	1.1699	1.2155	1.2625	1.3108	1.3605	1.4116	1.4641
5	1.0510	1.2166	1.2763	1.3382	1.4026	1.4693	1.5386	1.6105
6	1.0615	1.2653	1.3401	1.4185	1.5007	1.5869	1.6771	1.7716
7	1.0721	1.3159	1.4071	1.5036	1.6058	1.7138	1.8280	1.9487
8	1.0829	1.3686	1.4775	1.5938	1.7182	1.8509	1.9926	2.1436
9	1.0937	1.4233	1.5513	1.6895	1.8385	1.9990	2.1719	2.3580
10	1.1046	1.4802	1.6289	1.7908	1.9672	2.1589	2.3674	2.5937
11	1.1157	1.5394	1.7103	1.8983	2.1049	2.3316	2.5804	2.8531
12	1.1268	1.6010	1.7959	2.0122	2.2522	2.5182	2.8127	3.1384
13	1.1381	1.6651	1.8856	2.1329	2.4098	2.7196	3.0658	3.4523
14	1.1495	1.7317	1.9799	2.2609	2.5785	2.9372	3.3417	3.7975
15	1.1601	1.8009	2.0789	2.3966	2.7590	3.1722	3.6425	4.1772
16	1.1726	1.8730	2.1829	2.5404	2.9522	3.4259	3.9703	4.5950
17	1.1843	1.9479	2.2920	2.6928	3.1588	3.7000	4.3276	5.0545
18	1.1961	2.0258	2.4066	2.8543	3.3799	3.9960	4.717	5.5599
19	1.2081	2.1068	2.5270	3.0256	3.6165	4.3157	5.1417	6.1159
20	1.2202	2.1911	2.6533	3.2071	3.8697	4.6610	5.6044	6.7275

	11%	12%	14%	15%	16%	18%	20%	25%
1	1.1100	1.1200	1.1400	1.1500	1.1600	1.1800	1.2000	1.2500
2	1.2321	1.2544	1.2996	1.3225	1.3456	1.3924	1.4400	1.5625
3	1.3676	1.4049	1.4815	1.5209	1.5609	1.6430	1.7280	1.9531
4	1.5181	1.5735	1.6890	1.7490	1.8106	1.9388	2.0736	2.4414
5	1.6851	1.7623	1.9254	2.0114	2.1003	2.2878	2.4883	3.0518
6	1.8704	1.9738	2.1950	2.3131	2.4364	2.6996	2.9860	3.8147
7	2.0762	2.2107	2.5023	2.6600	2.8262	3.1855	3.5832	4.7684
8	2.3045	2.4760	2.8526	3.0590	3.2784	3.7589	4.2998	5.9605
9	2.5580	2.7731	3.2519	3.5179	3.8030	4.4355	5.1598	7.4506
10	2.8394	3.1058	3.7072	4.0456	4.4114	5.2338	6.1917	9.3132
11	3.1518	3.4785	4.2262	4.6524	5.1173	6.1759	7.4301	11.641
12	3.4985	3.8960	4.8179	5.3502	5.9360	7.2876	8.9161	14.552
13	3.8833	4.3635	5.4924	6.1528	6.8858	8.5994	10.699	18.190
14	4.3104	4.8871	6.2613	7.0757	7.9875	10.147	12.839	22.737
15	4.7846	5.4736	7.1379	8.1371	9.2655	11.973	15.407	28.422
16	5.3109	6.1304	8.1372	9.3576	10.748	14.129	18.488	35.527
17	5.8951	6.8660	9.2765	10.761	12.467	16.672	22.186	44.409
18	6.5436	7.6900	10.575	12.375	14.462	19.673	26.623	55.511
19	7.2633	8.6128	12.055	14.231	16.776	23.214	31.948	68.389
20	8.0623	9.6463	13.743	16.366	19.460	27.393	38.337	86.763

Table II
Present Value of $1[1]
$(1 + r)^{-n}$

Year (n)	1%	2%	3%	4%	5%	6%	7%	8%	9%	10%	11%	12%	13%	14%
1	0.9901	0.9804	0.9709	0.9615	0.9524	0.9434	0.9346	0.9259	0.9174	0.9091	0.9009	0.8929	0.8850	0.8772
2	0.9803	0.9612	0.9426	0.9246	0.9070	0.8900	0.8734	0.8573	0.8417	0.8264	0.8116	0.7972	0.7831	0.7695
3	0.9706	0.9423	0.9151	0.8890	0.8638	0.8396	0.8163	0.7938	0.7722	0.7513	0.7312	0.7118	0.6931	0.6750
4	0.9610	0.9238	0.8885	0.8548	0.8227	0.7921	0.7629	0.7350	0.7084	0.6830	0.6587	0.6355	0.6133	0.5921
5	0.9515	0.9057	0.8626	0.8219	0.7835	0.7473	0.7130	0.6806	0.6499	0.6209	0.5935	0.5674	0.5428	0.5194
6	0.9420	0.8880	0.8375	0.7903	0.7462	0.7050	0.6663	0.6302	0.5963	0.5645	0.5346	0.5066	0.4803	0.4556
7	0.9327	0.8706	0.8131	0.7599	0.7107	0.6651	0.6228	0.5835	0.5470	0.5132	0.4817	0.4523	0.4251	0.3996
8	0.9235	0.8535	0.7894	0.7307	0.6768	0.6274	0.5820	0.5403	0.5019	0.4665	0.4339	0.4039	0.3762	0.3506
9	0.9143	0.8368	0.7664	0.7026	0.6446	0.5919	0.5439	0.5002	0.4604	0.4241	0.3909	0.3606	0.3329	0.3075
10	0.9053	0.8203	0.7441	0.6756	0.6139	0.5584	0.5083	0.4632	0.4224	0.3855	0.3522	0.3220	0.2946	0.2697
11	0.8963	0.8043	0.7224	0.6496	0.5847	0.5268	0.4751	0.4289	0.3875	0.3505	0.3173	0.2875	0.2607	0.2366
12	0.8874	0.7885	0.7014	0.6246	0.5568	0.4970	0.4440	0.3971	0.3555	0.3186	0.2858	0.2567	0.2307	0.2076
13	0.8787	0.7730	0.6810	0.6006	0.5303	0.4688	0.4150	0.3677	0.3262	0.2897	0.2575	0.2292	0.2042	0.1821
14	0.8700	0.7579	0.6611	0.5775	0.5051	0.4423	0.3878	0.3405	0.2992	0.2633	0.2320	0.2046	0.1807	0.1597
15	0.8613	0.7430	0.6419	0.5553	0.4810	0.4173	0.3624	0.3152	0.2745	0.2394	0.2090	0.1827	0.1599	0.1401
16	0.8528	0.7284	0.6232	0.5339	0.4581	0.3936	0.3387	0.2919	0.2519	0.2176	0.1883	0.1631	0.1415	0.1229
17	0.8444	0.7142	0.6050	0.5134	0.4363	0.3714	0.3166	0.2703	0.2311	0.1978	0.1696	0.1456	0.1252	0.1078
18	0.8360	0.7002	0.5874	0.4936	0.4155	0.3503	0.2959	0.2502	0.2120	0.1799	0.1528	0.1300	0.1108	0.0946
19	0.8277	0.6864	0.5703	0.4746	0.3957	0.3305	0.2765	0.2317	0.1945	0.1635	0.1377	0.1161	0.0981	0.0829
20	0.8195	0.6730	0.5537	0.4564	0.3769	0.3118	0.2584	0.2145	0.1784	0.1486	0.1240	0.1037	0.0868	0.0728
21	0.8114	0.6598	0.5375	0.4388	0.3589	0.2942	0.2415	0.1987	0.1637	0.1351	0.1117	0.0926	0.0768	0.0638
22	0.8034	0.6468	0.5219	0.4220	0.3418	0.2775	0.2257	0.1839	0.1502	0.1228	0.1007	0.0826	0.0680	0.0560
23	0.7954	0.6342	0.5067	0.4057	0.3256	0.2618	0.2109	0.1703	0.1378	0.1117	0.0907	0.0738	0.0601	0.0491
24	0.7876	0.6217	0.4919	0.3901	0.3101	0.2470	0.1971	0.1577	0.1264	0.1015	0.0817	0.0659	0.0532	0.0431
25	0.7798	0.6095	0.4776	0.3751	0.2953	0.2330	0.1842	0.1460	0.1160	0.0923	0.0736	0.0588	0.0471	0.0378
26	0.7720	0.5976	0.4637	0.3607	0.2812	0.2198	0.1722	0.1352	0.1064	0.0839	0.0663	0.0525	0.0417	0.0331
27	0.7644	0.5859	0.4502	0.3468	0.2678	0.2074	0.1609	0.1252	0.0976	0.0763	0.0597	0.0469	0.0369	0.0291
28	0.7568	0.5744	0.4371	0.3335	0.2551	0.1956	0.1504	0.1159	0.0895	0.0693	0.0538	0.0419	0.0326	0.0255
29	0.7493	0.5631	0.4243	0.3207	0.2429	0.1846	0.1406	0.1073	0.0822	0.0630	0.0485	0.0374	0.0289	0.0224
30	0.7419	0.5521	0.4120	0.3083	0.2314	0.1741	0.1314	0.0994	0.0754	0.0573	0.0437	0.0334	0.0256	0.0196
35	0.7059	0.5000	0.3554	0.2534	0.1813	0.1301	0.0937	0.0676	0.0490	0.0356	0.0259	0.0189	0.0139	0.0102
40	0.6717	0.4529	0.3066	0.2083	0.1420	0.0972	0.0668	0.0460	0.0318	0.0221	0.0154	0.0107	0.0075	0.0053
45	0.6391	0.4102	0.2644	0.1712	0.1113	0.0727	0.0476	0.0313	0.0207	0.0137	0.0091	0.0061	0.0041	0.0027
50	0.6080	0.3715	0.2281	0.1407	0.0872	0.0543	0.0339	0.0213	0.0134	0.0085	0.0054	0.0035	0.0022	0.0014

[1]Prepared by R. B. How, Department of Agricultural Economics, Cornell University.

Table II
(Continued)

Year (n)	15%	16%	17%	18%	19%	20%	21%	22%	23%	24%	25%	26%	27%	28%
1	0.8696	0.8621	0.8547	0.8475	0.8403	0.8333	0.8264	0.8197	0.8130	0.8065	0.8000	0.7937	0.7874	0.7813
2	0.7561	0.7432	0.7305	0.7182	0.7062	0.6944	0.6830	0.6719	0.6610	0.6504	0.6400	0.6299	0.6200	0.6104
3	0.6575	0.6407	0.6244	0.6086	0.5934	0.5787	0.5645	0.5507	0.5374	0.5245	0.5120	0.4999	0.4882	0.4768
4	0.5718	0.5523	0.5337	0.5158	0.4987	0.4823	0.4665	0.4514	0.4369	0.4230	0.4096	0.3968	0.3844	0.3725
5	0.4972	0.4761	0.4561	0.4371	0.4190	0.4019	0.3855	0.3700	0.3552	0.3411	0.3277	0.3149	0.3027	0.2910
6	0.4323	0.4104	0.3898	0.3704	0.3521	0.3349	0.3186	0.3033	0.2888	0.2751	0.2621	0.2499	0.2383	0.2274
7	0.3759	0.3538	0.3332	0.3139	0.2959	0.2791	0.2633	0.2486	0.2348	0.2218	0.2097	0.1983	0.1877	0.1776
8	0.3269	0.3050	0.2848	0.2660	0.2487	0.2326	0.2176	0.2038	0.1909	0.1789	0.1678	0.1574	0.1478	0.1388
9	0.2843	0.2630	0.2434	0.2255	0.2090	0.1938	0.1799	0.1670	0.1552	0.1443	0.1342	0.1249	0.1164	0.1084
10	0.2472	0.2267	0.2080	0.1911	0.1756	0.1615	0.1486	0.1369	0.1262	0.1164	0.1074	0.0992	0.0916	0.0847
11	0.2149	0.1954	0.1778	0.1619	0.1476	0.1346	0.1228	0.1122	0.1026	0.0938	0.0859	0.0787	0.0721	0.0662
12	0.1869	0.1685	0.1520	0.1372	0.1240	0.1122	0.1015	0.0920	0.0834	0.0757	0.0687	0.0625	0.0568	0.0517
13	0.1625	0.1452	0.1299	0.1163	0.1042	0.0935	0.0839	0.0754	0.0678	0.0610	0.0550	0.0496	0.0447	0.0404
14	0.1413	0.1252	0.1110	0.0985	0.0876	0.0779	0.0693	0.0618	0.0551	0.0492	0.0440	0.0393	0.0352	0.0316
15	0.1229	0.1079	0.0949	0.0835	0.0736	0.0649	0.0573	0.0507	0.0448	0.0397	0.0352	0.0312	0.0277	0.0247
16	0.1069	0.0930	0.0811	0.0708	0.0618	0.0541	0.0474	0.0415	0.0364	0.0320	0.0281	0.0248	0.0218	0.0193
17	0.0929	0.0802	0.0693	0.0600	0.0520	0.0451	0.0391	0.0340	0.0296	0.0258	0.0225	0.0197	0.0172	0.0150
18	0.0808	0.0691	0.0592	0.0508	0.0437	0.0376	0.0323	0.0279	0.0241	0.0208	0.0180	0.0156	0.0135	0.0118
19	0.0703	0.0596	0.0506	0.0431	0.0367	0.0313	0.0267	0.0229	0.0196	0.0168	0.0144	0.0124	0.0107	0.0092
20	0.0611	0.0514	0.0433	0.0365	0.0308	0.0261	0.0221	0.0187	0.0159	0.0135	0.0115	0.0098	0.0084	0.0072
21	0.0531	0.0443	0.0370	0.0309	0.0259	0.0217	0.0183	0.0154	0.0129	0.0109	0.0092	0.0078	0.0066	0.0056
22	0.0462	0.0382	0.0316	0.0262	0.0218	0.0181	0.0151	0.0126	0.0105	0.0088	0.0074	0.0062	0.0052	0.0044
23	0.0402	0.0329	0.0270	0.0222	0.0183	0.0151	0.0125	0.0103	0.0086	0.0071	0.0059	0.0049	0.0041	0.0034
24	0.0349	0.0284	0.0231	0.0188	0.0154	0.0126	0.0103	0.0085	0.0070	0.0057	0.0047	0.0039	0.0032	0.0027
25	0.0304	0.0245	0.0197	0.0160	0.0129	0.0105	0.0085	0.0069	0.0057	0.0046	0.0038	0.0031	0.0025	0.0021
26	0.0264	0.0211	0.0169	0.0135	0.0109	0.0087	0.0070	0.0057	0.0046	0.0037	0.0030	0.0025	0.0020	0.0016
27	0.0230	0.0182	0.0144	0.0115	0.0091	0.0073	0.0058	0.0047	0.0037	0.0030	0.0024	0.0019	0.0016	0.0013
28	0.0200	0.0157	0.0123	0.0097	0.0077	0.0061	0.0048	0.0038	0.0030	0.0024	0.0019	0.0015	0.0012	0.0010
29	0.0174	0.0135	0.0105	0.0082	0.0064	0.0051	0.0040	0.0031	0.0025	0.0020	0.0015	0.0012	0.0010	0.0008
30	0.0151	0.0116	0.0090	0.0070	0.0054	0.0042	0.0033	0.0026	0.0020	0.0016	0.0012	0.0010	0.0008	0.0006
35	0.0075	0.0055	0.0041	0.0030	0.0023	0.0017	0.0013	0.0009	0.0007	0.0005	0.0004	0.0003	0.0002	0.0002
40	0.0037	0.0026	0.0019	0.0013	0.0010	0.0007	0.0005	0.0004	0.0002	0.0002	0.0001	0.0001	0.0001	0.0001
45	0.0019	0.0013	0.0009	0.0006	0.0004	0.0003	0.0002	0.0001	0.0001	0.0001	0.0000	0.0000	0.0000	0.0000
50	0.0009	0.0006	0.0004	0.0003	0.0002	0.0001	0.0001	0.0000	0.0000	0.0000				

Table II
(Continued)

Year (n)	29%	30%	35%	40%	45%	50%
1	0.7752	0.7692	0.7407	0.7143	0.6897	0.6667
2	0.6009	0.5917	0.5487	0.5102	0.4756	0.4444
3	0.4658	0.4552	0.4064	0.3644	0.3280	0.2963
4	0.3611	0.3501	0.3011	0.2603	0.2262	0.1975
5	0.2799	0.2693	0.2230	0.1859	0.1560	0.1317
6	0.2170	0.2072	0.1672	0.1328	0.1076	0.0878
7	0.1682	0.1594	0.1224	0.0949	0.0742	0.0585
8	0.1304	0.1226	0.0906	0.0678	0.0512	0.0390
9	0.1011	0.0943	0.0671	0.0484	0.0353	0.0260
10	0.0784	0.0725	0.0497	0.0346	0.0243	0.0173
11	0.0607	0.0558	0.0368	0.0247	0.0168	0.0116
12	0.0471	0.0429	0.0273	0.0176	0.0116	0.0077
13	0.0365	0.0330	0.0202	0.0126	0.0080	0.0051
14	0.0283	0.0253	0.0150	0.0090	0.0055	0.0034
15	0.0219	0.0195	0.0111	0.0064	0.0038	0.0023
16	0.0170	0.0150	0.0082	0.0046	0.0026	0.0015
17	0.0132	0.0116	0.0061	0.0033	0.0018	0.0010
18	0.0102	0.0089	0.0045	0.0023	0.0012	0.0007
19	0.0079	0.0068	0.0033	0.0017	0.0009	0.0005
20	0.0061	0.0053	0.0025	0.0012	0.0006	0.0003
21	0.0048	0.0040	0.0018	0.0009	0.0004	0.0002
22	0.0037	0.0031	0.0014	0.0006	0.0003	0.0001
23	0.0029	0.0024	0.0010	0.0004	0.0002	0.0001
24	0.0022	0.0018	0.0007	0.0003	0.0001	0.0001
25	0.0017	0.0014	0.0006	0.0002	0.0001	0.0000
26	0.0013	0.0011	0.0004	0.0002	0.0001	0.0000
27	0.0010	0.0008	0.0003	0.0001	0.0000	
28	0.0008	0.0006	0.0002	0.0001		
29	0.0006	0.0005	0.0002	0.0001		
30	0.0005	0.0004	0.0001	0.0000		
35	0.0001	0.0001	0.0000			
40	0.0000	0.0000				
45						
50						

Table III
Present Value of $1 Received Annually at the End of Each Year for n Years[1]

$$\frac{1 - (1 + r)^{-n}}{r}$$

Year (n)	1%	2%	3%	4%	5%	6%	7%
1	0.9901	0.9804	0.9709	0.9615	0.9524	0.9434	0.9346
2	1.9704	1.9416	1.9135	1.8861	1.8594	1.8334	1.8080
3	2.9410	2.8839	2.8286	2.7751	2.7232	2.6730	2.6243
4	3.9020	3.8077	3.7171	3.6299	3.5460	3.4651	3.3872
5	4.8534	4.7135	4.5797	4.4518	4.3295	4.2124	4.1002
6	5.7955	5.6014	5.4172	5.2421	5.0757	4.9173	4.7665
7	6.7282	6.4720	6.2303	6.0021	5.7864	5.5824	5.3893
8	7.6517	7.3255	7.0197	6.7327	6.4632	6.2098	5.9713
9	8.5660	8.1622	7.7861	7.4353	7.1078	6.8017	6.5152
10	9.4713	8.9826	8.5302	8.1109	7.7217	7.3601	7.0236
11	10.3676	9.7868	9.2526	8.7605	8.3064	7.8869	7.4987
12	11.2551	10.5753	10.9540	9.3851	8.8633	8.3838	7.9427
13	12.1337	11.3484	10.6350	9.9856	9.3936	8.8527	8.3576
14	13.0037	12.1062	11.2961	10.5631	9.8986	9.2950	8.7455
15	13.8651	12.8493	11.9379	11.1184	10.3797	9.7122	9.1079
16	14.7179	13.5777	12.5611	11.6523	10.8378	10.1059	9.4466
17	15.5623	14.2919	13.1661	12.1657	11.2741	10.4773	9.7632
18	16.3983	14.9920	13.7535	12.6593	11.6896	10.8276	10.0591
19	17.2260	15.6785	14.3238	13.1339	12.0853	11.1581	10.3356
20	18.0456	16.3514	14.8775	13.5903	12.4622	11.4699	10.5940
21	18.8570	17.0112	15.4150	14.0292	12.8212	11.7641	10.8355
22	19.6604	17.6580	15.9369	14.4511	13.1630	12.0416	11.0612
23	20.4558	18.2922	16.4436	14.8568	13.4886	12.3034	11.2722
24	21.2434	18.9139	16.9355	15.2470	13.7986	12.5504	11.4693
25	22.0232	19.5235	17.4131	15.6221	14.0939	12.7834	11.6536
26	22.7952	20.1210	17.8768	15.9828	14.3752	13.0032	11.8258
27	23.5596	20.7069	18.3270	16.3296	14.6430	13.2105	11.9867
28	24.3164	21.2813	18.7641	16.6631	14.8981	13.4062	12.1371
29	25.0658	21.8444	19.1885	16.9837	15.1411	13.5907	12.2777
30	25.8077	22.3965	19.6004	17.2920	15.3725	13.7648	12.4090
31	26.5423	22.9377	20.0004	17.5885	15.5928	13.9291	12.5318
32	27.2696	23.4683	20.3888	17.8736	15.8027	14.0840	12.6466
33	27.9897	23.9886	20.7658	18.1476	16.0025	14.2302	12.7538
34	28.7027	24.4986	21.1318	18.4112	16.1929	14.3681	12.8540
35	29.4086	24.9986	21.4872	18.6646	16.3742	14.4982	12.9477
40	32.8347	27.3555	23.1148	19.7928	17.1591	15.0463	13.3317
45	36.0945	29.4902	24.5187	20.7200	17.7741	15.4558	13.6055
50	39.1961	31.4236	25.7298	21.4822	18.2559	15.7619	13.8007

[1]Prepared by R. B. How, Department of Agricultural Economics, Cornell University.

Table III *(Continued)*

n	8%	9%	10%	11%	12%	13%	14%	15%	16%	17%	18%	19%	20%	21%
1	0.9259	0.9174	0.9091	0.9009	0.8929	0.8850	0.8772	0.8696	0.8621	0.8547	0.8475	0.8403	0.8333	0.8264
2	1.7833	1.7591	1.7355	1.7125	1.6901	1.6681	1.6467	1.6257	1.6052	1.5852	1.5656	1.5465	1.5278	1.5095
3	2.5771	2.5313	2.4869	2.4437	2.4018	2.3612	2.3216	2.2832	2.2459	2.2096	2.1743	2.1399	2.1065	2.0739
4	3.3121	3.2397	3.1699	3.1024	3.0374	2.9745	2.9137	2.8550	2.7982	2.7432	2.6901	2.6386	2.5887	2.5404
5	3.9927	3.8897	3.7908	3.6959	3.6048	3.5172	3.4331	3.3522	3.2743	3.1993	3.1272	3.0576	2.9906	2.9260
6	4.6229	4.4859	4.3553	4.2305	4.1114	3.9976	3.8887	3.7845	3.6847	3.5892	3.4976	3.4098	3.3255	3.2446
7	5.2064	5.0330	4.8684	4.7122	4.5638	4.4226	4.2883	4.1604	4.0386	3.9224	3.8115	3.7057	3.6046	3.5080
8	5.7466	5.5348	5.3349	5.1461	4.9676	4.7988	4.6389	4.4873	4.3436	4.2072	4.0776	3.9544	3.8372	3.7256
9	6.2469	5.9952	5.7590	5.5370	5.3282	5.1317	4.9464	4.7716	4.6065	4.4506	4.3030	4.1633	4.0310	3.9054
10	6.7101	6.4177	6.1446	5.8892	5.6502	5.4262	5.2161	5.0188	4.8332	4.6586	4.4941	4.3389	4.1925	4.0541
11	7.1390	6.8052	6.4951	6.2065	5.9377	5.6869	5.4527	5.2337	5.0286	4.8364	4.6560	4.4865	4.3271	4.1769
12	7.5361	7.1607	6.8137	6.4924	6.1944	5.9176	5.6603	5.4206	5.1971	4.9884	4.7932	4.6105	4.4392	4.2784
13	7.9038	7.4869	7.1034	6.7499	6.4236	6.1218	5.8424	5.5831	5.3423	5.1183	4.9095	4.7147	4.5327	4.3624
14	8.2442	7.7862	7.3667	6.9819	6.6282	6.3025	6.0021	5.7245	5.4675	5.2293	5.0081	4.8023	4.6106	4.4317
15	8.5595	8.0607	7.6061	7.1909	6.8109	6.4624	6.1422	5.8474	5.5755	5.3242	5.0916	4.8759	4.6755	4.4890
16	8.8514	8.3126	7.8237	7.3792	6.9740	6.6039	6.2651	5.9542	5.6685	5.4053	5.1624	4.9377	4.7296	4.5364
17	9.1216	8.5436	8.0216	7.5488	7.1196	6.7291	6.3729	6.0472	5.7487	5.4746	5.2223	4.9897	4.7746	4.5755
18	9.3719	8.7556	8.2014	7.7016	7.2497	6.8399	6.4674	6.1280	5.8178	5.5339	5.2732	5.0333	4.8122	4.6079
19	9.6036	8.9501	8.3649	7.8393	7.3658	6.9380	6.5504	6.1982	5.8775	5.5845	5.3162	5.0700	4.8435	4.6346
20	9.8181	9.1286	8.5136	7.9633	7.4694	7.0248	6.6231	6.2593	5.9288	5.6278	5.3528	5.1009	4.8696	4.6567
21	10.0168	9.2922	8.6487	8.0751	7.5620	7.1016	6.6870	6.3125	5.9731	5.6648	4.3837	5.1268	4.8913	4.6750
22	10.2007	9.4424	8.7715	8.1757	7.6446	7.1695	6.7429	6.3587	6.0113	5.6964	5.4099	5.1486	4.9094	4.6900
23	10.3711	9.5802	8.8832	8.2664	7.7184	7.2297	6.7921	6.3988	6.0442	5.7234	5.4321	5.1668	4.9245	4.7025
24	10.5288	9.7066	8.9847	8.3481	7.7843	7.2829	6.8351	6.4338	6.0726	5.7465	5.4510	5.1822	4.9371	4.7128
25	10.6748	9.8226	9.0770	8.4217	7.8431	7.3300	6.8729	6.4642	6.0971	5.7662	5.4669	5.1952	4.9476	4.7213
26	10.8100	9.9290	9.1610	8.4881	7.8957	7.3717	6.9061	6.4906	6.1182	5.7831	5.4804	5.2060	4.9563	4.7284
27	10.9352	10.0266	9.2372	8.5478	7.9426	7.4086	6.9352	6.5135	6.1364	5.7975	5.4919	5.2151	4.9636	4.7342
28	11.0511	10.1161	9.3066	8.6016	7.9844	7.4412	6.9607	6.5335	6.1520	5.8099	5.5016	5.2228	4.9697	4.7390
29	11.1584	10.1983	9.3696	8.6501	8.0218	7.4701	6.9830	6.5509	6.1656	5.8204	5.5098	5.2292	4.9747	4.7430
30	11.2578	10.2737	9.4269	8.6938	8.0552	7.4957	7.0027	6.5660	6.1772	5.8294	5.5168	5.2347	4.9789	4.7463
31	11.3498	10.3428	9.4790	8.7332	8.0850	7.5183	7.0199	6.5791	6.1872	5.8371	5.5227	5.2392	4.9824	4.7490
32	11.4350	10.4062	9.5264	8.7686	8.1116	7.5383	7.0350	6.5905	6.1959	5.8437	5.5277	5.2430	4.9854	4.7512
33	11.5139	10.4644	9.5694	8.8005	8.1354	7.5560	7.0482	6.6005	6.2034	5.8493	5.5320	5.2462	4.9878	4.7531
34	11.5869	10.5178	9.6086	8.8293	8.1566	7.5717	7.0599	6.6091	6.2098	5.8541	5.5356	5.2490	4.9898	4.7546
35	11.6546	10.5668	9.6442	8.8552	8.1755	7.5856	7.0700	6.6166	6.2153	5.8582	5.5386	5.2512	4.9915	4.7559
40	11.9246	10.7574	9.7791	8.9511	8.2438	7.6344	7.1050	6.6418	6.2335	5.8713	5.5482	5.2582	4.9966	4.7596
45	12.1084	10.8812	9.8628	9.0079	8.2825	7.6609	7.1232	6.6543	6.2421	5.8773	5.5523	5.2611	4.9986	4.7610
50	12.2335	10.9617	9.9148	9.0417	8.3045	7.6752	7.1327	6.6605	6.2463	5.8801	5.5541	5.2623	4.9995	4.7616

Table III *(Continued)*

n	22%	23%	24%	25%	26%	27%	28%	29%	30%	35%	40%	45%	50%
1	0.8197	0.8130	0.8065	0.8000	0.7937	0.7874	0.7813	0.7752	0.7692	0.7407	0.7143	0.6897	0.6667
2	1.4915	1.4740	1.4568	1.4400	1.4235	1.4074	1.3916	1.3761	1.3610	1.2894	1.2245	1.1653	1.1111
3	2.0422	2.0114	1.9813	1.9520	1.9234	1.8956	1.8684	1.8420	1.8161	1.6959	1.5889	1.4933	1.4074
4	2.4936	2.4483	2.4043	2.3616	2.3202	2.2800	2.2410	2.2031	2.1662	1.9970	1.8492	1.7195	1.6049
5	2.8636	2.8035	2.7454	2.6893	2.6351	2.5827	2.5320	2.4830	2.4356	2.2200	2.0352	1.8755	1.7366
6	3.1669	3.0923	3.0205	2.9514	2.8850	2.8210	2.7594	2.7000	2.6428	2.3852	2.1680	1.9831	1.8244
7	3.4155	3.3270	3.2423	3.1611	3.0833	3.0087	2.9370	2.8682	2.8021	2.5075	2.2628	2.0573	1.8829
8	3.6193	3.5179	3.4212	3.3289	3.2407	3.1564	3.0758	2.9986	2.9247	2.5982	2.3306	2.1085	1.9220
9	3.7863	3.6731	3.5655	3.4631	3.3657	3.2728	3.1842	3.0997	3.0190	2.6653	2.3790	2.1438	1.9480
10	3.9232	3.7993	3.6819	3.5705	3.4648	3.3644	3.2689	3.1781	3.0915	2.7150	2.4136	2.1681	1.9653
11	4.0354	3.9018	3.7757	3.6564	3.5435	3.4365	3.3351	3.2388	3.1473	2.7519	2.4383	2.1849	1.9769
12	4.1274	3.9852	3.8514	3.7251	3.6060	3.4933	3.3868	3.2859	3.1903	2.7792	2.4559	2.1965	1.9846
13	4.2028	4.0530	3.9124	3.7801	3.6555	3.5381	3.4272	3.3224	3.2233	2.7994	2.4685	2.2045	1.9897
14	4.2646	4.1082	3.9616	3.8241	3.6949	3.5733	3.4587	3.3507	3.2487	2.8144	2.4775	2.2100	1.9932
15	4.3152	4.1530	4.0013	3.8593	3.7261	3.6010	3.4834	3.3726	3.2682	2.8255	2.4839	2.2138	1.9954
16	4.3567	4.1894	4.0333	3.8874	3.7509	3.6228	3.5026	3.3896	3.2832	2.8337	2.4885	2.2164	1.9970
17	4.3908	4.2190	4.0591	3.9099	3.7705	3.6400	3.5177	3.4028	3.2948	2.8398	2.4918	2.2182	1.9980
18	4.4187	4.2431	4.0799	3.9279	3.7861	3.6536	3.5294	3.4130	3.3037	2.8443	2.4941	2.2195	1.9986
19	4.4415	4.2627	4.0967	3.9424	3.7985	3.6642	3.5386	3.4210	3.3105	2.8476	2.4958	2.2203	1.9991
20	4.4603	4.2786	4.1103	3.9539	3.8083	3.6726	3.5458	3.4271	3.3158	2.8501	2.4970	2.2209	1.9994
21	4.4756	4.2916	4.1212	3.9631	3.8162	3.6792	3.5514	3.4319	3.3198	2.8519	2.4979	2.2213	1.9996
22	4.4882	4.3021	4.1300	3.9705	3.8223	3.6844	3.5558	3.4356	3.3230	2.8533	2.4985	2.2216	1.9997
23	4.4985	4.3106	4.1371	3.9764	3.8273	3.6885	3.5592	3.4384	3.3254	2.8543	2.4989	2.2218	1.9998
24	4.5070	4.3176	4.1428	3.9811	3.8312	3.6918	3.5619	3.4406	3.3272	2.8550	2.4992	2.2219	1.9999
25	4.5139	4.3232	4.1474	3.9849	3.8342	3.6943	3.5640	3.4424	3.3286	2.8556	2.4994	2.2220	1.9999
26	4.5196	4.3278	4.1512	3.9879	3.8367	3.6963	3.5656	3.4437	3.3297	2.8560	2.4996	2.2221	2.0000
27	4.5243	4.3316	4.1542	3.9903	3.8387	3.6979	3.5669	3.4447	3.3305	2.8563	2.4997	2.2221	2.0000
28	4.5281	4.3346	4.1566	3.9923	4.8402	3.6991	3.5679	3.4455	3.3312	2.8565	2.4998	2.2222	2.0000
29	4.5312	4.3371	4.1585	3.9938	3.8414	3.7001	3.5687	3.4461	3.3316	2.8567	2.4999	2.2222	2.0000
30	4.5338	4.3391	4.1601	3.9950	3.8424	3.7009	3.5693	3.4466	3.3321	2.8568	2.4999	2.2222	2.0000
31	4.5359	4.3407	4.1614	3.9960	3.8432	3.7015	3.5697	3.4470	3.3324	2.8569	2.4999	2.2222	2.0000
32	4.5376	4.3421	4.1624	3.9968	3.8438	3.7019	3.5701	3.4473	3.3326	2.8570	2.5000	2.2222	2.0000
33	4.5390	4.3431	4.1632	3.9975	3.8443	3.7023	3.5704	3.4475	3.3328	2.8570	2.5000	2.2222	2.0000
34	4.5402	4.3440	4.1639	3.9980	3.8447	3.7026	3.5706	3.4477	3.3329	2.8570	2.5000	2.2222	2.0000
35	4.5411	4.3447	4.1644	3.9984	3.8450	3.7028	3.5708	3.4478	3.3330	2.8571	2.5000	2.2222	2.0000
40	4.5439	4.3467	4.1659	3.9995	3.8458	3.7034	3.5712	3.4482	3.3332	2.8571	2.5000	2.2222	2.0000
45	4.5449	4.3474	4.1664	3.9998	3.8460	3.7036	3.5714	3.4482	3.3333	2.8571	2.5000	2.2222	2.0000
50	4.5452	4.3477	4.1666	3.9999	3.8461	3.7037	3.5714	3.4483	3.3333	2.8571	2.5000	2.2222	2.0000

Table IV
e^{-rt} Values for Continuous Discounting

rt	0	.01	.02	.03	.04	.05	.06	.07	.08	.09
0	1.0000	.9900	.9802	.9704	.9608	.9512	.9418	.9324	.9231	.9139
.10	.9048	.8958	.8869	.8781	.8694	.8607	.8521	.8437	.8353	.8270
.20	.8187	.8106	.8025	.7945	.7866	.7788	.7711	.7634	.7558	.7483
.30	.7408	.7334	.7261	.7189	.7118	.7047	.6977	.6907	.6839	.6771
.40	.6703	.6636	.6570	.6505	.6440	.6376	.6313	.6250	.6188	.6126
.50	.6065	.6005	.5945	.5886	.5827	.5770	.5712	.5655	.5599	.5543
.60	.5488	.5434	.5379	.5326	.5273	.5220	.5169	.5117	.5066	.5016
.70	.4966	.4916	.4868	.4819	.4771	.4724	.4677	.4630	.4584	.4538
.80	.4493	.4449	.4404	.4360	.4317	.4274	.4232	.4190	.4148	.4107
.90	.4066	.4025	.3985	.3946	.3906	.3867	.3829	.3791	.3753	.3716
1.00	.3679	.3642	.3606	.3570	.3535	.3499	.3465	.3430	.3396	.3362
1.10	.3329	.3296	.3263	.3230	.3198	.3166	.3135	.3104	.3073	.3042
1.20	.3012	.2982	.2952	.2923	.2894	.2865	.2837	.2808	.2780	.2753
1.30	.2725	.2698	.2671	.2645	.2618	.2592	.2567	.2541	.2516	.2491
1.40	.2466	.2441	.2417	.2393	.2369	.2346	.2322	.2299	.2276	.2254
1.50	.2231	.2209	.2187	.2165	.2144	.2122	.2101	.2080	.2060	.2040
1.60	.2019	.1999	.1979	.1959	.1940	.1920	.1901	.1882	.1864	.1845
1.70	.1827	.1809	.1791	.1773	.1755	.1738	.1720	.1703	.1686	.1670
1.80	.1653	.1637	.1620	.1604	.1588	.1572	.1557	.1541	.1526	.1511
1.90	.1496	.1481	.1466	.1451	.1437	.1423	.1409	.1395	.1381	.1367
2.00	.1353	.1340	.1327	.1313	.1300	.1287	.1275	.1262	.1249	.1237
2.10	.1225	.1212	.1200	.1188	.1177	.1165	.1153	.1142	.1130	.1119
2.20	.1108	.1097	.1086	.1075	.1065	.1054	.1043	1033	.1023	.1013
2.30	.1003	.0993	.0983	.0973	.0963	.0954	.0944	.0935	.0926	.0916
2.40	.0907	.0898	.0889	.0880	.0872	.0863	.0854	.0846	.0837	.0829
2.50	.0821	.0813	.0805	.0797	.0789	.0781	.0773	0765	.0758	0750
2.60	.0743	.0735	.0728	.0721	.0714	.0707	.0699	.0693	.0686	.0679
2.70	.0672	.0665	.0659	.0652	.0646	.0639	.0633	.0627	.0620	.0614
2.80	.0608	.0602	.0596	.0590	.0584	.0578	.0573	.0567	.0561	.0556
2.90	.0550	.0545	.0539	.0534	.0529	.0523	.0518	.0513	.0508	.0503
3.00	.0498	.0493	.0488	.0483	.0478	.0476	.0469	.0464	.0460	.0455
3.10	.0450	.0446	.0442	.0437	.0433	.0429	.0424	.0420	.0416	.0412
3.20	.0408	.0404	.0400	.0396	.0392	.0388	.0384	.0380	.0376	.0373
3.30	.0369	.0365	.0362	.0358	.0354	.0351	.0347	.0344	.0340	.0337
3.40	.0334	.0330	.0327	.0324	.0321	.0317	.0314	.0311	.0308	0305
3.50	.0302	.0299	.0296	.0293	.0290	.0287	.0284	.0282	.0279	0276
3.60	.0273	.0271	.0268	.0265	.0263	.0260	.0257	.0255	.0252	.0250
3.70	.0247	.0245	.0242	.0240	.0238	.0235	.0233	.0231	.0228	.0226
3.80	.0224	.0221	.0219	.0217	.0215	.0213	.0211	.0209	.0207	.0204
3.90	.0202	.0200	.0198	.0196	.0194	.0193	.0191	.0189	.0187	.0185
4.00	.0183	.0181	.0180	.0178	.0176	.0174	.0172	.0171	.0169	.0167
4.10	.0166	.0164	.0162	.0161	.0159	.0158	.0156	.0155	.0153	.0151
4.20	.0150	.0148	.0147	.0146	.0144	.0143	.0141	.0140	.0138	.0137
4.30	.0136	.0134	.0133	.0132	.0130	.0129	.0128	.0127	.0125	.0124
4.40	.0123	.0122	.0120	.0120	.0118	.0117	.0116	.0114	.0113	.0112
4.50	.0111	.0110	.0109	.0108	.0107	.0106	.0105	.0104	.0103	.0102
4.60	.0101	.0100	.0099	.0098	.0097	.0096	.0095	.0094	.0093	.0092
4.70	.0091	.0090	.0089	.0089	.0087	.0087	.0086	.0085	.0084	.0083
4.80	.0082	.0081	.0081	.0080	.0079	.0078	.0078	0077	.0076	.0075
4.90	.0074	.0074	.0073	.0072	.0072	.0071	.0070	.0069	.0069	.0068

Table V
Present Value of Depreciation Charges, Sum-of-the-Year's-Digits Method, No Salvage*

n	3%	4%	5%	6%	7%	8%	9%	10%	11%	12%	13%	14%	15%	20%	25%	30%	35%	40%
1	0.9709	0.9615	0.9524	0.9434	0.9346	0.9259	0.9174	0.9091	0.9009	0.8929	0.8850	0.8772	0.8696	0.8333	0.8000	0.7692	0.7407	0.7143
2	0.9614	0.9492	0.9373	0.9256	0.9142	0.9031	0.8922	0.8815	0.8711	0.8610	0.8510	0.8413	0.8318	0.7870	0.7467	0.7101	0.6767	0.6463
3	0.9522	0.9371	0.9225	0.9083	0.8945	0.8810	0.8680	0.8552	0.8429	0.8308	0.8190	0.8076	0.7964	0.7446	0.6987	0.6577	0.6210	0.5879
4	0.9430	0.9253	0.9081	0.8915	0.8754	0.8598	0.8448	0.8301	0.8160	0.8022	0.7889	0.7759	0.7633	0.7056	0.6554	0.6113	0.5723	0.5377
5	0.9340	0.9136	0.8940	0.8752	0.8570	0.8394	0.8225	0.8061	0.7904	0.7751	0.7604	0.7462	0.7324	0.6698	0.6162	0.5699	0.5295	0.4941
6	0.9251	0.9022	0.8803	0.8593	0.8391	0.8197	0.8011	0.7832	0.7660	0.7494	0.7335	0.7181	0.7033	0.6368	0.5807	0.5329	0.4918	0.4562
7	0.9163	0.8910	0.8669	0.8438	0.8218	0.8007	0.7806	0.7613	0.7428	0.7251	0.7081	0.6918	0.6761	0.6063	0.5484	0.4997	0.4584	0.4230
8	0.9077	0.8800	0.8538	0.8288	0.8050	0.7824	0.7609	0.7403	0.7207	0.7019	0.6840	0.6669	0.6505	0.5782	0.5190	0.4699	0.4287	0.3937
9	0.8992	0.8693	0.8410	0.8142	0.7888	0.7648	0.7419	0.7202	0.6996	0.6800	0.6613	0.6434	0.6264	0.5521	0.4922	0.4430	0.4022	0.3678
10	0.8908	0.8587	0.8285	0.8000	0.7731	0.7477	0.7237	0.7010	0.6795	0.6591	0.6397	0.6213	0.6038	0.5280	0.4676	0.4187	0.3784	0.3448
11	0.8825	0.8483	0.8162	0.7861	0.7579	0.7313	0.7062	0.6826	0.6603	0.6392	0.6192	0.6004	0.5825	0.5055	0.4451	0.3966	0.3571	0.3243
12	0.8744	0.8381	0.8043	0.7727	0.7431	0.7154	0.6894	0.6649	0.6419	0.6203	0.5998	0.5806	0.5623	0.4847	0.4244	0.3765	0.3378	0.3059
13	0.8663	0.8281	0.7926	0.7596	0.7288	0.7000	0.6732	0.6480	0.6244	0.6022	0.5814	0.5618	0.5434	0.4652	0.4053	0.3581	0.3203	0.2893
14	0.8584	0.8183	0.7812	0.7468	0.7149	0.6852	0.6576	0.6317	0.6076	0.5851	0.5639	0.5441	0.5254	0.4471	0.3877	0.3413	0.3044	0.2743
15	0.8506	0.8087	0.7701	0.7344	0.7014	0.6709	0.6425	0.6162	0.5916	0.5687	0.5473	0.5273	0.5085	0.4302	0.3714	0.3259	0.2899	0.2608
20	0.8131	0.7631	0.7179	0.6770	0.6399	0.6061	0.5752	0.5470	0.5211	0.4972	0.4753	0.4550	0.4362	0.3602	0.3056	0.2648	0.2333	0.2084
25	0.7781	0.7214	0.6711	0.6265	0.5867	0.5510	0.5189	0.4899	0.4637	0.4399	0.4182	0.3984	0.3802	0.3085	0.2586	0.2223	0.1947	0.1731
30	0.7455	0.6832	0.6291	0.5819	0.5404	0.5038	0.4714	0.4424	0.4165	0.3933	0.3723	0.3533	0.3360	0.2690	0.2237	0.1912	0.1668	0.1478
35	0.7150	0.6482	0.5913	0.5424	0.5001	0.4632	0.4309	0.4025	0.3773	0.3548	0.3347	0.3167	0.3004	0.2382	0.1968	0.1675	0.1458	0.1290
40	0.6864	0.6161	0.5571	0.5072	0.4646	0.4280	0.3962	0.3685	0.3442	0.3227	0.3036	0.2865	0.2712	0.2134	0.1756	0.1491	0.1294	0.1143
45	0.6596	0.5865	0.5261	0.4758	0.4333	0.3972	0.3663	0.3395	0.3161	0.2956	0.2775	0.2614	0.2470	0.1932	0.1585	0.1342	0.1163	0.1027
50	0.6345	0.5592	0.4979	0.4476	0.4056	0.3703	0.3402	0.3144	0.2920	0.2725	0.2554	0.2402	0.2266	0.1765	0.1443	0.1220	0.1056	0.0931

Table VI
Present Value of Depreciation Charges, Double Declining Balance Method With Switchover to Straight Line, No Salvage*

n	3%	4%	5%	6%	7%	8%	9%	10%	11%	12%	13%	14%	15%	20%	25%	30%	35%	40%
3	0.9584	0.9453	0.9325	0.9200	0.9079	0.8960	0.8845	0.8732	0.8622	0.8515	0.8410	0.8308	0.8208	0.7742	0.7324	0.6949	0.6609	0.6301
4	0.9465	0.9299	0.9138	0.8982	0.8830	0.8684	0.8542	0.8404	0.8271	0.8141	0.8016	0.7893	0.7775	0.7229	0.6752	0.6332	0.5960	0.5628
5	0.9355	0.9156	0.8965	0.8781	0.8604	0.8433	0.8269	0.8110	0.7957	0.7809	0.7666	0.7528	0.7394	0.6788	0.6270	0.5821	0.5431	0.5088
6	0.9243	0.9013	0.8793	0.8583	0.8381	0.8188	0.8003	0.7825	0.7655	0.7491	0.7333	0.7182	0.7036	0.6382	0.5834	0.5370	0.4971	0.4627
7	0.9137	0.8878	0.8632	0.8398	0.8174	0.7961	0.7758	0.7564	0.7379	0.7202	0.7032	0.6870	0.6714	0.6025	0.5458	0.4985	0.4585	0.4243
8	0.9031	0.8743	0.8472	0.8214	0.7971	0.7740	0.7520	0.7312	0.7114	0.6925	0.6745	0.6574	0.6411	0.5695	0.5117	0.4642	0.4245	0.3910
9	0.8929	0.8615	0.8320	0.8042	0.7780	0.7533	0.7299	0.7078	0.6869	0.6671	0.6483	0.6305	0.6135	0.5401	0.4818	0.4344	0.3954	0.3627
10	0.8827	0.8487	0.8169	0.7872	0.7593	0.7331	0.7085	0.6853	0.6634	0.6428	0.6234	0.6050	0.5876	0.5129	0.4545	0.4077	0.3695	0.3378
11	0.8728	0.8364	0.8026	0.7710	0.7416	0.7141	0.6884	0.6643	0.6417	0.6204	0.6004	0.5816	0.5638	0.4884	0.4302	0.3842	0.3469	0.3163
12	0.8630	0.8242	0.7884	0.7552	0.7244	0.6957	0.6690	0.6441	0.6208	0.5990	0.5786	0.5594	0.5414	0.4657	0.4081	0.3629	0.3267	0.2971
13	0.8535	0.8125	0.7749	0.7401	0.7080	0.6783	0.6507	0.6252	0.6013	0.5791	0.5584	0.5390	0.5209	0.4451	0.3882	0.3440	0.3088	0.2802
14	0.8440	0.8009	0.7615	0.7253	0.6920	0.6614	0.6331	0.6069	0.5827	0.5602	0.5392	0.5197	0.5014	0.4260	0.3699	0.3268	0.2927	0.2651
15	0.8348	0.7897	0.7487	0.7112	0.6769	0.6454	0.6165	0.5899	0.5652	0.5425	0.5214	0.5017	0.4835	0.4085	0.3534	0.3113	0.2782	0.2516
20	0.7910	0.7371	0.6893	0.6466	0.6085	0.5742	0.5433	0.5154	0.4900	0.4669	0.4459	0.4265	0.4088	0.3382	0.2884	0.2515	0.2231	0.2005
25	0.7508	0.6901	0.6375	0.5916	0.5514	0.5159	0.4845	0.4565	0.4315	0.4090	0.3887	0.3703	0.3535	0.2884	0.2437	0.2111	0.1864	0.1668
30	0.7139	0.6479	0.5920	0.5443	0.5032	0.4675	0.4364	0.4091	0.3849	0.3634	0.3442	0.3269	0.3113	0.2514	0.2111	0.1821	0.1601	0.1429
35	0.6799	0.6100	0.5520	0.5034	0.4622	0.4271	0.3967	0.3704	0.3473	0.3269	0.3088	0.2926	0.2781	0.2230	0.1863	0.1601	0.1404	0.1250
40	0.6486	0.5758	0.5166	0.4678	0.4271	0.3928	0.3635	0.3383	0.3163	0.2971	0.2801	0.2649	0.2514	0.2004	0.1668	0.1429	0.1250	0.1111
45	0.6197	0.5449	0.4852	0.4367	0.3968	0.3635	0.3354	0.3113	0.2904	0.2723	0.2563	0.2421	0.2294	0.1820	0.1510	0.1290	0.1127	0.1000
50	0.5930	0.5169	0.4571	0.4093	0.3704	0.3383	0.3113	0.2883	0.2685	0.2513	0.2363	0.2229	0.2111	0.1668	0.1380	0.1177	0.1026	0.0909

*Prepared by Ted C. and W. Harry Schaffer

TABLE VII

PRESENT VALUE OF ACCELLERATED COST RECOVERY

Rapid ACRS	1%	2%	3%	4%	5%	6%	7%	8%
3 year	.9792	.9590	.9395	.9206	.9024	.8847	.8676	.8510
5 year	.9696	.9406	.9129	.8864	.8611	.8369	.8137	.7915
10 year	.9492	.9021	.8585	.8179	.7802	.7451	.7124	.6818
15 year*	.9354	.8772	.8246	.7769	.7337	.6943	.6584	.6256

	9%	10%	11%	12%	13%	14%	15%	16%
3 year	.8349	.8193	.8042	.7895	.7753	.7614	.7480	.7350
5 year	.7702	.7498	.7302	.7114	.6934	.6760	.6593	.6433
10 year	.6532	.6265	.6014	.5779	.5558	.5351	.5155	.4971
15 year	.5955	.5679	.5425	.5190	.4973	.4773	.4586	.4413

	17%	18%	19%	20%	21%	22%	23%	24%
3 year	.7223	.7100	.6980	.6863	.6750	.6640	.6533	.6428
5 year	.6279	.6130	.5987	.5850	.5717	.5589	.5466	.5346
10 year	.4798	.4634	.4479	.4333	.4194	.4063	.3938	.3819
15 year	.4252	.4101	.3961	.3829	.3705	.3589	.3480	.3377

	25%	26%	27%	28%	29%	30%	31%	32%
3 year	.6326	.6227	.6131	.6037	.5945	.5856	.5769	.5684
5 year	.5231	.5120	.5013	.4909	.4809	.4712	.4619	.4528
10 year	.3707	.3600	.3498	.3401	.3309	.3221	.3136	.3055
15 year	.3280	.3189	.3102	.3020	.2942	.2868	.2797	.2730

*15 year real estate. Half-year convention does not apply.